D0452148

Disorienting Sexuality

NATIONAL UNIVERSITY
LIBRARY SAN DIEGO

Disorienting Sexuality

Psychoanalytic Reappraisals of Sexual Identities

Edited by
Thomas Domenici
Ronnie C. Lesser

Foreword by
Adrienne Harris

Routledge
New York London

Published in 1995 by
Routledge
29 West 35th Street
New York, NY 10001

Published in Great Britain by
Routledge
11 New Fetter Lane
London EC4P 4EE

Copyright © 1995 by Routledge

Printed in the United States of America on acid-free paper.

All rights reserved. No part of this book may be reprinted or reproduced or utilized in any form or by any electronic, mechanical, or other means, now known or hereafter invented, including photocopying and recording or in any information storage or retrieval system, without permission in writing from the publishers.

Library of Congress Cataloging-in-Publication Data
Disorienting sexuality: psychoanalytic reappraisals of sexual identities/
edited by Thomas Domenici, Ronnie C. Lesser; foreword
p. cm.
Includes bibliographical references and index.
ISBN 0-415-91197-4 (hbk.)—ISBN 0-415-91198-2 (pbk)
1. Sex (Psychology) 2. Pschoanalysis. 3. Homosexuality.
4. Gender identity. I. Domenici, Thomas. II. Lesser, Ronnie C.
BF175.5.S48D57 1995
155.3—dc20 95-38513
CIP

This Book is dedicated to
Angelina Amorello,
Josephine Steo,
and in loving memory of
my grandfather Thomas Steo
and a much missed friend Gordon MacMahon
—T. Domenici

For Erica
—R.C. Lesser

Contents

Acknowledgments

WE ARE GRATEFUL TO ALL the people who gave us professional and personal assistance in the planning and execution of the December 4, 1993 conference, "Perspectives on Homosexuality: An Open Dialogue," and in compiling this book. We would like to first jointly express our gratitude to those who have helped us both, and then acknowledge others separately.

First, we want to acknowledge Bernard Kalinkowitz for the inspiration and support which made the conference possible. We want to especially thank Adrienne Harris for providing the help and encouragement necessary to bring the conference to fruition, and for her extensive help with the book. We also appreciate those faculty, graduates, and candidates of the New York University Postdoctoral Program in Psychotherapy and Psychoanalysis who helped and supported us with the conference.

Most importantly, we want to thank all those who participated in the conference and in this book. Their contributions are greatly appreciated.

We also want to express our appreciation to our editor, Maureen MacGrogan, for her enthusiastic support of this project, and to Alison Shonkwiler, for providing us with information and support.

Thomas Domenici

I WANT TO PARTICULARLY THANK Jessica Benjamin for being a true mentor during the last five years; providing tutorage, supervision, and guidance with respect, encouragement, support, and steadfast friendship, making this long and at times lonely journey much easier. I give my heartfelt gratitude to Emmanuel Ghent, Joseph Natterson, Barry Miller, and David V. Foster for making this journey possible. I want to express appreciation to Stephen Mitchell, Doris Silverman, Lynne Kwalwasser, and Barbara Cadow for an opportunity to learn through their expert supervision.

I want to especially thank my daughters, Jacqueline and Anne-Marie, in whom I have great pride and respect, for their love and esteem and their strength of character. I want to thank my family: my mother, grandmother, aunts and uncles and especially my cousins (who, in the Italian tradition, are more like sisters and brothers) for their confidence. And I thank my friends: Cathy Adams, Richard Bozanich, T. R. Burton, Sue Chenoweth, Barbara Cadow, Mike Hill, Joan Petty, Mark Thompson; and particularly Nancy Faranda, Paula Maxwell, Janice, Denny, and Greg Morrison, and Judy, Mike, and Stephen Stahl for their consistent love, urging and generosity.

I want to thank my patients for their trust and willingness to allow me to learn from, and share in, their struggles to create a meaning-filled life.

I want to also thank my co-editor, Ronnie Lesser, and those in my study group, Jessica Benjamin, Janice Crawford, Susan Rita Gair, Barbara Newman, and Janet Pfunder, for reading my paper and providing insightful critiques, and for being part of an exciting and safe place to struggle with new ideas. Many thanks to Sam Berlind for rehabilitating my aching back with great Shiatsu, interesting conversation, and friendship; and a special thanks to Donald Murray for trusting me while we "danced with demons."

Ronnie C. Lesser

I WANT TO ACKNOWLEDGE and thank the following people: Adrienne Harris, whose boundless generosity, help, encouragement, and support have been so important to me; Jay Greenberg, for his suggestions for getting the book going; April Martin, for encouraging and nurturing my writing; Ruth Imber, for her warmth, belief in me, and for her patience, fortitude, and gentle touch in doing internal redecorating; Reuven Closter, Robin Fried, Steve Goldman, and April Martin, whose friendship means so much to me; Muriel Lesser, for fostering my creativity; Mel and Lea Schoenberg, for being such a supportive second family; and Erica Schoenberg, whose love enriches my life in ways that words are too meager to describe.

Thanks also to the members of my study group: Diane Burhenne, Ann D'Ercole, Debbie Gold, Erica Schoenberg, and Melanie Suchet (and the members of the original group, Thomas Domenici, Martin Stephen Frommer, and Carole Vance) for stimulating discussions and good times.

My appreciation also goes to Ann D'Ercole, Thomas Domenici, Adrienne Harris, April Martin, Erica Schoenberg, and Sue Shapiro for their helpful comments on earlier drafts of my chapter, and Adrienne Harris, Erica Schoenberg, April Martin, and Zina Steinberg for comments on the introduction.

Foreword

THIS BOOK IS THE OUTCOME of the determined and courageous efforts of gay and lesbian analysts to enter into and alter the psychoanalytic institutions, theories, and practices in which homosexuality and homosexual persons have been so ill-considered and ill-treated, in all senses of that term. This particular project had its genesis at the New York University Postdoctoral Program in Psychotherapy and Psychoanalysis, emerging in a quite unique conjunction of the strong and always radical vision of the program's founder, Bernie Kalinkowitz, and a group of articulate candidates who formed a Committee for Gay and Lesbian Concerns in 1993. Of course, this process was occurring in the larger and longer context of a quarter century of gay liberation and highly developed theoretical and historical work on homosexuality, most recently in the emergence of queer theory.

To characterize the appearance of a group practicing identity politics in psychoanalysis in 1993 as "courageous" is to immediately mark the uniqueness and the entrenched difficulties in considering homosexuality within psychoanalysis. What is commonplace in most institutional settings is and has been still radical and resisted within psychoanalysis. To understand the power of psychoanalysis' investment in orthodoxies of desire and identity is one of the tasks of this book. To understand this investment, to deconstruct it and to move from the margins, is the necessary and belated project that has inspired all the authors in this volume. One of the unique features of the work presented here is its capacity to attend to questions of identity and sexuality concerning both the analyst and the analysand.

This book is the outcome of and evolves from an earlier development at New York University in the Postdoctoral Program, a conference, "Perspectives on Homosexuality: An Open Dialogue," which the two editors of this volume, Tom Domenici and Ronnie Lesser, took primary responsibility in organizing. They were encouraged, challenged, and deeply supported by Bernie Kalinkowitz. He was an analyst and teacher whose life and work were committed to a respect for difference and the encouragement of distinct and particular voices and experiences in analytic training. It is a measure of his deeply democratic spirit that he would welcome but did not coopt the spirited demand which developed not from senior or even junior faculty or graduates but from students, from analysts in sensitive and vulnerable positions within their institute. I think it is entirely compatible with Kalinkowitz's life commitments that he would have both encouraged and protected the challenging spirit that the Committee for Gay and Lesbian Concerns manifested. He died a year before the conference, but the great response to that meeting and its rich intellectual and clinical offerings would have meant a great deal to him.

Yet Kalinkowitz's authorizing of a critical and emergent gay and lesbian presence in his training program and the committee's creative reaction tell only part of the story. The need for gay and lesbian analysts to have a voice in the discourses on sexuality and identity in psychoanalysis has been deeply felt, but it is indisputably long overdue. At the 1994 winter meeting of the American Psychoanalytic Association, at a panel devoted to the discussion of the acceptance for analytic training at the medical institutes of openly gay and lesbian analysts, rather strikingly, participants at the panel said there was no problem for any such admissions. Before the history gets lost in a rush to repair or rewrite it, it must be said, and a number of chapters in this book do just so, that the pain and anger of many gay and lesbian analysts over experiences in their training or in search of training are fundamental to the work of this book and to its critical stance.

This book also records the angry protests of experiences of erasure, silence, homophobia, misunderstanding, and disrespect which have a long and shameful history in many institutions and writings within our field. Amidst a very developed modern tradition of research, literary and artistic work, and theorizing in and by homosexual persons, gay and lesbian voices in psychoanalysis have had undue difficulties in establishing conditions for work on questions of sexuality, of homosexuality, and of homophobia.

The concerns of gay and lesbian analysts have been directed both to questions of training and questions of treatment. Becoming a psychoanalyst is a loving attachment one hopes is destined to last a lifetime. Even amidst contemporary conditions of assault, economic challenge to, and misunderstanding of psychoanalysis, many analysts over a number of generations feel blessed to be developing and working within this discipline. How to love a practice, a body of thought, theories, or institutions which do not appear to offer love and respect in return? Added to these disappointments is a concern for the impact of what all analysts are taught on the clinical practice with gay and lesbian patients. How is it possible to practice with tools that appear to disfigure the patient rather than help or understand?

So in the heady moment when some would proclaim this history of rejection and distortion happily concluded and with the appearance of this book so strong in its theorizing, its clinical insights, its placement in history, I would still want to inquire as to why psychoanalysis has been so recalcitrant and so impenetrable to internal criticism in regard to homosexuality. In the humanities, in cultural studies, in the academy in so many domains, a gay and lesbian presence has been visible and groundbreaking in the deconstruction and revisioning of much of the standard canonical texts. It is striking that gay and lesbian intellectuals and scholars—Judith Butler, Michel Foucault, Monique Wittig, John D'Emilio, John Boswell, to name only a few very central figures—have developed among the most robust and creative intellectual projects in contemporary scholarship. Many of these thinkers, perhaps most significantly Judith Butler, have made powerful use of psychoanalysis.

In turning to clinical practice and to theoretical work within psychoanalysis, the conversations and discourse become fragile and riddled with anxiety and misrecognition. Why so? Many of the essays in this volume touch on and comment on this conundrum. As many of the contributors to this volume suggest, I would look for some answers to this question in the insights of Foucault in regard to the interdependence of structures of power and structures of knowledge. Institutional/ideological/intellectual structures within any culture, apparently designed only to reflect and observe and learn, mask their role and power in constructing the very objects they study. The role of the observer in the construction of the observed is of course a feature of much twentieth-century scientific thinking in the physical and the social sciences. Foucault's spin on this concept is to stress the need to mystify and disguise this constructive intervention.

Psychoanalysis is an integral part of the very processes of identity formation and the deployment of desire that it was developed to react to. The massive, far-reaching structure involved in the term "psychoanalysis" is paradoxically dispersed and abstract within social life and at the same time highly concentrated in particular institutions and formations which generate powerful constitutive forces in securing and regulating identity, desire, and individuality. Inevitably, this complex tangible and intangible world of theory and practice will be strongly contested.

Psychoanalysis is our most complex, deeply subtle tool for thinking about mind, body, desire, and social connection. It is a recording device and a blueprint for the constitution of intrapsychic and interpersonal life. So it is the most hopeful and elaborate site for asking transforming questions about these matters. Butler's understanding of this situation has led to her appreciation that any act of interrogation of theory from the margins reveals that theory's constitutive power and thus must challenge its hegemony by challenging its foundational claims. I believe that this is the deep hope of this book. Psychoanalytic theory and its practices have carried ideology, prejudice, and conforming pressures. The liberatory and conservative impulses within psychoanalysis are inextricably intertwined and have been since its earliest formations. A number of essays here trace this contradiction, but are unique in that they do so from *within* psychoanalysis. Epistemological power, interpretive power, and political power are interwoven and mutually co-constructing. Marginalized and stigmatized voices in this situation are being welcomed and being resisted. It has been challenging and inspiring to read and follow the scholars in this volume as they trace their unique and individual paths through this complex mazeway.

Another crucial aspect in the critique gay and lesbian analysts have articulated concerns access to training. No practice considers character in quite the deep way psychoanalysis does. The analytic instrument is the whole thinking, feeling apparatus of personality, the whole range of capacities to engage with and react to others who are trained to act and interact in prescribed ways. This condition leaves the profession enormously susceptible to cruelties, to the exercise of prejudice and homophobia, all spruced up in neutral sounding terms like technique and analyzability. Given this history and its persistence, though often in more covert form, in current theory, it is a signal act of courage for gay and lesbian analysts to insist on a voice and an open presence. Heterosexuality is the usually unquestioned, unremarkable fact of character or desire. Homosexuality is the marked, the particularized, the to-be-interrogated form. Many of the authors in this volume live within this contradiction; focusing questions and attention on homophobia and homosexuality still preserves one of the phenomena so deeply under attack —the privilege of orthodoxy and of heterosexuality.

This must be a historically necessary moment in our development; difficult, exciting, demanding. I would like to hold out for the utopian vision that is one legacy of psychoanalysis and one current strand in modern gender theory, namely that all identities and forms of desire are mutually interdependent upon and constructed through their supposed others or opposites. I believe this volume points towards a discourse on sexuality and identity in which, without erasing difference or idealizing particular forms of personhood, there could truly be "free association," that revolutionary ideal of our practice. Any and all genders, sexualities, and desires (thus opening the discourse to much more variegated experiences as sexual beings than the limiting binary category scheme of homosexual/heterosexual) would be analyzable for constructive, organizing, and reparative capacities as well as for their defensive roles in neurosis. At the same time, all forms of identity and love could be a matter of wonder, fascination, and respect.

Adrienne Harris, Ph.D.
Co-Director, New York University
Postdoctoral Program in Psychotherapy
and Psychoanalysis

Introduction

Thomas Domenici and Ronnie C. Lesser

IN THE PROCESS OF BUILDING theory within a hierarchical, universalizing, and normalizing medical discourse, psychoanalysts have not only marginalized groups of people, but now find themselves in danger of being marginalized. We believe that psychoanalysis has an opportunity to revitalize itself as a mode of treatment if it moves toward contextualizing theory by taking cultural and historical factors into account. *Disorienting Sexuality*'s project is to make this move by contesting and revitalizing the psychoanalytic theory of sexuality, a theory marked by essentialist assumptions and bias.

I. The Essentialist, Anti-Homosexual Turn in Psychoanalysis

In the late nineteenth century Krafft-Ebing defined the normal functioning of the sexual instinct as those processes that lead to procreation. He believed that non-procreative sexuality must be regarded as perversion. In 1881, Albert Moll wrote:

> from a teleological point of view, that is from the point of view of the reproduction of the species, we consider natural the urge that the normal man feels for woman . . . we can hardly establish a connection between man's genital organs and his urge for women except from a teleological point of view. Otherwise, one does not see why men should be urged to have connections with women since ejaculation of the sperm can be brought about in quite other ways. (Davidson 1987)

Anything that was not propagational, such as homosexuality, was considered a sign of neurological degeneracy.

In his first major work with regard to sexuality, "Three Essays on the Theory of Sexuality" (1905), Freud argued that the biological essentialism of

Albert Moll and Krafft-Ebing gave a false picture of sexuality. In the first of the "Three Essays," he dismantled the connections between both the sexual instinct and the object, and the sexual instinct and the aim. If there is no natural object and no natural aim to the instinct, then deviations from genital intercourse cannot be called perverse. Unfortunately, Freud defused this radical move with two theoretical turns.

First, Freud introduced the Oedipal Complex as the universal structure-building event, conceptualizing both heterosexuality and homosexuality as by-products of the identificatory process. While viewing sexuality as decisively influenced by familial configurations and interrelations refuted essentialism, Freud's universalizing of the Oedipal Complex meant rejecting the historicity of sexual practices and categories. Homosexuality was no longer seen as neurological/genetic degeneracy, but was now viewed as oedipally structured, and as fixed an identity as heterosexuality.

Second, Freud used a Darwinian evolutionary model of psychosexual development which organized all human activity in relation to the survival of the species. By defining "normal" sexuality as procreative, sexuality was essentialized and homosexuality was pathologized. According to Robert Padgug (1979):

> Such a view necessitates the location of sexuality within the individual as a fixed essence, leading to a classic division of individual and society and to a variety of psychological determinism, and, often enough, to a full-blown biological determinism as well. These in turn involve the enshrinement of contemporary sexual categories as universal, static, and permanent, suitable for the analysis of all human beings and all societies.

What occurred after Freud can best be described as an anti-homosexual turn in psychoanalytic theory. Building on Freud's own essentialism, his positing of both homosexuality and heterosexuality as fixed essences, psychoanalysts discarded his more radical and tolerant ideas about homosexuality and moved toward the preoedipalization of homosexuality. Object Relations theorists, such as Klein and Fairbairn, argued that homosexuality was not oedipally structured but rooted in preoedipal (hierarchically inferior) conflicts, oral fixations, and narcissism. Freudians, such as Nunberg and Bergler, also argued that Freud was wrong with regard to the oedipal status of homosexuality, and that in all cases homosexuality is preoedipally determined, inferior to heterosexuality, and rooted in a mistaken gender identity and defective superego which can not control primitive impulses (Lewes 1988).

Anti-homosexual theory building went in another direction as well when it followed Freud's lead in "Psychogenesis of A Case of Female Homosexuality" (1920). Here Freud posited that his lesbian patient had to turn into a man to love another woman. Following this model, analysts theorized a gendered split between identification and desire (O'Connor and Ryan 1993). Identification and desire came to be viewed as opposed: one cannot have and be the same sex at the same time. By positing identification and desire as binary opposites, the normative structure of heterosexuality was buttressed and essentialized.

Until recently the anti-homosexual tenor within psychoanalytic theory has remained largely uncontested. We believe that attention must be paid to this turn by investigating the following questions: How have cultural attitudes about homosexuality affected psychoanalytic theory? What need do psychoanalysts fulfill in upholding conventional, white, middle-class definitions of both sexuality and gender, vaunting them as universal truths? Why has psychoanalytic theory taken homosexuality and heterosexuality as foundational aspects of being, ignoring historical and cultural contexts? What defensive purposes has this reification served? Why is psychoanalysis so resistant to both recognizing and changing its anti-homosexual views?

II. Foucault and "Queer" Theories: A Move Toward Revitalizing Psychoanalytic Theory

Central to many current challenges to normalization, hierarchization, essentialism, and dichotomization in psychoanalytic theory is Foucault's analysis of knowledge and power. Following Nietzsche, Foucault questioned the existence of universal, absolute truth. In so doing, he argued that while might made right in the past, modern times are marked by the power behind knowledge, i.e., the power of truth construction. Knowledge does its work through various language mechanisms such as dichotomy and hierarchy. An example of such structuralization is the categorization of people as "normal" and "abnormal." Those who are deemed "abnormal" (e.g., criminals, mentally ill, perverts) and the behaviors that are taken to define "abnormality" are historically and culturally constructed. What is typically studied is not the "normal," but the "abnormal." Those who are defined as normal, the truth constructors, avoid scrutiny and become the absent norm (Sampson 1993).

Taking Sartre's dictum "Existence precedes essence," Foucault argued that the world does not contain transcendent meaning, but is constructed through language. While Sartre believed we all had the freedom to act, Foucault questioned the limitlessness of this freedom. Realizing that people are limited by the society that creates them, he turned to language as the structuralizing force within knowledge. What now could be said is that language precedes existence: beings come into existence through language.

In *The History of Sexuality*, Foucault described the process by which sex became the key to self-understanding and liberation, as well as the means through which medical, psychiatric, and government experts intervened into sexuality and family life. Power, he argued, does not operate primarily by denying sexual expression, but by creating the forms that modern sexuality takes. He focused on how social control is maintained by marginalizing and medicalizing "deviance." This diverts attention from tolerated "abnormalities" within the "normal" (e.g., marital rape, incest). In shifting our attention away from repression to the relations between power and sex, he freed us from thinking of the truth of the individual as being in his or her sexuality. Truth is not the form of some fixed, static, and individualistic identity, but is constituted by a myriad of social relationships and practices in which the individual is engaged.

Queer Theory, according to Michael Warner (1993), following Foucault, represents dissatisfaction with and protestation against the idea of the "normal," and the logic of toleration. Not a theory about "queers," it is an attempt to move theory to its critical edges by reconsidering the definitions and purposes of the putative norm. In contrast to multiculturalism, it has the effect of pointing out a wide field of normalization rather than intolerance as the site of violence. Multiculturalism presupposes an ethnic organization of identity rooted in family, language, and cultural traditions which define the norm, and relies on notions of authenticity, tolerance, culture, and shared meanings as the source of identity. Queer theory does not fit with this modernist trend. Perhaps the greatest shared value between feminism, multiculturalism, and queer theory is their creation of noise, or interference: their efforts to put difference into "play."

An important question that follows is how one creates change. Foucault saw organized reform as doing more to stabilize power than change it. Change comes about through transformation, reversals of the system and rituals that order things. The struggle in Queer Theory is to create change by putting the "normal" and the "abnormal" back into play. It is our belief that psychoanalysis, which has the most rigorous language about abnormality and sexuality, can be revitalized by using ideas from both Foucault and Queer Theory.

Historically, the psychoanalytic discourse has viewed sexuality as the key to self understanding, leading psychoanalysts to assume that in order to liberate ourselves from personal "abnormalities," we must uncover the truth of our sexuality. From the point of view being discussed here, this is seen as a move toward normalization, rather than liberation.

Freedom is not in discovering or being able to determine who we are, but in rebelling against those ways in which we are already defined, categorized, and classified. This move toward freedom gives voice to those on the margins. These voices are the sources of resistance, the creative subjects of the present. What becomes central is an effort to discover differerences and to view them as resources rather than threats.

III. Marginalized Voices: The Influence of Identity Movements

Since the 1960s, identity movements (e.g., movements of women, African-Americans, gay men and lesbians) have challenged academe by exposing the extent to which they have been omitted from prevailing theoretical models (Sampson 1993). By unmasking the biases behind paradigms hitherto regarded as objective, identity movements have revealed the extent to which all epistemology is discourse-specific. They have also insisted that the exclusion of cultural and sexual diversity from Western theoretical models serves to enhance the power of dominant groups. By taking themselves as the standard (much as the makers of Crayola crayons came up with a light-colored crayon they called "flesh" when we were children), dominant groups have constructed narratives of minorities which bolster their own needs, values, interests, self-esteem, and perspectives. These narratives are often posed as dichotomies in which the master term (e.g., male, reason, self, heterosexual) is defined as possessing certain qualities which its opposing term lacks. The negative term is used by the master term to represent everything that it would like to believe itself not to be: In psychoanalysis, for example, "normal" heterosexuals are emphatically not homosexual, perverse, developmentally arrested, or identified with the wrong sex. Dominant groups have the power not only to construct "serviceable" others, but also to define how these others think and feel about themselves: For dominated groups what is said about them becomes the reality of their lives. Those who have the power to say and think also have the power to construct the world in their image (Sampson 1993). (Of course this is not simply a top-down relationship since dominated groups also influence the identity of dominant groups.)

This book is an attempt by lesbian, gay, and heterosexual psychoanalysts to reshape the psychoanalytic discourse on sexuality in a new image. The shared vision of each author is one which respects diversity, does not privilege one form of sexuality over another, confronts the uses of categorization, hierarchization, and the use of the "abnormal" within psychoanalytic theory, is suspicious of the power plays which underlie essentialist assumptions, and views gay, lesbian, and heterosexual identities as historical and cultural productions. Rooted in the gay, lesbian, and feminist movements, Foucauldian theory, as well as social constructivist and postmodern critiques of sexuality, the views presented in this book, however, are not monolithic. Some contributors keep the structure of psychoanalytic theory largely intact, while adding gay and lesbian voices; others redeploy psychoanalytic concepts to suit new, more radical purposes; others attempt to transform theory, radicalizing our visions of both sexuality and gender.

The voices not heard in this book are those of anti-homosexual psychoanalysts. This editorial decision was not without vociferous opposition from those who believed us to be inhibiting free speech, an issue to which those of us who have experienced exclusion cannot fail to be sensitive. Our decision was to have this book focus on views of sexuality which respect diversity, recognizing that the psychoanalytic literature is already replete with anti-homosexual papers which need no boost from us.

Critiques of sexuality come late to psychoanalysis: while feminists have transformed the psychoanalytic discourse on gender in recent years, exposing biases against women and formulating new theories of gender, there has been relative silence about the extent of anti-homosexual bias in both psychoanalytic theory and practice. Psychoanalysis has been able to remain largely immune from the challenges posed by gay and lesbian scholars in other fields. This has meant that a steady stream of anti-homosexual books and articles have been and continue to be published, deriding homosexuality as a pathology or developmental arrest to be modified whenever possible. Often this bias is more subtle and cloaked in assurances of tolerance and open-mindedness. Because there are few viable alternatives, anti-homosexual books and articles continue to be used for training purposes. Psychoanalysts who are trained with biased theories cannot help but bring these prejudices into the consulting room, causing harm to gay and lesbian analysands.

Challenges to psychoanalysis's biased view of sexuality come late to psychoanalysis in large part because of the power that psychoanalytic institutes have to silence opposition and to harm lesbian and gay psychoanalysts who come out. This power is wielded both in a way that is unique to psychoanalysis and in a way that is common to all institutions. First, psychoanalysts use their privileged position as interpreters of reality and truth to label those who speak out against anti-homosexuality in psychoanalytic theory and practice as paranoid, political, under the throes of a powerful transference distortion, or insufficiently analyzed. It is hard to fight psychoanalysts who see themselves as objective purveyors of truth.

The second method is the use of power by institutions to silence opposition. Psychoanalytic institutes do this through threats of reprisals: ostracism, demotion, loss of sources of referrals, or denial of advancement (see Bert Schaffner's chapter in this book for a poignant description of his being denied advancement at his institute). Although there are more gay and lesbian psychoanalysts who are open about their homosexuality today than ever before, many still fear disclosing their homosexuality. It is our view that psychoanalytic theory and practice will not change until gay and lesbian psychoanalysts can openly speak and express our discontent and create new theoretical conceptualizations. This will lead not only to theoretical change, but to changes in power within psychoanalytic institutes. Anti-homosexual psychoanalysts for too long have had the power to negatively affect the way gay and lesbian psychoanalysts and patients think and feel about ourselves. The psychoanalytic construction of a developmentally arrested, perverse, gender-disordered homosexual has gone a long way in reproducing and generating new biases against gay and lesbian people in popular culture. It is our hope that this book makes a contribution toward effecting changes in all these areas.

While it is important to add the voices of gay and lesbian analysts to the psychoanalytic discourse on sexuality, we also want to articulate some of the thorny philosophical and political problems raised by so apparently straightforward a project. These problems can be put into relief by thinking about the sections of this book: two written by gay and lesbian psychoanalysts and a third theoretical section written by psychoanalysts of undeclared sexuality (who might be assumed by the reader to all be heterosexual). While intended to fulfill the important political task of supporting gay and lesbian analysts in coming out, the division also reproduces the dichotomy homosexual/heterosexual, a dichotomy that we are trying to deconstruct. At the same time, the arbitrary nature of such a dichotomy is highlighted by the fact that two of the contributors to the putatively heterosexual section are lesbian themselves. How meaningful are these categories?

Consider the different gay and lesbian psychoanalysts who could potentially be included in the gay and lesbian section: those who feel that they've always been exclusively gay or lesbian and remember feeling this way from early childhood, those who believe that they are attracted to people on the basis of characteristics other than sex, those who are presently having sexual relations with members of the same sex but previously have had sex with a person of the opposite sex and do not preclude that possibility from again arising in the future, those who have sex with members of the same sex but have exclusively heterosexual fantasies, and a myriad of other permutations. This range presumably exists among the heterosexual psychoanalysts as well. Diversity among people in how they "do" sexuality challenges the meaningfulness of thinking of sexuality through binary, stable categories.

Note the assumptions that underlie such seemingly "natural" categories as "gay," "lesbian," and "heterosexual": that a person's sexuality expresses an essential truth about her; that these categories are ahistorical, rather than particular, ephemeral styles we moderns have assumed for organizing part of our experience; that these so-called "sexual identities" are coherent, stable, and necessary; that being "gay" or "lesbian" can be contrasted with its binary opposite, "heterosexual," in ways that are both "natural" and meaningful, and not defensive.

Recent work in gay and lesbian studies throws essentialist assumptions about sexuality into disarray, raising important questions as to why psychoanalysis, a method designed to look beneath the surface to expose hidden meanings, utilizing historical material to do so, has taken historical, cultural productions as facts. Indeed, modern, heterosexual, white, middle-class psychoanalysts seem to be of the opinion that their own sexual and gender arrangements are both ahistorical and universal truths: anything different is a deviation which signifies pathology and requires explanation and change.

In a history of homosexuality in New York, Chauncey (1994) has provided evidence not only that the categories "heterosexual" and "homosexual" were products of the late nineteenth century but also that they changed in the middle class at least two generations before they changed in much of Euro-American and African-American working class culture. Prior to World War I, the gay male world was not divided into homosexual and heterosexual: men could have sex with other men and not consider themselves "queer" as long as they conformed to conventional gender stereotypes. Passionate, tender relationships between men did not preclude the possibility of similar relationships with women. Only in the 1930s–1950s did the now common conventional division replace this, and this change was uneven, marked by class and ethnic differences. Chauncey sees this change as a reaction to the growth and visibility of gay life during the twenties and thirties that seemed to arouse the fear that normative gender and sexual arrangements would be disrupted. The heterosexual world began to police and rigidify its own boundaries, outlawing the gender non-conformity of the queers, and defining how normal men should dress, walk, talk, and relate to each other.

Rather than being tied to developmental constants, both sexuality and gender are historical constructions which serve to create boundaries between what is forbidden and allowable, defining both deviance and normality. By taking historical constructions about gender and sexuality as natural facts, psychoanalysis contributes to the process of naturalizing these differences, instead of trying to understand the defensive and political purposes they serve.

The historian Joan Scott (1993) described the importance identity politics plays in adding the voices of those who had previously been omitted from conventional narratives in the field of history (e.g., women, gay men and lesbians, minorities). Including them has

> provided evidence for a world of alternative values and practices whose existence gives the lie to hegemonic constructions of social worlds, whether these constructions vaunt the political superiority of white men, the coherence and unity of selves, the naturalness of heterosexual monogamy, or the inevitability of scientific progress and economic development. (Scott 1993, 399)

Yet to include these omitted voices must not preclude the possibility of examining the practices and beliefs that led both to their prior exclusion and to their very construction as categories in the first place. We must change our focus

> from one bent on naturalizing experience through a belief in the unmediated relationship between words and things, to one that takes all categories of analysis as contextual, contested, and contingent. How have the categories of representation and analysis—such as class, race, gender, relations of production, biology, identity, subjectivity, agency, experience, even culture—achieved their foundational status? What have been the objects of their articulation? These questions deny the fixity of anything appearing as a foundation, focusing on the history of foundationalist concepts, always themselves contested and political. (Scott 1993, 411)

IV. Disorienting Sexuality

In the first section, "New Voices: Gay and Lesbian Psychoanalysts," lesbian and gay psychoanalysts write on both theoretical and clinical issues which are central to dismantling the prejudices that affect the treatment of all patients.

Lee Crespi, in "Some Thoughts on the Role of Mourning in the Development of a Positive Lesbian Identity," explores some of the losses that lesbians must come to terms with in their lives as a result of being gay. Crespi illustrates how the analyst can facilitate the necessary mourning process by presenting some of the clinical manifestations of problems that are related to unresolved mourning. Crespi also presents some of the countertransference issues that come into play when working with lesbian patients.

Thomas Domenici, in "Exploding the Myth of Sexual Psychopathology: A Deconstruction of Fairbairn's Anti-Homosexual Theory," takes a Butlerian approach to Fairbairn's object relational theory of the development of object choice. At a time when Fairbairn is being regarded as one of the most significant psychoanalytic theorists in the past fifty years by many relationally oriented psychoanalysts, Domenici is problematizing some of the most central ideas in Fairbairn's theory. These ideas led Fairbairn, and object relations theorists who followed him, to regard homosexuality as a severe psychopathology. Domenici then makes a move toward a relational understanding of development which does not hold to anti-homosexual theorizing.

Martin Stephen Frommer explores both the causes and clinical consequences of the "Countertransference Obscurity in the Psychoanalytic Treatment of Homosexual Patients" in his essay. Countertransferential phenomena are frequently examined from the vantage point of a heterosexist bias embedded both in psychoanalytic theory and in the analyst's way of thinking about and responding to his/her gay patients. Frommer examines the effects of the analyst's unrecognized countertransference on the course of treatment, emphasizing the analyst's failure to address the social context of the homosexual patient and issues of shame.

Ronnie C. Lesser, in "Objectivity as Masquerade," argues that anti-homosexuality is ubiquitous in contemporary psychoanalysis. She explores the ways that this bias is hidden by analysts through their utilization of "The Myth of the Objective Analyst" and "The Myth of the Objective Theory." Lesser argues that psychoanalysis's tolerance and enjoyment of anti-homosexuality is tied to its view of gay men and lesbians as sub-human specimens. Some of the defensive, destructive, and political purposes this derogation serves are explored by Lesser.

Maggie Magee and Diana C. Miller, in "Psychoanalysis and Women's Experience of 'Coming Out': The Necessity of Becoming a 'Bee-Charmer'," use cases by Freud and Khan, as well as Fannie Flagg's novel *Fried Green*

Tomatoes at the Whistle Stop Cafe, to discuss the process of "Coming Out." Flagg's heroine Idgie is a "Bee-Charmer" who manages the stinging names, confusion, and anxieties associated with her homosexual identity. This is discussed with a view toward the treatment of homosexual patients where these and other anxieties can threaten, confound, and frighten the movement of both analyst and patient.

David Schwartz, in "Current Psychoanalytic Discourses on Sexuality: Tripping Over the Body," looks at how the concept of "sexual orientation" is deployed and how important psychoanalytic principles are contradicted by inherent assumptions. He discusses the serious consequences of these moves for both psychoanalytic theory and practice. Schwartz illustrates the problematic aspects of the concept of sexual orientation by examining writings from three different groups of contemporary psychoanalysts who have concerned themselves with sexuality.

In the second section of the book, "Rethinking Sexuality: Theoretical Perspectives," psychoanalysts bring different perspectives to the task of creating new understandings of sexuality. Historically, psychoanalytic theory has implicitly or explicitly concerned itself with what is normal and what is abnormal as well as with what is biologically essential and directed and what is learned. Schafer (1992) writes:

> No longer is psychoanalysis a theory of instinct-ridden organisms, turbulent unconscious dynamics, and the like. All aspects of development are to be seen as being profoundly influenced by learning in a context of object relations that are, on the one hand, biologically essential and biologically directed and, on the other hand, culturally molded and historically conditioned.

The papers in this section respect diversity, reject essentialist assumptions, and situate sexuality within object relations informed by history and culture.

Muriel Dimen, in "On 'Our Nature': Prolegomenon to a Relational Theory of Sexuality," asserts that a psychoanalytic theory of sexuality requires giving up the discourse of nature in which the normal, the healthy, and the moral pursue one another in a wickedly circular rhetoric that leaves no space for the ambiguity of desire.

Robert May returns to one of Freud's most influential papers, "Three Essays on the Theory of Sexuality" (1905), in "Re-Reading Freud on Homosexuality." May starts with a consideration of how and why American orthodox psychoanalysis went astray in relation to homosexuality and then considers Freud's "Three Essays," highlighting the way in which Freud was constantly undermining categories. May argues that psychoanalysis is best characterized by this endless undoing of certainty.

Noreen O'Connor, in "Passionate Differences: Lesbianism, Post-Modernism, and Psychoanalysis," explores the relationship between a postmodernist view of human subjectivity and a view of subjectivity in psychoanalytic theory and practice. The analysis of lesbianism highlights the closure which characterizes much psychoanalytic writing. O'Connor holds that post-modernism can offer a framework for a more open theoretical and practical development, and uses clinical material to illustrate her argument.

Richard Rutkin, in "Psychoanalysis with Gay and Lesbian People: An Interpersonal Perspective," discusses an interpersonal psychoanalytic conceptualization of analytic treatment and highlights particular issues that pertain to the psychoanalysis of people who are homosexual. Rutkin pays special attention to the relationship between the analyst and the patient and discusses transference and countertransference factors that might ensue.

Roy Schafer, in "The Evolution of My Views on Nonnormative Sexual Practices," asserts that anti-homosexual psychoanalytic theorizing revolves mainly around false, prejudicial, dualistic assumptions about psychosexual development, gender differences, and sexual orientations and performances. Schafer maintains that by using an arbitrary evolutionary ethic, Freud reinforced value-laden, conventional dichotomizing of masculine and feminine, active and passive, etc. Freud thereby legitimized analysts' unrecognized moralistic attitudes and practices, and he compromised the truly analytic attitude he otherwise exemplified of sustained, nonjudgmental curiosity. Schafer includes an account of his gradual emancipation from the homophobic presuppositions instilled by his cultural background and psychoanalytic training.

Erica Schoenberg's paper, "Psychoanalytic Theories of Lesbian Desire: A Social Constructionist Critique," is a social contructionist interrogation of psychoanalytic theories of lesbians, particularly the work of Joyce McDougall, revealing it to be prejudice masquerading as science. Rather than impartially describing natural laws of "normal" sexuality, Schoenberg argues that the literature on lesbianism is a political product instrumental in maintaining the status quo by pathologizing difference.

•

Lesbian and gay psychoanalysts have experienced discrimination and bias at many different levels in psychoanalytic institutes. This is slowly changing: While prior to 1984 there were no openly lesbian or gay psychoanalysts in training at medical institutes, today openly gay and lesbian candidates have been accepted for training at many institutes. It is not known how many institutes still discriminate against gay and lesbian applicants. What is certain is that institutes have a long way to go toward ridding themselves of bias against homosexuality. The third section of the book, "Lesbian and Gay Psychoanalysts: Their Encounters with Anti-Homosexuality," presents three narratives about discrimination and bias against gay men and lesbians in psychoanalytic training.

Jack Drescher, who in 1988 was among the first openly gay men admitted to a psychoanalytic institute for training, argues in "Anti-Homosexual Bias in Training," that anti-homosexual bias in psychoanalytic training is based upon misinterpretations of Freud's theory by psychoanalysts such as Rado. He believes that psychoanalytic clinical theory, combined with demonizing social myths, led to prejudices against lesbian and gay men that resemble anti-Semitism. Anecdotes illustrate biases and the evolution of a "don't ask, don't tell" policy within psychoanalysis.

In "The Difficulty of Being a Gay Psychoanalyst During the Last Fifty Years," Stephen B. Goldman interviews Dr. Bertram Schaffner. Dr. Schaffner gives us an historical perspective for understanding discrimination against gay psychoanalysts within psychoanalytic institutes during the past fifty years.

April Martin, in "A View From Both Sides: Coming Out as a Lesbian Psychoanalyst," gives us an account of her personal experiences in coming out while a candidate in psychoanalytic training in the late seventies.

In his concluding remarks, "The Shaping of Psychoanalytic Theory and Practice by Cultural and Personal Biases About Sexuality," Mark J. Blechner focuses on several significant issues raised by the papers. These include: 1) the special issues of the development of gay and lesbian individuals in a homophobic society; 2) the misunderstanding and misinterpretation of this experience by psychoanalysts, and some possible correctives; 3) the relation of sexual orientation and gender identity; 4) the role of language, culture, empirical data, and biology in these issues; 5) how psychoanalytic theory and practice are related to the mores and taboos of the culture, with special attention given to the related histories of psychoanalytic attitudes toward women and toward homosexuality; 6) the different forms of hatred, bias, and ignorance in the psychoanalytic treatment of homosexuals; and 7) some alternative directions that psychoanalytic theory and practice might take in the future.

Freud's vision was one of human struggle in diversity. His vision was lost, as he feared it would be, with the medicalization of psychoanalysis. The papers in this book offer an opportunity for psychoanalysis to simultaneously discover a way back to Freud's original radical vision, and to go beyond it.

Lesbians and gay men who did not conceal their homosexuality have been excluded from medical psychoanalytic institutes and hence the psychoanalytic discourse for nearly one hundred years. This exclusion is now changing: As a result, much of the anti-homosexual rhetoric in psychoanalytic theory will now be challenged. In contesting anti-homosexuality we seek to contest and disorient all sexuality. Our goals are threefold: (1) to confront the use of categorization, hierarchization, and the use of the "abnormal" within psychoanalytic theory; (2) to offer new theoretical approaches to understanding sexuality; and (3) to help transform theory into clinical practice.

This is not an effort to replace identity and community, but to hold a tension in place, a tension between the fixity of all sexual identities and the possibility of fluidity. It is our belief that as homosexuality is reconsidered, all sexuality and its discontents will be revisioned. In making this move it is our hope to bring psychoanalysis into its second century with a discourse that moves toward creativity, fluidity, flexibility, and diversity, and away from one that stresses hierarchy, prejudice, rigidity, and pathology.

References Cited

Chauncey, G. 1994. *Gay New York*. N.Y.: Basic Books.

Davidson, A. I. 1987. "How To Do The History of Psychoanalysis: A Rereading of Freud's Three Essays on The Theory of Sexuality." In *The Trials of Psychoanalysis*, ed. by F. Meltzer. Chicago: University of Chicago Press.

Foucault, M. 1970. *The Order of Things: An Archeology of the Human Sciences*. N.Y.: Vintage.

Foucault, M. 1972. *Power/Knowledge*. N.Y.: Pantheon.

———. 1978. *The History of Sexuality; Vol. I. An Introduction*: N.Y.: Pantheon.

Freud, S. 1905. "Three Essays on Sexuality." *The Standard Edition of the Complete Psychological Works of Sigmund Freud* 7: 123–243. London: Hogarth, 1953.

———. 1920. "Psychogenesis of a Case of Female Homosexuality." *Standard Edition*, 18: 145–72.

Lewes, K. 1988. *The Psychoanalytic Theory of Male Homosexuality*. N.Y.: Simon and Schuster.

O'Connor, N., and Ryan, J. 1993. *Wild Desires and Mistaken Identitities*. N.Y.: Columbia University Press.

Padgug, R.A. "Sexual Matters: On Conceptualizing Sexuality in History." *Radical History Review* 20: 16.

Sampson, E. 1993. *Celebrating The Other: A Dialogic Account of Human Nature*. Boulder: Westview Press.

Schafer, R. 1992. *Retelling a Life: Narration and Dialogue in Psychoanalysis*. N.Y.: Basic Books.

Scott, J. 1993. "The Evidence of Experience." In (Eds. Abelove, H.; Barale, M.; Halperin, D.) *The Lesbian and Gay Studies Reader*. N.Y.: Routledge.

Warner, M., ed. 1993. *Fear of a Queer Planet: Queer Politics and Social Theory*. Minn: University of Minnesota Press.

Part 1

New Voices

Gay and Lesbian Psychoanalysts

1

Some Thoughts on the Role of Mourning in the Development of a Positive Lesbian Identity

Lee Crespi

UNTIL RECENTLY THE LIMITED NUMBER of psychoanalytic writings concerning lesbians focused on questions of etiology and the nature of the underlying pathology that resulted in a lesbian orientation (see Magee and Miller 1993 for a complete review of the literature). More recent contributions have attempted to challenge these earlier works and either depathologize lesbianism or deconstruct the concept of sexual orientation (Burch 1993; Lesser 1993; O'Connor and Ryan 1993). While this debate is important and challenging, it leaves out a great deal about the phenomenological experiences of lesbian patients and their analysts in doing the day-to-day work of analysis, an area in need of greater investigation. Although these issues are raised in private settings, supervision, and gay and lesbian organized conferences, they remain outside the mainstream of psychoanalytic discourse. As a result, clinicians are often left without a context in which to place the material of their lesbian patients in order to better understand them and their needs in treatment.

With this in mind, the purpose of this paper is to explore the idea that just as it is necessary for heterosexuals to mourn aspects of their homosexuality, as part of the normal developmental process, it is necessary for lesbians to mourn aspects of heterosexuality in order to allow for a more integrated self and to establish a positive lesbian identity.[1] Moreover, this mourning, when it appears in analysis, should be understood to be a normal developmental process which should not be confused with sexual orientation conflict. Therefore, it is the additional aim of this paper to illustrate through clinical examples, some of the manifestations of the mourning process as they may appear in the clinical setting.

Mourning and Development

Freud (1923) recognized mourning as a pivotal developmental process when he expanded his theory of identification with the lost object first presented in "Mourning and Melancholia" (1917). He proposed that identification and mourning are integrally related, both to each other and to the formation of ego structure. He posited that in the resolution of the Oedipal Conflict mourning of the relinquished love object results in identification with that object, and ultimately results in the formation of the superego.

> When it happens that a person has to give up a sexual object, there quite often ensues an alteration of his ego which can only be described as a setting up of the object inside the ego, *as occurs in melancholia*. . . . (Freud 1923, 29; emphasis added)

Mourning plays a central role in Object Relations Theory as well. Emotional and psychological development are achieved through the related processes of mourning and integration. Beginning with the loss of the mother's breast and on through the separation and individuation process, the individual undergoes repeated experiences of relinquishing fantasies as well as actual infantile dependencies in the move toward greater autonomy and independence. In order for this to occur, conflictual ambivalent ties to early objects must be resolved, and the lost objects must be mourned so that aspects of them can be internalized and integrated as parts of the internal Self and Object world. According to Melanie Klein (1958), as a result of this mourning and integration process, perception is brought more in line with reality, resulting in a better relationship between the internal and external world.

More recently, Judith Butler (1993) also placed mourning at the core of certain developmental processes when she expanded on Freud's discussion of melancholic identifications as the origin of gender identity. She questioned whether rigidification of gender identity might be understood to be the result of a failure to adequately mourn the same-sexed Oedipal love object which must be relinquished or "foreclosed" by the prohibition against homosexuality (Butler 1993).

This dynamic mourning, identification, and integration process continues throughout life, and at each significant developmental passage is reworked and renegotiated. At adolescence, the conflicts of the earlier separation stage are revisited, and the individual must mourn the loss of childhood dependence in order to establish the beginnings of her adult identity. Forming a committed relationship requires that the individual mourn the loss of potential fantasied partners and the narcissistic pleasures which are given up in exchange for partnership and intimacy. In a similar fashion, career choice, childbearing, midlife, and aging all require mourning of lost opportunities, choices, fantasies, dependencies, and grandiosity.

For the very young child this mourning process takes place in the context of a maternal holding environment which Winnicott (1960) defined as a "complex psychological field, determined by the awareness and the empathy of the mother" in which the infant's "ego changes over from an unintegrated state to a structured integration." As the individual grows, society becomes an extension of the maternal holding environment through projection and transference. Using Kohut's model of self-objects, one may say that a "self sustaining function is performed by those objects who by their presence or activity evoke and maintain the self" (Wolf, 1988). The social structure performs this function through the family, in which expectations are defined and role models are presented. Folklore, religion, history and fashion also define social expectations by providing the images that guide certain choices. Institutional validation also provides another source of influence and direction for developmental choices and losses, the most obvious being the institution of marriage.[2]

Usually, intrapsychic obstacles to navigating normal developmental passages arise primarily as a result of an individual's inability to mourn, to tolerate her ambivalent feelings toward her objects, or to relinquish omnipotent fantasies, due to internal deficits or conflicts. However, in addition to any such personal barriers which may exist, lesbians, because their life choices and passages are not mirrored or socially sanctioned (Buloff and Osterman 1993) are provided little or no external structure to aid in the mourning process or to facilitate integration. As a result, certain problems may arise and need to be addressed in analysis. I will be giving some examples of these problems throughout this paper.

The Impact of Internalized Homophobia

Lesbians develop an identity in a world that at best denies and at worst reviles homosexuality. A world in which the necessary and stage-appropriate mourning process becomes hampered by issues of internalized homophobia. Internalized homophobia is a concept introduced in the 1970s (Weinberg 1972) to identify the various forms of pernicious self attack that homosexuals experience through interaction and identification with the culture which generally promotes an anti-homosexual attitude. This creates in the individual a sense of badness that transforms mourning into depression.

Freud (1917) differentiated between mourning and melancholia primarily on the basis of the presence of lowered self-esteem, self-reproach, and self-reviling in patients exhibiting melancholia. Freud was referring to the effects of superego attacks resulting from anger at the lost object with which an identification has been made. Self-hatred resulting from internalized homophobia feeds a punitive superego and it is the rare individual whose superego is unaffected by her experience of being gay. As a result, an individual may utilize various defenses consistent with her personality to ward off self-attack. For example, we may see doubt or compartmentalization in obsessives, denial and confusion in hysterics, projection and hostility in borderlines, and so on. The greater the degree of internalized homophobia, the more rigid the defenses, thus leaving the individual less able to work through the grieving process. As a result, the interaction between internalized homophobia and the emotional pain involved in unresolved mourning can lead to *increased* self-hatred and depression. This may then result in greater rigidity and bravado, or alternatively in repudiation of one's homosexuality. This raises important treatment issues.

Clinical Issues

One key issue which stands out is the need for the analyst to distinguish between conflicts about sexuality and the process of mourning. Some patients do have genuine conflicts about their sexuality and their sexual object choices, and these conflicts should be treated as such. Likewise, the patient's mourning process needs to be facilitated through identifying it and encouraging a full range of the expression of feelings. I believe that serious problems arise when the analyst misinterprets the normal mourning process as a conflict about the patient's sexual orientation. This inaccurate interpretation can impede the patient's progress toward integration and thwart development of a unified self. This will lead to overcompliance and depression, or to anger and a negative therapeutic reaction.

Mistaking normal mourning for conflict often reflects the analyst's conscious or unconscious assumptions that if the patient is expressing pain or grief or even anger about being gay, this means she has the desire to change, and it would be better to do so. This brings to mind a story told to me about a lesbian who was talking to her elderly Jewish grandmother about being gay. She was trying to explain that she had struggled long and hard with it, and that it was a difficult and painful process. Her grandmother replied, "Nu, so if it's so hard, why do it?"

Once the distinction between conflict and mourning is made, the question of *what* needs to be mourned can be addressed.

Self-Regard and the Ego Ideal

According to Freud,

> Mourning is regularly the reaction to the loss of a loved person, or to the loss of some abstraction which has taken the place of one, such as fatherland, liberty, *an ideal* and so on. (1917, 243; emphasis added)

This loss of an ideal may be thought of in terms of the role that heterosexuality plays in our culture. As the means of procreation and perpetuation of the species, heterosexuality is not only deemed necessary but is raised to the level of the holy, the legal, or an indication of one's status and place in the world. It is a measure of one's success, the basis of all social structure and stability, and in general not only the ideal outcome of all human development, but indeed, the only acceptable outcome. It follows that in recognizing or choosing homosexuality, the individual is forced to renounce any hope of ever reaching the ideal state. It is difficult therefore to describe the enormity of the loss that a man or woman faces in being gay. This loss has the potential to become the basis for self-rejection. It will be felt not only in relation to the external world but in one's internal world in which the self becomes degraded in relation to the ego ideal (Epstein 1993).

Heterosexual Relationships

Most lesbians have had heterosexual experiences and many lesbians have had one or more serious and extended heterosexual relationships, including satisfying sexual relations, loving attachments, and at times marriage and children. For many lesbians who have had these experiences, their homosexual object choice is driven predominantly by their emotional "fit" with women, which does not preclude sexual desire but rather encompasses it. However, their experiences with men are also reflective of some degree of heterosexual emotional and/or sexual interest. Whatever the multiplicity of factors which predominate in a woman's homosexual choice, the components of her self that continue to desire closeness with men, either physically or emotionally, need to be addressed so as to meet those needs, either directly through family relationships and friendships or indirectly through sublimation. To the degree they cannot be met they will need to be mourned. These heterosexual needs can be confusing to both patient and analyst and even can be experienced by the patient as a threat, much as heterosexual patients feel threatened when they experience awareness of their homosexual desires.

For example, recently a lesbian patient who had been active heterosexually until her late twenties presented the following situation. She had received a phone call from a man whom she used to know who wanted to get together for dinner. She found herself experiencing an old difficulty in not being able to say no to him, despite the fact that she did not like him, thinking of him as unstable and somewhat frightening. She had previously discussed how in her past relations with men she had often found herself unable to stop their sexual advances. Although she enjoyed sex with these men, she felt she allowed herself to get into situations which she later regretted, because of either the circumstances or the people involved. This incident revived concerns about whether her homosexuality was a defense against her impulsiveness with men. The patient had spent many sessions exploring various aspects of her feelings about men and women and the meaning to her of her object choices. O'Connor and Ryan (1993) attribute the propensity for self-doubt and uncertainty about sexual identity that some lesbians experience to the universal assumption of heterosexuality. The lesbian or gay man must "discover" her or his own sexuality in relation to this assumption and is therefore subject to questioning it. For the above-mentioned woman, this incident crystallized a remaining question about her sexuality. Suppose it was a defensive reaction? What then? She struggled with this for a while. What did she want to do about it? Whatever defensive functions had been served by her homosexuality had long ago been understood. She was no longer impulsive in her relations with men or women. She had no wish to change her sexual orientation. What was making her anxious was not knowing what to do with her *heterosexual* feelings. She did not want a relationship with a man although she sometimes desired sex with them. She was happily progressing in her current lesbian relationship and felt no need to disrupt it. We then explored the possibility that she needed to mourn the loss of physical relationships with men. This struck the patient as emotionally correct. She found she no longer had any difficulty refusing the unwanted invitation. It had the additional effect of restoring her sense that she was *choosing* her sexuality rather than being a lesbian by default.

Physical Security

A second element of heterosexuality that may need to be mourned by lesbians is the loss of a physically safe and socially sanctioned self-identity. Being a lesbian means giving up many powerful and important aspects of heterosexual life, including the status and respectability that marriage provides as well as the social mobility and physical safety that being with a man confers. In a recent *New York Times* article, a lesbian described the feelings of exposure that she felt when paying her bills in a small New England town with a check that bore her name and the name of her partner (Graff 1993). This article reflected a concern felt by many lesbians who reside or have second homes in rural areas. Unconscious fears of attack and retaliation by internal objects may often resonate with external physical risk. Many will attest to the ever-present sense of potential danger that lurks side by side with feelings of relief and gratitude in being accepted into a rural community where people own guns.

Social Losses

In regard to the social losses, there are certain events, such as attending a heterosexual wedding, that may be counted upon to trigger disguised forms of grief reactions. I have repeatedly observed in both individuals and couples an almost predictable depressive reaction manifested in the form of fighting or withdrawing and distancing from others following attendance at a wedding. This can occur in even the most progressive families where the lesbian couple may be acknowledged and accepted—in fact, sometimes even more so in these families because the individual or couple may be unprepared for the bad feelings that do surface. This reaction needs to be understood as resulting from the confrontation with the powerful confluence of social, institutional, and familial celebration of the heterosexual union and the reawakening of the sense of loss that one experiences in no longer having access to that form of sanction and approbation.

Traveling on vacation can also, at times, trigger unexpected feelings of depression. For example, another patient, a highly successful businesswoman who came from a socially prominent family, had been accustomed to spending her summers in the relatively mixed (straight and gay) social setting of the Hamptons, a beach community in New York. She and her lover, along with another couple, took their vacation at a tennis camp. This woman was completely unprepared for how painfully isolated and vulnerable she felt in a resort where they were a distinct minority. When understood in analysis, such experiences can provide an opportunity for the patient to acknowledge feelings related to being gay of which she may be unaware.

Parenthood

A third area in which mourning plays a significant role is in the decision and attempt to have a child. Prior to about ten years ago, the only lesbians who had children were those who had previously been married. For lesbians who desired to have children, the choice was either to renounce their relationships with women and marry men—often unhappily—or to be childless. In the last ten years, however, owing to the increased sense of self-esteem and entitlement brought about by the Gay Rights movement, coupled with advances in the availability of donor insemination and adoption, more and more lesbians are choosing to have children. As a result, new issues have arisen.

The decision to have a child is encouraged to varying degrees by the social climate, as mentioned earlier. In general, however, it is always viewed positively in the context of a heterosexual marriage. It is, after all, the purpose of heterosexuality itself. To decide to have a child outside of a heterosexual marriage, as we saw in the 1992 Republican Presidential Campaign, is to invite harsh criticism and rebuke. In addition, internalized homophobia may be stimulated, leading to self-attack and depression.

I have observed that it is necessary for lesbians who decide to have children, whether through adoption or insemination, to mourn the fact that they cannot make a baby with their partners. This is not unlike what couples who are infertile must address, but will encompass additional components as well. The absence of gender-defined roles in a lesbian relationship, despite providing an advantage of greater flexibility, can also create conflict. For example, questions of competition and jealousy can be more challenging to negotiate and may place additional stress on the relationship.

The following case examples demonstrate some of the feelings that may arise relating to mourning and having children. Couple one had been trying donor insemination for two years. Jane had been unable to conceive. The ongoing anxiety, physical and emotional stress, and repeated disappointments resulting from trying to become pregnant and failing had placed enormous pressure on their relationship, as often occurs with heterosexual couples who are having difficulties conceiving. This was then exacerbated when Jane told her lover Sara that she wanted to adopt rather than have Sara try to inseminate as they had originally planned. Sara experienced this as a negation of her role in the relationship and as proof that Jane did not really love her. What emerged was that Jane was unable to accept being in what she felt to be a secondary role in relation to the child. In addition, she unconsciously resented Sara for not being able to give her the baby that she wanted. Sara on the other hand felt impotent in the face of Jane's inability to conceive, and then was further wounded by Jane's rejection of her own wish to conceive. As a result, each woman lost her belief in the other's ability to love her.

The second couple came to therapy for help in deciding whether to have a known or an unknown donor and, if known, whom to choose from several possible choices. It soon became apparent that although Diane and Angela were ostensibly committed—they were, after all, planning to have a child—they remained unsettled about their commitment. This was largely due to Diane's feeling that as a result of her being gay she was a failure in relation to her highly competitive family. As a defense, she would become very critical and attacking of Angela, who would respond by distancing, generally in the form of fantasizing aloud about moving to another part of the country.

With each of these couples, we pursued questions related to mourning and, more specifically, to their mourning of their inability to make a baby together through their lovemaking. We were able to examine issues related to gender identification and parental identifications as well as anger and grief about the fact that no matter how accepting of their having children they, their families, and their communities were, they could not conceive by themselves. Shortly following these discussions, both couples became pregnant. Whether the pregnancies were indeed the direct result of the therapeutic intervention or merely a happy coincidence, I leave to the reader to decide.

Family Rejection

A great many lesbians who maintain close ties with their families of origin are treated with full acceptance of their relationships. Others, however, are not so fortunate. They may be unable to reveal their sexual preference to their families at all because they know they will be rejected. They may, in fact, be estranged, or they may exist in a kind of limbo in which their families are aware that they are gay but exhibit some form of denial such as refusing to welcome their partner into their house. As a result, the need to come to terms with the loss of family love or the love of an individual parent becomes a crucial step in individuation and the ability to form satisfying committed relationships. The feeling of being a disappointment or failure, as with Diane in the previous example, can also become an obstacle to self-acceptance.

Relationship Problems

As described earlier in relation to Diane and Angela, another arena in which unresolved mourning can be a factor is in the ability to make and sustain a commitment. Most lesbians, like most heterosexual women, seek committed long-term relationships. In addition to the issues usually associated with commitment problems, some lesbians, while seeking a monogamous relationship, resist committing themselves to one because to do so would mean committing to homosexuality.

Another manifestation of this problem is the ongoing conviction expressed by some women that despite the formation of a committed relationship, "I am not really a lesbian, I just happen to be in love with another woman." Similarly, this can present as a sexual problem, in which a woman may be experiencing inhibitions or may be unable to be more active in initiating or participating in sex, also as a way of resisting acknowledgement of her homosexuality.

Countertransference Issues

Earlier in this paper I emphasized the potentially destructive consequences that can result when the analyst mistakes mourning for conflict about sexuality. This is frequently the result of the analyst's countertransference to the patient's homosexuality. I am not addressing here the analyst who subscribes to the theory that all homosexuality is pathological and should be cured in analysis, although this position can also be understood as countertransferential (Kwawer 1980; Lewes 1988; Mitchell, 1981). For the purpose of this paper, I am addressing those situations in which the analyst believes herself to be neutral in regard to her patient's homosexuality. In his paper on Homosexuality and Psychoanalysis, Frommer (1993) contends that "analysts who adopt a surface neutrality toward their patients' homosexuality are often guided by hidden countertransference."

Countertransference is communicated to the patient in many subtle ways, through silence as well as through interpretation and choice of questions. Most gay patients have an understandable resistance to expressing the full range of their distress in analysis when they sense that it will be misinterpreted or used as leverage in attempting to convert them. Countertransferences to the patient's homosexuality can take a number of forms.

Sexual Issues

The presence of unresolved homosexual feelings in the heterosexual analyst is one important source of countertransference. This may lead to envy of the patient's homosexuality and a need to destroy it. It may result in an unconscious wish to be the object of the patient's desire or conversely to anxiety about being that object. For a male analyst, anger at not being the patient's sexual object may be stimulated along with fantasies of seduction and conquest.

Parentalism

A parental countertransference toward the patient may lead the analyst to feel that although she herself is not biased against homosexuality per se, she wishes to spare the patient the pain of a lifestyle that would be difficult. A woman in her early twenties, aware of strong homosexual feelings, sought analysis with an older woman analyst in order to understand these feelings before acting on them. After several months of treatment, she became involved with another young woman. She reported that when she told her analyst, who until this point had presented herself as neutral and interested only in helping the patient figure this out for herself, the analyst began weeping.

Denial of Social Reality

Unlike the analyst who wishes to protect the patient from the hardships of homosexuality, some "liberal" analysts naively insist that an individual can be immune to the negative pressures of a homophobic society if she is secure in herself. Any painful reactions the patient may have to external homophobia are then treated as resulting from projections of her own conflictual feelings. This often will include reactions the patient may have to the analyst's unconscious feelings. In confronting the analyst with her feelings that the analyst is trying to influence her, the patient is told that this too stems from the patient's own wishes.

Projective Identification

Another countertransference problem is that which results when the patient projects her unresolved homophobia onto the analyst and induces it in the analyst through projective identification. The patient presents aspects of her relationships and lifestyle in such a cynical and negatively tinged manner as to induce in the analyst a distorted sense of the reality of the patient's relationships. This is done by the patient as a defense against resolving her own feelings about her homosexuality.

Countertransference in the Lesbian Analyst

Lesbian analysts working with lesbian clients also face some specific countertransference pitfalls. Overidentification with the patient can lead to a stance that avoids genuine confrontation of identity issues that remain unresolved for the analysts. On the other hand, the lesbian analyst's own unresolved internalized homophobia and superego problems may manifest in a tendency to be hypercritical and to overpathologize in an effort to defend against possible identification with her lesbian patients.

Mourning and the Analyst

A last note on mourning and countertransference. Sometimes it is the analyst who needs to mourn the loss of her expectations that the patient will meet the analyst's idea of normalcy and be cured of her homosexuality. The patient who chooses to follow her sexual desires in a direction other than that which the analyst believes in or wishes for the patient will engender feelings of loss in that analyst. This loss needs to be mourned in order for the analyst to continue to be useful to the patient.

To close with a final word from Freud,

> It is well worth noting that, although grief involves grave departures from the normal attitude to life, it never occurs to us to regard it as a morbid condition. . . . We rest assured that after a lapse of time it will be overcome, and we look upon any interference with it as inadvisable or even harmful. (1917, 243)

Notes

1. By "positive lesbian identity" I refer not to a fixed entity but to something that differs for each woman. Whether an individual considers her homosexuality to be a significant component of her overall identity, or merely marginal, her feelings about her lesbianism will invariably impact on the other components of her identity to an extent that will be significant.
2. An example of the ways in which the social structure influences and guides the individual through what are generally thought of as developmentally and internally determined choices can be seen in the fluctuations in childbearing norms in the United States. In the fifty years since World War II there has been a marked reduction in the number of children per family, as well as a significant increase in the age of first-time parents in middle-class families.

References Cited

Buloff, B. and Osterman, M. 1993. The Unmirrored Self. Presented at The Women's Therapy Center Institute, New York.

Burch, B. 1993. Heterosexuality, Bisexuality, and Lesbianism: Psychoanalytic Views of Women's Sexual Object Choice. *The Psychoanalytic Review* 80: 1, 83–99.

Butler, J. 1993. Feminist Post-Modernism and Melancholia. Paper presented at "Psychoanalysis 1993: Diversity and Integration," American Psychological Association, Division 39, Spring Meeting, New York, 1993.

Epstein, L. 1993. Personal communication to author.

Frommer, M. 1993. Homosexuality and Psychoanalysis: Technical Considerations Revisited. *Psychoanalytic Dialogues* 4: 2, 215–233.

Freud, S. 1917. Mourning and Melancholia. *Standard Edition*, 14. London: Hogarth, 1957.

———. 1923. The Ego and The Id. *Standard Edition*, 19. London: Hogarth, 1957.

Graff, E.J. 1993. The Double-Bed Principle. *The New York Times*, Section 6, Sunday, October 17, 1993.

Klein, M. 1958. On the Development of Mental Functioning. *Envy and Gratitude*. London: Hogarth, 1975.

Kwawer, J. 1980. Transference and Countertransference in Homosexuality: Changing Psychoanalytic Views. *American Journal of Psychotherapy* 34: 72–80.

Lesser, R. 1993. The Psychoanalytic Construction of the Female Homosexual. Paper presented at "Diversity and Integration," American Psychological Association, Division 39, Spring Meeting, New York, 1993.

Lewes, K. 1988. *The Psychoanalytic Theory of Male Homosexuality*. New York: Simon and Schuster.

Magee, M. and Miller, D. 1993. "She Forswore Her Womanhood": Psychoanalytic Views of Female Homosexuality. *Clinical Social Work Journal* 20: 67–87.

Mitchell, S. 1981. The Psychoanalytic Treatment of Homosexuality: Some Technical Considerations. *International Review of Psychanalysis* 8: 63–80.

O'Connor, N. and Ryan, J. 1993. *Wild Desires and Mistaken Identities: Lesbianism and Psychoanalysis*. New York: Columbia University Press.

Weinberg, G. 1972. *Society and the Healthy Homosexual*. New York: Grune and Stratton.

Winnicott, D.W. 1960. The Theory of the Parent-Infant Relationship. In *The Maturational Processes and the Facilitating Environment*. New York: International Universities Press, 1965.

Wolf, E. 1988. *Treating the Self: Elements of Clinical Self Psychology*. New York: Guilford Press.

2

Exploding the Myth of Sexual Psychopathology

A Deconstruction of Fairbairn's Anti-Homosexual Theory

Thomas Domenici

Hamlet:	Denmark's a prison.
Rosencrantz:	We think not so, my lord.
Hamlet:	Why, then, t'is none to you; for there is nothing either good or bad, but thinking makes it so. To me it is a prison.
Rosencrantz:	Why, then, your ambitions makes it one.

—*Hamlet*, act 2, scene 2

THROUGHOUT THE HISTORY OF PSYCHOANALYSIS, theorists have disguised theorem as fact and set the discourse for heterosexual and homosexual object choice in terms of normal and abnormal development. However, "theories are not fact, observations, or descriptions—they are organizational schemes, ways of arranging and shaping facts, observations and descriptions" (Mitchell 1988). Often as new attitudes arise, they are forced to fit within, or are sacrificed to maintain, old theories; or when new theories do arise they are made to conform to old attitudes. Seldom are there major paradigm shifts. Rather, the changes that do occur are the products of both the pressure of current politics and cultural anxieties and are burdened by past ideologies and power structures.

The organizational scheme upon which much of the psychoanalytic theory of object choice is based is phallocentric, misogynistic, copulocentric, and therefore anti-homosexual in nature. This reification and normalization of a male-female split in power is based upon (1) reproductive functions, (2) the reification of gender and the subsequent idealization of masculinity and devaluation of femininity, and (3) the insistence on the biologistic view of heterosexuality as healthy and homosexuality as an arrest, delay, fixation, or confusion of gender identification. However, this very theory could itself be viewed as based in pathological processes if it were not for the fact that these assumptions form the base upon which psychoanalytic theory rests.

I do not believe that Freud was personally anti-homosexual (Abelove 1993). In fact he developed a "new attitude" toward homosexuality, which challenged the then newly evolving biologically based sexology (Davidson 1987). However, owing to his adherence to a copulocentric, evolutionary-based value system (Schafer 1992), generations of anti-homosexual analysts (Lewes 1988) have advanced prejudicial ideas throughout psychoanalytic theory. For example, as theorists, such as W.D.R. Fairbairn, moved toward a relational theory, where sex and aggression are considered the by-products of object relations and intimacy is considered primary, homosexuality came to be depicted as much more pathological than in Freud's theory.

Because my own interest is in relational theory and the evolution of theory that is not based in anti-homosexuality, my focus is on deconstructing Fairbairn's object relations theory in an effort to develop a different understanding of *all* object choice. I propose that psychoanalytic theory might hold the view that object choice and gendered identities are social constructions, based in some form of psychic compromise; that all object choice and gender identities are to be understood not merely as accomplishments but as problematic, trauma-based, defensive psychic constructions. Psychoanalysts can thus move toward an understanding of the defensive nature of such maneuvers as well as the perverse struggle for power involved in *all* masculinity, in *all* object choice, and examine their effects on object relations.

Currently, an effort is being made by some psychoanalysts to dislodge anti-homosexual prejudices from psychoanalytic theory. By providing an understanding of the historically constructed, intrapsychic processes to which these prejudices attach themselves, I hope to help derealize the suffocating grip anti-homosexual prejudices have on the immediate. I will first deconstruct heretofore unchallenged assumptions underlying Fairbairn's relational theory; second, suggest the defensive processes that are normalized by these assumptions; and third, open a discourse on the psychic processes involved in anti-homosexuality, especially transference/countertransference enactments that support explicit or implicit anti-homosexual collusions between both heterosexual and homosexual analysts and analysands. I take as basic assumptions that homosexuality and heterosexuality are variants of the human need for relationships; that any belief that devalues homosexuality and idealizes heterosexuality is "copulocentric" in nature; that masculinity and femininity are psychosocially-constructed categories in dialectic tension, informing and transforming each other; that any theory that privileges masculinity is misogynistic; and that any theory that biologizes sex and marries it to gender is phallocentic in nature. I also take as a basic assumption that hierarchical oppositions, based in paranoid schizoid intrapsychic process, will always tend toward reestablishing themselves.

Classical Theory and Homosexuality

During the second half of the nineteenth century there was a virtual explosion of medical discussions about sexual perversion, an immense verbosity (Foucault 1978) which incited a new discourse. Sexologists, such as Albert Moll and Richard Krafft-Ebing, used the Christian conceptualization of sexuality as sinful (perverse) when it is not propagational and developed a medical conceptualization of the sexual instinct as natural and biological. Homosexuality was then considered to be a sign of nervous degeneracy. Perverse heterosexual incest, rape, and pedophilia, ironically, remained within the realm of biological legitimacy.

Freud first entered the discourse in 1896 when he created an alliance between psychoanalysis and sexology, equating neurosis with a pathologically repressed or a "negative" state of sexual perversion (Davidson 1987). His first major effort within the discourse was in 1905 when he published the "Three Essays on the Theory of Sexuality." Despite the fact that Freud decenters heterosexuality in the essay, I see his effect in general as not having overthrown the old Christian or the newly developing biological paradigm but rather as having added psychology or learning to the essentialism of the discourse. In so doing, he enriched and deepened the discourse, which in turn helped to support the Christian conceptualization of sexuality as "copulocentric."

Early in the first essay, Freud stated that the prevailing assumptions about childhood sexuality and the attraction of one sex for the opposite sex "give a very false picture of the true situation." He overturned the theory that homosexuality indicated nervous degeneracy and then argued that having to decide whether homosexuality was innate or acquired was a mistake, since neither explained the nature of inversion. He concluded,

> It has been brought to our notice that we have been in the habit of regarding the connection between the sexual instinct and the sexual object as more intimate than it in fact is. . . . We are thus warned to loosen the bond that exists in our thought between instinct and object. It seems probable that the sexual instinct is in the first instance independent of its object; nor is its origin likely to be due to its object attractions. (Freud 1905, 147–48)

Before Freud, instinct and object were married, one to the other. Yet in this essay Freud argued that the sexual object and instinct are merely soldered together. He then moved on to consider instinct and aim, arguing that the sexual instinct is made up of components, of a multiplicity of erotogenic zones and aims, which led to his claim that neither the erotogenic zone of the genitals nor the aim of copulation bear any privileged connection to the sexual instinct. Genital intercourse is not part of the content of the instinct, but rather is also soldered to it. In making this argument, Davidson (1987) points out that Freud undermines the position that inversion is pathological. If there is no natural object and no natural aim to the sexual instinct, then deviations from genital intercourse cannot be given the status of perverse.

As one reads Freud's "Three Essays" and witnesses this overturning of the conceptual apparatus of perversion, one is struck by his contradictory and ambiguous remarks. First, Freud dismantles Krafft-Ebing's notions on perversion and then doubles back and talks about fixations and the instinctual weakness of the genital zone which can fail and result in perversion. In effect, Freud reintroduces the concept of perversion that he just argued was untenable. If we accept Freud's arguments that neither specific aim nor specific object has any constitutive bond with the sexual instinct, then the only way to maintain a concept of unnatural functional deviations is to accept as natural the goal of uniformity of behavior. But Freud claimed that well-entrenched uniformity actually masks the operations of the sexual instinct, operations which show us that the idea of the natural function of the instinct has no basis whatsoever (Freud 1905, 148). Schafer (1992), however, writes that "Freud adhered to a biological, evolutionary model . . . [which] requires the assumption that individual human beings are destined to be links in the chain of survival, and this assumption necessarily implies that genital sexuality is the culmination of psychosexual development" (68). I maintain that Freud had developed a "new attitude," shown clearly through his personal feelings with regard to homosexuality (Abelove 1993). Yet Freud's new theory was actually a reconceptualization based in psychosexual development, with copulation as a developmental end point.

Freud was not alone in his new attitude toward homosexuality. Brill in 1913 wrote that "homosexuality may occur in persons just as healthy as normal heterosexual persons" and claimed that from his experience with his homosexual patients he could not connect homosexuality with any necessary emotional disturbance. In 1939 Glover wrote, "In many cases, apart from the denial of heterosexual genital and reproductive functions, the manifestation of homosexual love feelings and the attitude to the love object cannot be distinguished from those associated with normal heterosexual love." All of this is quite consistent with Freud's attitude regarding homosexuality as a non-pathological aspect of a person's personality.

In 1914, Ferenczi began to take a step in another direction. In his "Nosology of Male Homosexuality," he wrote of his concern with the impoverishment of friendship in Western culture, which he thought was a result of the general disdain and loathing felt for homosexuality. "Men have lost their mutual affection and amiability. Instead there prevails among men decided apathy, resistance and love of disputation. I quite seriously believe that the men of today are one and all *obsessively* heterosexual" (emphasis added). This line of inquiry was not followed up on within psychoanalysis.

In 1940, in "An Outline of Psychoanalysis," Freud wrote about homosexuality in his discussion of bisexuality. He argued that everyone is bisexual and that in either a manifest or latent fashion, the libido is distributed over objects of both sexes. He further remarked that where bisexuality is manifest, there is no conflict between these two trends, but that where bisexuality is latent there is irreconcilable conflict in which a person's heterosexuality will not put up with any homosexuality, and vice versa. "There is no greater danger for a man's heterosexual function than its being disturbed by his latent homosexuality."

Freud thus dismantled the nineteenth-century conception of perversion based in Judeo-Christian traditions and opened the possibility of seeing homosexuality as an element of diversity rather than perversity. Yet, when he developed his new theory of sexuality along a developmental hierarchy and maintained the primacy of genital intercourse, he again problematized difference as perverse rather than diverse. As Schafer (1992) writes, "In Freud's evolutionary based value system, where nature has a procreative plan, non-procreative pleasures become part of the system of foreplay, otherwise they are perversions, or in the case of homosexuality, an inversion." Although Freud was not anti-homosexual, his "copulocentric" theory laid the groundwork upon which generations of anti-homosexual prejudices, disguised as fact, were advanced and woven into the fabric of the psychoanalytic discourse (Lewes 1988).

Relational Theory and Homosexuality

In relational theories, social relations are considered biologically rooted, genetically encoded, rather than forming an overlay upon a more basic template of sexuality and aggression. Here the connection between instinct and object that Freud dismantled is reconstructed through the genome. Freud's system is uprooted and turned on its head; the object is primary, sexuality and aggression are powerful responses, generated within a biologically mandated relational matrix from which they derive meaning.

Object relations theory originating with Klein moved the object into the system of instinct using the Jungian notion of phylogenetic inheritance. She argued that the species-specific images of the breast, penis, baby, mother, explosion, poison, and so forth were inherent to the instinct (1932, 195). Although she struggled with how to link the object to drive, she, like Freud, emphasized internal, constitutional sources, such that real others serve primarily to ameliorate anxiety arising from persecutory fantasies of internal origins (Mitchell 1981).

Fairbairn took issue with Klein's notion of phylogenetically determined internal objects. For Klein fantasy is the most basic activity of the mind (Segal 1964), and the internal world of the infant is the source of both horror and comfort. Fairbairn contended that internal objects are not primary—are not biologically determined. Rather, fantasy is the by-product of failed relations, an escape from relations. Whereas Klein argued that the earliest psychic processes involve aggression, projection, and persecution, Fairbairn saw these as not being involved until later.

Fairbairn's psychoanalytic theory is a dynamic theory of universal object relations in which, due to frustrating interactions between infants and caretakers, ego splitting occurs, resulting in a tripartite psychic structure. Whereas Klein understood splitting as a resistance toward the integration of good and bad, Fairbairn (1944) posited an infant psyche that was whole and in relationship to a preambivalent object. Once the infant experiences the object as frustrating, the psyche is split into good and bad, resulting in a split of the infant's libidinal ego. The instinct is object-seeking and suffering is rooted in inadequate parenting. The bad object is the one that is disappointing; it is felt in its absence and unresponsiveness to be rejecting. The child, in an effort to maintain the goodness of parental figures, internalizes the bad aspects of the parents. This process entails a splitting of the ego since a portion of the libidinal ego remains attached to the bad object. This internalized bad object is then further split into the exciting object (which becomes the libidinal ego) and the rejecting object (which becomes the anti-libidinal ego).

In the adult, the libidinal ego remains involved with a hope for infantile dependency, unfulfilled promises, enticements, and potentials for satisfying contact which is never attained and therefore remains in a constant state of longing. The anti-libidinal ego is the part of the ego that becomes the repository for hate, destructiveness, and rage. This hate is directed internally toward the libidinal ego for its naive hope of intimacy with others and toward external objects, attacking anyone who offers the possibility for relatedness. The libidinal and anti-libidinal egos are said to be observed by the third aspect of the ego, called the central ego, which itself is split from the libidinal and anti-libidinal egos.

Internally, this internalized badness leads to both a feeling of helplessness and despair and a fantasy of omnipotent control. The child now experiences itself as unconditionally bad but can become good through identification with its good parents, thus developing a second process of internalization, or what Fairbairn called the "moral defense." The initial step involves the internalization of the badness, on which the good object is superimposed, leading to the development of a superego—a system of self-accusation and perfectionistic striving. Fairbairn's approach stressed a defensive but purely object-relational approach to internal objects that represent compensatory substitutes for, and a secondary retreat from, disturbances or relations with real people (Mitchell 1981). In this system, psychopathology is defined in terms of the quality and quantity of the central ego (a component of which is the superego) available for external relations; the extent of psychopathology is dependent upon the extent to which the ego is tied to primary objects; the type of pathology depends upon the kind of object that is introjected and projected. Health is the capacity for a rich and intimate mutual relatedness; intimacy is crucial and primary.

With intimacy as primary, Fairbairn redefined human motivation. He argued that libidinal energy is object-seeking, that pleasure is the means to that end, and that libidinal energy is part of the ego and its structure, rather than the ego being structured and libidinal energy coming from the id. In so doing, he argued that the human psyche is able to use energy in object-seeking ways rather than in activities that differ from the energy that drives them. Behavior, according to Fairbairn, is not derived from a set of directionless tensions seeking release through various bodily pleasures which become altered into socially acceptable behaviors. Rather, behavior is derived fundamentally from the search for and maintenance of contacts with others. The various erotogenic zones do not produce tension that demand release but rather provide *pathways* that afford techniques for seeking objects. In classical theory the development of genital primacy is crucial, and relatedness is derivative. When Fairbairn made intimacy primary, he maintained that the possibility of "genital functioning" becomes the consequence of the ability to relate with mutuality. Relations are primary; the zones are *simply instruments* of those relations. "It is not the libidinal attitude which determines the object-relationship, but the object-relationship which determines the libidinal attitude" (Fairbairn 1941, 34).

If we were to maintain a purely neutral position with regard to the object chosen in the object relationship, would we not argue that it is not the libidinal attitude which determines the object relationship but the object relationship which determines the libidinal attitude within same-sex and opposite-sex relations? Would not intimacy be crucial, regardless of the sex of the object, and erotogenic zones simply the instruments of those relations; *pathways* to the establishment of intimate relations? Genital functioning or the lack of it, regardless of the sex of the object, would become the consequence of one's ability to relate with or without mutuality. Exclusive heterosexuality that results from an inability to establish homosexual relations or vice versa would then be seen as a sign of psychopathology; disturbed same-sex or opposite-sex object relations. Fairbairn, however, did not take this turn; rather he structured anti-homosexuality and made it necessary for heterosexual functioning and mental health.

How does Fairbairn explain the development of object choice? What is suggested is that *all* sexuality, experiences, and fantasies derive from more basic needs and feelings, the by-product of failed object relations. Both parents in the preoedipal phase are embodied as one object in the structure of the exciting object and the rejecting object which, according to Fairbairn

(1944), "plays an important part in determining the psychosexual attitude of the individual." An ambivalent attitude is maintained toward each parent; thus, a positive, inverted, and mixed oedipal situation can exist. However, in Fairbairn's words, "for *simplicity's sake*" the child converts one parent into the exciting object and the other into the rejecting object. Fairbairn seemed to break from relational events for simplicity's sake.

In the Oedipal phase, Fairbairn held, psychic representations of the parents are split according to gender, and the opposite-sex parent is fused with the exciting object—the libidinal ego—making him/her the desired object of choice. The same-sex parent is fused with the rejecting object, the anti-libidinal ego, the object of hate. If this fusion is "normal" and ensures heterosexuality, then heterosexuality is ensured by gendered self-hate, same-sex hate—homophobia and anti-homosexuality—what Ferenczi referred to as obsessive heterosexuality.

Fairbairn argued that if preoedipal object relations are not severely disturbed, the child will identify with the same-sex parent, the now anti-libidinal object, and establish a superego through the moral defense: incorporating the parent's goodness and their choice of object. Here object choice becomes a by-product of a second system of identification, and, most importantly, superego development is assumed to be dependent on and incorporates both parental goodness and their choice of object, one going with the other. It is important to understand that desire, incestuous or otherwise, does not drive Fairbairn's system of oedipal identifications. Rather, the child represses all preoedipal ambivalence, using guilt as a defense against "bad" internal objects. "Guilt originates on the principle that the child finds it more tolerable to regard himself as conditionally (i.e., morally) bad than to regard his parents as unconditionally (i.e., libidinally) bad." Fairbairn used a Christian metaphor to further explain this repression of preoedipal internalized objects which sounds like a description of the rejecting and exciting objects: "It is better to be a sinner in a world ruled by God than to live in a world ruled by the Devil. . . . God's in Heaven . . . there is always a hope of redemption." Although Fairbairn arrives at bisexual desire constructed through a relational matrix, all is repressed by the moral defense, itself a libidinal and anti-libidinal structure.

However, according to Fairbairn, if object relations are severely disturbed, the moral defense and same-sex identification does not occur, resulting in impaired superego development, leading to psychopathy, a heterosexual who is a psychopath, or a homosexual, all of whom are psychopaths. This led Fairbairn (1946) to write that homosexual behavior is an expression of one of the most severe pathologies and that heterosexual intercourse is the natural and normal expression of mental health. He argued that homosexuals are not capable of healthy relations because "the sexual pervert is not psychoneurotic, but a psychopath" (291).

In that 1946 article, submitted to the Scottish Advisory Council on "The Treatment and Rehabilitation of Sexual Offenders," Fairbairn, unlike Freud, argued that homosexuality must not simply be regarded as a perverse expression of natural sexuality. Psychoneurotics, he explained, would rather suffer than give natural expression to tendencies the homosexual capitalizes upon instead of repressing. The homosexual refuses to conform to society, to lead a normal sexual life, to comply with cultural standards. Instead, homosexuals form groups of their own within the community. Fairbairn maintained that the distress homosexuals feel is from their forfeiture of social and material advantages rather than from guilt or remorse and that typically they resent society's attitude toward them. Ultimately, the homosexual does not want "cure," but acceptance. Therefore, homosexuality is the natural sexual expression of a psychopathic personality.

His recommendation to the Scottish Advisory Council was not to imprison homosexuals, but rather to remove them from society and put them into settlement camps.[1] Homosexuals should not receive psychotherapy, since this will generally not be effective; rather they should be rehabilitated. They should be put in controlled environments with a view toward a gradual approximation of the life of the community at large. Fairbairn also saw these settlements as a unique opportunity for social experimentation and a scientific study of social relations.

Fairbairn was obviously anti-homosexual. His ideological convictions ran counter to his most profound and brilliant analytic insights. His psychosocial theory led him to both the particular import of the preoedipal paternal figure (which I will discuss later) and the understanding that sexual desire was not instinctual but socially constructed within a relational matrix. Rather than taking his conceptualization of sexuality with its structural ambivalence to the next step, he broke from preoedipal structure, putting a lid (the moral defense) on all oedipal and preoedipal desire.[2] However, Fairbairn contradicted himself when he referenced the devil (rejecting object) and God (exciting object) and suggested the moral defense is something other than a continuation of preoedipal processes. Rather than hypothesizing a break from established preoedipal processes, I suggest their continuation following the preoedipal phase. I believe that there is evidence within Fairbairn's writings to support my proposition.

Using Fairbairn's understanding of the structuralization of the ego, can we give an alternative explanation (other than "for simplicity's sake") for the fusion of the same-sex parent with the rejecting object and the establishment of the moral defense? Is there a relational explanation for the establishment of heterosexual desire that then also explains the necessity for a self-critical (anti-libidinal), perfectionistic (libidinal) superego?

Fairbairn argued that the boy child maintains an ambivalent attitude toward each parent; in the Oedipal phase both parents are embodied in the structure of the exciting and rejecting object. At this time the father is *first* recognized as a separate object. Although Fairbairn felt that incestuous desires do not play a part in the oedipal phase, he contradicted himself, when he stated (1944) that the child has a need for both parents and that these needs become a need for the father's penis and a need for the mother's vagina: "The strength of these physical needs for his parent's genitals varies, however, in inverse proportion to the satisfaction of his emotional needs. . . . The latter needs are never satisfied. Consequently, some measure of ambivalence necessarily develops in relation to his mother's vagina and his father's penis."[3] Fairbairn then states: "His father thus first presents himself to the child as a parent without breasts; and this is one of the chief reasons that his relationship with his father has to be established so much more on an emotional plane than his relationship with his mother" (122). Clearly, heterosexually speaking, in relation to the father the terrain is far more difficult for the boy than the girl. The girl must navigate through this relationship in the face of the incest taboo; in addition, the boy must confront the homosexual taboo.

Fairbairn states that "the oedipal situation is not really an external situation at all, but an internal situation." Fairbairn had argued that psychic structure is the result of relational events, yet here in the oedipal he retreats to the internal world. I believe that if we accept Fairbairn's proposition that the instinct is object seeking and that the psyche is structured through failed relations, the oedipal is as much an external situation as the preoedipal.

Then, to continue Fairbairn's logic, in the oedipal phase the boy's homosexual incestuous desire, both object and aim, are rejected by the father. This rejecting father is then fused with the rejecting object, the anti-libidinal ego, now structurally anti-homosexual. Alternatively, the boy's incestuous heterosexual desire (the aim) is encouraged by the father but frustrated. Mother-as-object is denied by the father, making her the exciting object, and tied to the libidinal ego. Perhaps the maternal object remains partially libidinal and anti-libidinal and is then repressed by a newly formed paternal object that is either purely anti-libidinal or both libidinal and anti-libidinal. Either way, what structures the newly forming superego is the internalization of the "law": the paternal object which creates internalized ambivalence, where objects are split and structured as good and bad. Regardless of whether the maternal and paternal objects are purely libidinal and anti-libidinal or remain a mixture of both, the superego is structured in part by the repudiation of homosexual desire. In this process the boy first realizes that he cannot "have" father and moves toward "being" father, an identification born in object love and resulting in rejection. Not being able to "be" father, the boy moves toward becoming "like" the father. In so doing, the boy further identifies with the father, another identification born in object love which now results in frustration. What results is a superego built upon identifications with the aggressor, born of frustrations and prohibitions.

Like Freud, Fairbairn posits an oedipal situation arising from bisexual desire. Whereas Freud argued for constitutional dispositions (masculinity, femininity), Fairbairn argued that bisexual desire (for the father's penis and mother's vagina) is the result of failed relations. I believe this is why Fairbairn is so important. Whereas Freudians, Kleinians, and currently the French School (Harris 1991) rely on biologically determined dispositions, Fairbairn's theory, up until this point, relies on the social construction of desire through relational events. Fairbairn was concerned with the social construction of the "sexual disposition"—heterosexual, bisexual, homosexual—dispositions (personalities) that are constructed preoedipally, modified in the oedipal phase and then repressed by the superego which then purposes desire through the moral defense. Although I agree that his theory is a model of a type of heterosexual desire, I believe that repression of all preoedipal and oedipal desire by a moral superego can only lead to an empty, passionless type of heterosexuality.

In Kernberg's (1988) view, there are three important factors to passionate sexual love. The first is skin eroticism, which is the result of gratifying (valued) bodily stimulation in early dyadic relations. The second is the important component of aggression in sex play. And third is the understanding that the perverse components of sexual play—fellatio, cunnilingus, anal penetration, as well as exhibitionistic, voyeuristic, sadistic, and masochistic sexual games—maintain their erotic intensity because they activate unconscious fantasies regarding oedipal and pre-oedipal relations. He states: "A corollary of this idea is that the traditional psychoanalytic view of perversion needs to be reexamined, and that the definition of perversion as a pathological psychological structure may have to be revised. I think perversions should be defined more narrowly as the obligatory, habitual restriction of sexual fantasies and activities to one particular sexual component" (1988, 65). In this light, I argue that Fairbairn's theory, as it is, gives us a model for a melancholic, perverse, anti-homosexual heterosexuality.

A Butlerian Approach to Fairbairn's Anti-Homosexual Heterosexuality

Judith Butler (1990) provides an analysis of the Freudian notion of masculine and feminine primary, constitutional dispositions which drive object choice. My intent is to use a similar analysis of Fairbairn's notion of a socially constructed heterosexual personality. Butler, using Freud's (1917, 1923a, b) thesis on the psychic processes involved in melancholia and gender identity formation, examines gender identity as a melancholic experience. Butler explains that according to Freud gender identity becomes a structure of the ego through the act of identification. The ego incorporates into its structure that which it loved and lost. When ambivalence existed in the lost relationship it becomes internalized as a self-critical disposition of the ego and ego ideal (superego). I will argue that Fairbairn's type of superego is also "melancholic," perhaps more severely melancholic.

In "The Ego and the Id" (1923a) Freud argued that it may be that the sole manner in which the id can give up an object is through melancholic incorporation, a process that actually preserves the object cathexis. Melancholia, Freud maintained, becomes the precondition for mourning. Mourning and melancholia are no longer oppositions but are integrally related. Freud remarks that the ego ideal, born of melancholic incorporation, is the solution to the Oedipal complex and the successful consolidation of masculinity and femininity, serving as an interior agency of sanctions, taboos, and sublimated desire.

Butler (1990) argues that the incest taboo initiates a loss of a love object for the ego, which recuperates through the internalization of the tabooed object of desire. In the case of heterosexual union, it is the specific object that is denied; aim, both loving and hating, is deflected from that object onto another. In the case of homosexual union, both object and aim require renunciation and become subject to melancholic internalization. This bisexual libidinal disposition was suggested by Freud when he questioned his own assumption that a son's identification with his father is only born out of rivalry. Perhaps the boy must choose not only between two object choices but between two sexual dispositions: masculinity and femininity. That the boy usually chooses heterosexuality, according to Butler, could be explained by the fear of castration, the fear of feminization associated with male homosexuality within heterosexual cultures. It is not primarily the heterosexual lust that must be punished and sublimated but the homosexual cathexis. When Freud suggests that it may be primary bisexuality rather than oedipal rivalry which produces the boy's identification with the father, he makes suspect the exclusive primacy of the maternal cathexis and, consequently, the primary heterosexuality of the boy's cathexis.

Butler argues that regardless of whether the boy repudiates the mother owing to the oedipal drama or because of his bisexual cathexis, this repudiation leads to an identification with the father. According to Freud, this repudiation becomes the founding moment of gender consolidation. The boy internalizes the lost mother through identification with her and displaces his heterosexual attachment. In so doing, he fortifies his attachment to his father, consolidating his masculinity. If, however, he also renounces heterosexual aim, he internalizes his mother and sets up a feminine superego which dissolves masculinity and consolidates feminine libidinal dispositions. Interestingly, as Butler points out, in such a system there is no homosexuality: only opposites attract. Freud's bisexuality is two heterosexual desires within one psyche; the libidinal cathexis to father is feminine and to mother it is masculine. Masculine consolidation cannot occur with father as love object.

Butler points out that in Freud's system of gender identity formation, through the taboo on incest and homosexuality one internalizes same-sexed object love, both aim and object, and thus preserves unresolved, ambivalent, same-sexed object relations. Thus, the stricter and more stable the gender affinity and the more rigid the need and demand for gender boundaries, the less resolved the original loss. If gender identity remains melancholic, consistent obsessive application of taboos in the production and disposition of sexual desire will maintain compulsive heterosexuality. Thus, Butler argues, dispositions (masculine or feminine) are not primary sexual facts of the psyche, but are produced by the law imposed by one's culture: the prohibition against homosexuality and the incest taboo: "The dispositions which are presumed to be primary or constitutive fact of sexual life are effects of a law, which, internalized, produces and regulates discrete gender identity and heterosexuality" (1990).

Gender, Butler argues, is socially constructed and not the result of primary dispositions. The incest taboo and the taboo against homosexuality presume an original desire localized in the notion of primary dispositions, which, owing to the repression of homosexual libido, produce displaced heterosexual desire. Freud's sexual dispositions are said to be prediscursive, temporally primary, and ontologically discrete drives which have a meaning before their emergence into language and culture. Culture deflects these desires from their original meanings; thus desire is a series of displacements producing heterosexuality. In the Freudian system, homosexuality, then, is a sign of failed repression, displacement, and development rather than produced by culture, by the very law that is said to repress it.

Using the work of Abraham and Torok (1980), Butler then differentiates between introjection, where the object is not only lost but acknowledged as lost serving the work of mourning, and incorporation which denotes a magical resolution of loss and which maintains the state of disavowal or suspended grief.

Through introjection, the possibility of metaphorical signification is founded; incorporation is anti-metaphorical, the loss remains unnameable, disavowed. Melancholic gender identity, where there is a fixity, is the result and maintenance of incorporative, antimetaphorical processes. Incorporation literalizes the body and so appears as facticity; the body comes to bear "sex" as a literal truth and pleasure becomes localized and prohibited to certain erotogenic zones. Literalization forfeits the imaginary and with it an imaginable homosexuality.

In the case of heterosexual identity established through the heterosexual incest taboo, loss is borne as grief; object is lost and aim is displaced. In the case of heterosexual identity established through the homosexual taboo, loss is sustained through a melancholic structure. "The object is not only lost but the desire fully denied such that 'I never lost that person and I never loved that person, indeed never felt that kind of love at all'" (Butler 1990). Women-as-object become for the melancholic heterosexual male the sign that he not only never felt homosexual desire but also that there is no grief over its loss; women-as-object become necessary for the maintenance of such denial. This disavowed male homosexuality culminates in a heightened or consolidated masculinity, one which maintains the feminine as the unthinkable.

Butler problematizes the assumption that gender is a primary disposition which leads to heterosexual desire. She argues that gender is socially constructed by the law imposed by one's culture: prohibitions against homosexuality and incest. However, these taboos presume the existence of both homosexual and incestuous desires which are said to be prior to the law. In so doing, Butler is arguing that from a state of ambivalence both heterosexual and homosexual incestuous desire is produced by the very law that forbids them. However, Butler argues, homosexual desire becomes that which is denied, making it part of a melancholic incorporative process, while heterosexual desire is displaced.

Although sexuality, in Fairbairn's theory, is not primary, it remains a component part of psychic structure. Structural ambivalence, bisexual desire, which was suggested by Freud, is central to Fairbairn's theory of endopsychic structure. As stated earlier, the boy internalizes the father's rejection of his desire. Thus the father becomes the rejecting object, the anti-libidinal ego, the anti-homosexual ego, and the mother becomes the exciting object, the libidinal ego. As Butler has argued, this anti-homosexual ego is a melancholic ego and for the boy ambivalent same-sex object relations are internalized through the process of incorporation. However, the libidinal ego, the maternal object, is also a melancholic ego; in Fairbairn's theory heterosexual incestuous desires are also not displaced.

Interestingly, while both the libidinal and anti-libidinal ego are repressed by the ego ideal, the libidinal ego is further repressed by the anti-libidinal ego, resulting in a greater measure of repression. And this dual attack upon the object of the libidinal ego, the primary maternal object, does nothing to loosen its melancholic tie. To the contrary, this dual attack actually serves to perpetuate the attachment to the primary maternal object, perhaps even strengthening it. To Fairbairn, this obstinate attachment of the libidinal ego to the exciting object and its reluctance to renounce its object constitutes a formidable source of resistance. In this lies the key to psychopathology.

Clearly then, it would have to be argued, the stronger the anti-libidinal ego, the greater the attachment of the libidinal ego to the exciting object, the primary maternal object, and therefore the greater the anti-homosexuality, the greater the psychopathology. The stricter and more stable the anti-homosexuality or heterophilia and the more rigid the need and demand for the strict enforcement of taboos, the less resolved are the oedipal losses. Vice versa, if the central ego weakens, and the need that emerges is for the primary maternal object, the greater will be the need for the strengthening of the anti-homosexual ego, the anti-libidinal ego.

What then structures heterosexuality is not the displacement of the heterosexual incestuous desire, but the renunciation of homosexual desire, which holds in repression the primary maternal object. Anti-homosexuality, an aspect of the anti-libidinal ego, helps repress the primary maternal object. It is this melancholic superego of sanctions, taboos, and perfectionistic strivings that is built upon the melancholic incorporative solution of oedipal desires which consolidates heterosexuality. It is the identification with the rejecting anti-homosexual father that holds maternal identifications in place. Thus, heterosexuality is not only a product of a melancholic superego that disavows primary maternal identifications but disavows homosexuality. Therefore, heterosexuality becomes both obsessional and compulsive, maintained by the strength of anti-homosexual thoughts and ensured by heterosexual behavior. To be anti-homosexual denies the possibility of homosexual desire or the possibility of homosexual relatedness; to act heterosexually denies homosexuality. In this type of melancholic sexual identity which disavows homosexual desire and literalizes the body, sex becomes a literal truth and pleasure becomes localized and rigidly defined. Or as Fairbairn (1946) states: "Genital intercourse becomes the sign of mental health."

This type of superego-directed heterosexuality, which is called "normal," may be typical but is it "healthy"? It is this "normal" melancholic, obsessive-compulsive heterosexuality, that not only legitimizes the privileging of masculinity and makes it the domain of the male, through literalization, but of necessity allocates femininity to women and marries this dualism to heterosexual object choice. In other words, being feminine, being the object of desire, "signifies" the desire of the other, which is the object of heterosexual masculine desire and the site of masculine self-elaboration, the site of penetration. In masculinity, men, the subject of desire, are dependent on those who are the object. This is an interdependency developed between subject and object for signification, the Hegelian structure of failed reciprocity between master and slave. Butler asks if masculinity and femininity are a masquerade to disguise bisexual possibilities that might otherwise disrupt a seamless construction of a heterosexual femininity—to which I add a heterosexual masculinity. A woman who has lost her desire for the vagina or her identification with the father through a melancholic process becomes psychically dependent on men, in that this woman can only have power through reflection, through being penetrated, a form of masochism. Men who have lost or disavowed their desire for the penis and are phobic to being penetrated, men who have lost their identification with the mother through a melancholic process, become psychically dependent on their power being reflected through penetration, a form of sadism.

From this melancholic system emerges compulsive heterosexuality, a heterosexuality that cannot tolerate any hint of homosexuality (Freud 1940). For homosexuality represents for the anti-homosexual a loss of power, privilege, hierarchical structure, and a loss of self. This melancholic compulsive heterosexuality depends on sadomasochistic power dynamics, in that the paternal object attacks and represses the maternal object. This is an anti-homosexuality that, as Freud argued in the Schreber case (1911), depends upon paranoiac processes and primitive defenses (Grotstein 1985). In this system, heterosexuality is dependent on the maintenance of sadomasochistic power dynamics and homosexuality comes to represent the loss of individuation. This system is dependent on misogyny and anti-homosexual prejudices where homosexuality is both present and forbidden. To be clear, not all heterosexuality is dependent on anti-homosexuality, heterophilia, and sadomasochistic power dynamics. Heterosexuality that is based on a system of eroticization which favors opposite-sexed attractions and is not rigid, and allows for multiple gendered and sexual self experiences, need not be anti-homosexual or heterophilic. However, where there is a fixity in sexual identity, a literalization of the body, and anti-homosexual and sadomasochistic power dynamics are employed to ensure sexual functioning, then the psyche is structured by splitting, *idealization* (exciting objects), and *devaluation* (rejecting objects), and through incorporative mechanisms.

Universal claims and generalization are clearly problematic, but, as O'Connor and Ryan (1993) have said, "If any generalization might be appropriate, it would be in the area of the structuring of lesbian oppression, rather than anything supposedly inherent in lesbians." This applies to the structuring of all homosexual oppression: what I call anti-homosexuality. And I would argue that presently in Western Judeo-Christian cultures it is upon this structure that prejudices are superimposed. Misogyny, anti-Semitism, racism, etc. are products of a weakened ego, a paranoid ego that splits good and bad, a melancholic ego and superego based in the incorporation of the rejecting object and the exciting object—the moral defense. Prejudices are dependent upon the projection of the bad object as an unconditionally bad other (the Devil: the rejected object which is morally bad) and the introjection of the good object (God: the frustrating and therefore exciting object), making oneself only conditionally bad. Thus, owing to cultural proscriptions and prohibitions, it is upon this first anti-libidinal, anti-homosexual- or heterophilic-structured superego that all other prejudices are structured and maintained.

Grotstein (1985) states that splitting is basic to all future defense mechanisms and in and of itself is not pathological. Differentiation is only possible through splitting. Pathological splitting, however, is the process by which one aspect of the split object is idealized, and the other aspect of the split is devalued. This process, the process upon which Fairbairn maintained that heterosexuality is guaranteed, weakens the ego, and other primitive defenses—such as denial, omnipotence, omniscience, fusion, paranoid fears of being poisoned or destroyed, projection of the bad object, and introjection of the good object—are relied upon to maintain psychic equilibrium. It is through an awareness of oneself being biologically "sexed," the culturally determined and ascribed meanings of gender, and these pathological defenses that the renunciation of both bi-genderedness (masculinity and femininity) and bisexuality (desire for the penis and vagina) is established and then in adulthood maintained. It is upon these pathological defenses, which result from not-good-enough maternal and paternal dyadic figures, that anti-homosexual prejudices rest. A Fairbairnian structure fuses one parent with the anti-libidinal ego and the other with the libidinal ego, then projects this bad object, a destructive, hating, unrelated object, onto one "form of desire" (homosexual) and introjects the good object, or "form of desire," and claims a unity of desire.

Alternatively, Butler (1990) points to a system of identification that emerges from psychoanalytic theory in which "multiple and coexisting identifications produce conflicts, convergences, and innovative dissonances within gender configurations which contest the fixity of masculine and feminine placements with respect to the paternal law. In effect, the possibility of multiple identifications (which are not finally reducible to primary or founding identifications that are fixed within masculine and feminine positions) suggest that the Law is not deterministic and that 'the' law may not even be singular" (67). Although Butler does not describe it as such, this system could result from a gendered and sexual self that is established through a mourning process: a grieving for the loss of both the homosexual and heterosexual object that is derived through the "law" displacing both the heterosexual and homosexual aim, thus making them both metaphorical and imaginable.[4]

In summary, Fairbairn's model of heterosexual identity formation may be a model which sometimes structures heterosexual desire. However, his model more specifically lends itself to an understanding of anti-homosexuality and heterophilia in men. Herein a paternal figure is not experienced as present until the oedipal phase and is then experienced as rejecting, resulting in a type of narcissistic psychopathology (Kaftal 1991) that structures anti-homosexuality and heterophilia in *both* heterosexual and homosexual men. What was thought to be the psychopathology of homosexual men can very well be the "primitive process" of anti-homosexuality in both heterosexual and homosexual men.

A Move Toward a Different View of Development[5]

I maintain that there is the possibility of there being present a primary but not exclusive preoedipal paternal figure. By positing the existence of nonexclusive primary internalized paternal relations along with, but separate from, primary internalized maternal relations, a system of endopsychic dyadic internalized relations develops within which a system of desire is born. This system would then inform gender awareness and transform the oedipal situation, which would lead to superego formation.

Fairbairn argued that both the male and female child have an exclusive primary maternal object. The father is not seen as a separate object until the oedipal stage. Fairbairn (1944), as stated earlier, contradicts himself theoretically when he astutely acknowledges this differentiation on the part of the child: "His father thus first presents himself to the child as a parent without breasts; and this is one of the chief reasons that his relationship with his father has to be established so much more on an emotional plane than his relationship with his mother" (122). This is an obvious reference to both the person of the father as a separate, external relational figure and the differentiated internal experience of the infant. Fairbairn could have taken this observation and moved into complex and interesting directions, but instead he denudes the dyadic father through a system of layering and fusion, thus positing the exclusivity of the primary maternal figure, a view which ignores the distinct import (Benjamin 1988; Kaftal 1991) of the preoedipal paternal figure.

Although issues of object choice and anti-homosexuality are not addressed in psychoanalytic literature, there is both a documentation (Abeline 1980; Benjamin 1988; Blos 1974) and an underestimation of the importance of the preverbal dyadic relation between the paternal figure and son. Without such a relationship the boy is raised with a pervasive experience of *otherness*, which sets the stage for complex narcissistic psychopathology, aggression, threats, and competitiveness between men—what Ferenczi referred to as obessive heterosexuality—rather than affection, support, and cooperation (Kaftal 1991). If this paternal dyadic relationship is failed, "not good enough," then an anti-homosexual attitude—hate, destructiveness, and rage—results and supports attacks on those who offer the possibility or hope of intimacy between men. Further, what results is the exclusive and primary maternal object-relational endopsychic structure which Fairbairn clearly described—a structure that sets the stage for complex narcissistic psychopathology which effects relations between men, but also, as I have argued, for an obsessive-compulsive heterosexuality that affects relations between these men and women. This anti-homosexual attitude can take the form of intraphysic and interpersonal anti-homosexuality in the adult heterosexual or homosexual man.

Infant research shows (Stern 1985) that the infant can differentiate mother from other and that this differentiation results in a complicated system of object-relational endopsychic processes. One set of dyadic relations are internalized through the process of identification with the maternal figure, and another set of dyadic relations are internalized with regard to the paternal figure. This model, based upon differentiated objects, can incorporate Fairbairn's ideas regarding the instinct as object seeking and the social construction of intraphysic structure through relational events. Yet it sets aspects of the ego that relate to the dyadic paternal internalized relations apart from the dyadic maternal internalized relations.

As stated earlier, Fairbairn held that this system of internalization continues and that in the Oedipal stage the boy child must identify with the father and in so doing develops both the superego and proper object choice. In Fairbairn's model, if disidentification with the mother does not occur, the boy is believed to not have separated from mother, remained dependent on a primary identification, and will not develop a superego. Jessica Benjamin (1991), however, posits instead that the boy does not have to disidentify with the mother to separate from her and identify with the father. Identification with the mother can be maintained and be an integrated part of the identification with the father.

Benjamin assumes that identification with the maternal object precedes identification with the paternal object. Rather, I would argue that identification is a process dependent on the differentiation and internalization of both the maternal and paternal objects. Identification becomes possible only when differentiation occurs, when the paternal object can be background to the maternal object and vice versa, which in turn leads to the object being experienced as external.

Mikkel Borch-Jacobsen (1988) argues that identification is a primordial tendency: "What comes first is a tendency toward identification, a primordial tendency which gives rise to a desire. . . . Identification brings the desiring subject into being, and not the other way around." Identification predates the subject which is born of this mimetic tendency. Benjamin (1991) states, however, that "identification becomes an important basis of the love of the other: it is not so much the opposite of object love as an important precursor and ongoing constituent of it."

Therefore, rather than necessary for superego development, disidentification with the mother or father is a defensive process, possibly resulting in a type of hypermasculinized or hyperfeminized character structure. This is an assumption that may provide the opening which is needed to begin a psychoanalytic dialogue on the violence of men toward women. Perhaps the identificatory process and superego development can best be understood in terms of the maintenance of a state of tension between a multiplicity of dyadic maternal and paternal relations and the triadic maternal and paternal internalized relations and identifications: "Multiple identifications . . . can constitute a nonhierarchical configuration of shifting and overlapping identifications that call into question the primacy of any univocal gender attribute" (Butler 1990).

Feminist critics, while problematizing hierarchy by focusing on maternal identifications, have tended to reinforce the binary heterosexist framework of gender as masculine or feminine. For example, the idea of "gender identity disorder" as formulated by Coates, Friedman, and Wolfe (1991) is clearly an example of the feminist heterosexist problemization of gender. The focus falls on boys and girls who are cross-gender identified. A gender identity disordered boy is said to have not separated (disidentified) from his mother which would allow him to identity with his father. His identification with his mother leads to a desire (literally) to have his penis removed. Could we not argue that what might have occurred is a renunciation of an identification with the father rather than a failure to disidentify with the mother? It is argued that for the boy, identification with the father, dependent on a renunciation of identifications with the mother, is valued and leads to proper gender-identity formation and heterosexual object choice. If instead we assume that maintaining an identification with father and mother is important to the separation and individuation process (making the child "like" and "not like" each parent), then disidentification with *either* would be problematic. Then, gender-identity disorder would include hypermasculinity (a disidentification with mother) and hyperfemininity (a disidentification with father) in either boy or girl. The problematizing of just hyperfemininity in boys and hypermasculinity in girls supports culture-bound prejudices. Hypermasculinity in boys due to a renunciation of identifications with the mother may be the bedrock for male violence against women.[6]

I argue, as does Benjamin, that the internalization of maternal and paternal dyadic relations into the internal world is a precursor to the oedipal situation when they are set in tension with each other. In this case, neither of the two identifications needs to be renounced; rather, an ambivalent attitude is tolerated toward each, using each in an effort to separate from the other, thus resulting in a fluid superego (Goldner 1991; Harris 1991) that integrates multiple-object relations and allows flexibility between the superego and ego.

I suggest that the oedipal complex begins when intrapsychic triangulation occurs, identificatory love and rivalry are set in motion, and exclusion (the primal scene) becomes part of awareness. Oedipal resolution occurs when this state of tension and exclusion can be tolerated and not resolved. Further, oedipal failure occurs when splitting takes over and idealization and devaluation determine maternal and paternal identifications and adult object choice. That culture supports one outcome over another does not lessen the defensive nature of the splitting, but rather supports its denial. As I have stated earlier, such defensive splitting has also structured culturally sanctioned misogyny which has been uncritically incorporated into psychoanalytic theory.

It has been assumed that for the male, masculinity, which is idealized, ensures his heterosexuality, and femininity, which is typically devalued, ensures female heterosexuality; homosexuality results from some system of trauma-based misidentification (Friedman 1988). Recently, many of the unchallenged assumptions about this system of gender identification have been problematized and brilliantly deconstructed by Benjamin (1991), Dimen (1991), Goldner (1991), and Harris (1991), providing a much richer and in-depth understanding of gender.

Dimen (1991) calls to question the notion that it is through gender that difference first emerges from sameness. She argues that rather it is the self-other distinction, amongst other things, that "registers the figure of absolute difference against a ground of seamless sameness." Here, gender seals the distinction rather than creates it, as suggested by the French School. Dimen juxtaposes difference and sameness and gives them equal weight, generating a paradox and possibly accounting for the strange and familiar, the "like" and "not-like" of recognition one finds in desire and in love. Having opened the possibility that psychic structure may rest on something other than the recognition of sex difference, Dimen has opened gender identity to "play."

Harris (1991) calls attention to the fact that while the French psychoanalytic school called attention to and critiqued Lacanian phallic monism (Chassequet-Smirgel 1966), it has put in its place biologically based feminine and masculine drives, securing "difference" in the biological and defining perversion as that which refuses "difference." Harris suggests a Winnicottian notion of play as normal versus rigidity as pathological where perversion is the enactment of a rigidly programmatic and fetishistic gender identity and object relation—a refusal of fluidity in respect to sex and identity. Both Dimen and Harris challenge the exclusivity of the primary maternal object. Instead of gender difference, maternal and paternal object differentiation and identification provide the basis for differentiation, thus creating the internal space for gender identity and object-relations "play." Again, a renunciation of either would collapse this space, leading to rigidity, literalization, and perversion.

Goldner (1991) takes an important next step when she challenges the notion that internally consistent gender identity is desirable if at all possible and that psychoanalytic theory uncritically absorbed the culturally mandated ideals of gender coherence, consistency, conformity, and identity which creates a universal pathogenic false-self system. What she suggests instead as a goal in analytic treatment is the ability to tolerate the ambiguity and instability of gender categories or, as I contend, a multiplicity of identifications and identitied selves.

Benjamin (1988, 1991), building on the feminist discussion of gender as a binary opposition, problematizes the conceptualization of gender as polarity, as opposites. Although Benjamin has not included a consideration of homosexuality in her critique of the psychoanalytic theory of gender, her reformulation is "in some ways much more far-reaching than that of other feminist psychoanalytic writers" (O'Connor and Ryan 1993). Noting the way psychoanalytic theory has constructed "mother as object of attachment," "father as subject of liberation," "women as objects of desire," and "men as subjects of desire," she points out that sexual agency is cast only in

phallic terms, a construction of sexuality which leaves women without a representation of female desire and agency. She posits that in the classic oedipal model, gender identity is established through the simultaneous identification with the same-sexed parent and repudiation of the opposite-sexed parent. The repudiation of the opposite sex forecloses more differentiated forms of identification and so interferes with the ability to tolerate and appreciate difference. As the boy defensively disidentifies with his mother, primitive identifications are left intact, requiring further defenses to enforce rigid gender boundaries. Difference becomes that which must be defensively excluded rather than experienced. What is appreciated is likeness and sameness.

Benjamin also suggests a formulation of gender in which the preoedipal identifications are, as Fast (1984) called it, over-inclusive, offering the possibility of continued cross-gender identifications. In this case the inevitable oedipal splitting of gender identifications can later be modified by the reintegration of those cross-sex identifications, thus supporting differentiation without primitive defenses. She argues that what is necessary for recognition and mutuality is being able to integrate what is "like" and what is "non-like" rather than having them simply split apart and placed in opposition. In her conceptualization, identifications with the masculinity and femininity of both parents can be maintained.

What then of superego development? According to Freud (1923b, 1933), the formation of the superego is a corollary of the resolution of the Oedipus complex, where through the renunciation of loving and hostile oedipal wishes the child transforms its cathexis of its parents into identifications with them, thus internalizing prohibition. The threat of castration spurs the development of the superego. Since the castration complex prepares the girl for the oedipal complex, she is said to remain trapped in it. Thus she never develops a "mature" superego and therefore never attains the strength and independence of men. In this process, object choice is formalized. This formulation led analysts after Freud to equate male heterosexuality with proper same-sex identifications and male homosexuality with confused opposite-sex identifications. A corollary to this is that male homosexuals have the "weaker" type female superego, are feminine, and are searching for the masculinity they never achieved.

Loewald (1962) writes of superego formation in terms of separation, loss, and mourning rather than renunciation which, interestingly, prefigures Butler's (1990) ideas about gender melancholia. Mourning is not the process

of disidentification but both a gradual relinquishment of lost objects and also an internalization of aspects of the objects. In the oedipal phase, when the parents are usually present, the loss or separation is not an actual separation but rather a separation promoted by the parents interpersonally and by the child intrapsychically. I would argue that in this way separation and individuation occurs as the child realizes identifications with both parents, thus making it both "like" and "not like" each parent. This entire process is predicated on each parent's ability to allow the child to use them as either the homosexual or heterosexual object. In so doing, the child uses the parents to bridge the potential space which is developing as the child masters triadic (oedipal) relations, thus securing an ego and superego that is "organism like" rather than "structure like"; a superego which can tolerate a system of erotics which is not based in and then fixated upon the perfectionistic and self-accusatory processes Fairbairn (1944) sees as necessary, but rather a superego which, as Loewald (1962) argues, can mature over the life span.

Fairbairn's model of superego development is not a process which intrapsychically results from a gradual maturation of the superego through a complex process of alternating identifications, separations, mourning, and individuation. Rather it is a conformity-valued trauma-based system built upon gender splitting, repression, and intrapsychic defensive fusions, and on the dissociation of previous identifications and desires which ultimately leads to "sexual" melancholia. Culture then comes to support this system and, in so doing, this melancholia blocks rather than facilitates mourning. It is a system which responds to external demands for conformity (Fairbairn 1946) and intraphysic anxieties which promote mandatory exclusive same-sex identifications and compulsory heterosexuality.

Loewald (1962) also writes of another aspect of superego development: the incorporation of parental projective fantasies of the child's narcissistic perfection as well as infantile projective fantasies of the parent's omnipotent perfection. These fantasies, although important for the beginning of superego development, Loewald agrues, *must be* gradually cleared and modified in accordance with a more realistic comprehension of the potentialities and limitations of the object relation involved.

It is interesting that the so-called "cure" for the homosexuality of anti-homosexual adult male homosexuals is based on the fortification of the very type of superego Loewald claims must be cleared and modified. Because of culturally mandated heterosexuality and the marginalization of women and other minorities, heterosexuality becomes for the anti-homosexual homo-

sexual male that which symbolizes narcissistic perfection, and the omnipotent parent is the idealized anti-homosexual or heterophilic heterosexual analyst. Through unanalyzed transference-countertransference enactments, a severe, rigid and easily threatened superego is fortified; sadomasochistic dynamics within both the analytic dyad and heterosexual relations are by necessity maintained in order to ensure heterosexual functioning. As an anti-homosexual heterosexual psychoanalyst instructed me, "An anti-homosexual heterophilic heterosexual psychoanalyst is the only type of analyst an anti-homosexual homosexual man should be in treatment with." Here collusion is called treatment.

A case that illustrates such dynamics is the "cure of Alan" in "Defense Analysis in Self Psychology: A Developmental View," by Trop and Stolorow (1992)[7] and the underlying unanalyzed sadomasochistic dynamics that are brought to light and discussed by Mitchell (1992) in his commentary on the article. Mitchell points out that during the ten-year analysis sadomasochistic dynamics, both within and outside of the analysis, remain active. What Mitchell does not discuss, and what I am arguing, is that Alan's heterosexuality is tied to the idealization of his heterophilic analyst and tied to sadomasochistic power dynamics which incorporate the need to control and objectify both his analyst and women. These cures, based on the idealization of the analyst and the maintenance of sadomasochistic anti-homosexual dynamics, usually fail when the analysis is terminated (Isay 1989) or when the superego matures.

By moving from the genome, sexual dimorphism, ego, and superego rigidity to explain heterosexuality, we can get back to the notion that drives, whether they are sexual and aggressive or relational, always get embroiled in conflict, fantasy, identity, narcissism, passionate object-relating, and reparation (Chodorow 1992). I have deconstructed Fairbairn's notion of layering and fusion and posited a more complex idea based on splitting, differentiation, and tensions. In so doing, we can move to more complex, experience-near, explanations which do not stand on hierarchal assumptions that privilege the oedipal or preoedipal, the maternal or paternal, masculinity or femininity, homosexuality or heterosexuality, but rather value each in a system of socially constructed categories which dialectically help to inform and transform the others. What is created is a state of psychic tensions, centering the ability to tolerate ambiguity, or the more Winnicottian notion of "the ability to play," as desirable.

Perhaps we can look to gender theorists such as Benjamin, Butler, Chodorow, Demin, Fast, Goldner, Harris, and others for a system of identification in which there are multiple and coexisting identifications. This system could include but not determine a sexual self that is established through a mourning process, contesting the fixity of both heterosexuality and homosexuality; a grieving for the loss of both the homosexual and heterosexual object displacing both the heterosexual and homosexual aim, thus making them both metaphorical and imaginable. In such a system, gender and sexual identities are not co-determined but rather co-exist. Sexual desire could then play in a gendered transitional space, and gendered identities could play in the transitional space of sexual desire. I believe this possibility lies in a space occupied by the often ignored dyadic (preoedipal) paternal figure.

Notes

1. Richard Plant, in the *Pink Triangle* (1988) discusses the history of homosexuality in Nazi Germany. In 1933, homosexuals, called "deviant psychopaths," were among the first men housed at the newly opened camp outside Munich at Dachau. Rudolf Hoess used this opportunity for social experimentation. He started a program called "Salvation through Work" in an effort to "straighten them out."
2. Richard Friedman (1988), borrowing from Fairbairn and "identity theory," argued that preoedipal desire is tied to all adult object choice. He argues that gender identity is determined by preoedipal parental relations and that once gender identity is structured (masculine, feminine), homosexual and heterosexual desire is directed. This was an important move in psychoanalytic theorizing in that it gave an understanding of adult homosexuality as nondefensive and not psychopathic, a position which countered that of Fairbairn (1946) and later Socarides (1988). Adult homosexual and heterosexual object choice were now structurally equivalent. Homosexual object choice, according to Friedman, was no longer something that should or could be cured. In effect, Friedman tied the preoedipal to the oedipal—a move Fairbairn resisted—through the structure of gender identity. However, interestingly, homosexual desire according to Friedman cannot exist within the psyche of the heterosexual, and vice versa, and homosexual object choice is based in confused gender identity and heterosexual object choice is based in proper gender identity.
3. This is a system of eroticization that is based in frustration. Desire is often formulated in terms of frustration, failure, and loss. Although I agree that this is a form of erotic desire, could desire also be influenced by and based upon a maternal or paternal relationship that is experienced as sensually satisfying, creative, spontaneous, expansive, warm, aggressive, nurturing, etc., and that is valued but not idealized or devalued? Could these valued maternal or paternal

eroticized dyadic relations then be the basis for a different type of oedipal complex, the triangulation in love relations? If so, then we have various possibilities for adult eroticization. Adult sexual desire could be proactive, based in an infant's valued relations, idealized relations, and devalued relations, or it may be reactive owing to overwhelmingly troubled relations which "explode" the possibility of adult heterosexual or homosexual relations.

4. See Lee Crespi's paper, "Some Thoughts on the Role of Mourning in the Development of a Positive Lesbian Identity," in this volume.
5. I do not hold to the idea that the paternal object must be male and the maternal object must be female. Men and women can be maternal or paternal objects. When I want to be specific to a male object I will refer to him as father. Also, the following discussion will focus on the male child since my clinical work has been with mostly heterosexual and homosexual adult men and how their anti-homosexuality affected their relations with both men and women; perhaps the discussion of anti-homosexuality in women and its effects can best be discussed by someone with more psychoanalytic experience with women.
6. Forty-two percent of all women killed in the United States are killed by their husbands or boyfriends; every fifteen seconds a women is beaten by her husband or boyfriend.
7. For greater detail see Martin Stephen Frommer's paper, "Countertransference Obscurity in the Psychoanalytic Treatment of Homosexual Patients," in this volume.

References Cited

Abeline, E. 1980. "Triangulation, the Role of the Father, and the Origins of Core Gender Identity During Rapprochement Subphase." In *Rapprochement: The Critical Subphase of Separation-Individuation*, ed. by R.F. Lax, S. Bach, and J.A. Burland. New York: Jason Aronson.

Abelove, H. 1993. "Freud, Male Homosexuality, and the Americans." In *The Lesbian and Gay Studies Reader*, ed. by H. Abelove, M.A. Barale, and D.M. Halperin. New York: Routledge.

Abraham, N. and Torok, M. 1980. "Introjection-Incorporation: Mourning or Melancholia." In *Psychoanalysis in France*, ed. by Serge Lebovici and Daniel Widlocher. New York: International University Press.

Benjamin, J. 1988. *Bonds of Love*. New York: Pantheon Books.

———. 1991. "Father and Daughter: Identification with Difference: A Contribution to Gender Heterodoxy." *Psychoanalytic Dialogues* 1 (3): 277–300.

Blos, P. 1974. "The Genealogy of the Ego Ideal." *Psychoanalytic Study of the Child* 29: 43–88.

Borch-Jacobsen, M. 1988. *The Freudian Subject*. Stanford. CA: Stanford University Press.

Brill, A. 1913. "The Conception of Homosexuality." *JAMA* 61 (5): 335–40.

Butler, J. 1990. *Gender Trouble*. New York: Routledge.

Coates, S.; Friedman, R.C.; and Wolfe, S. 1991. "The Etiology of Boyhood Gender Identity Disorder: A Model for Integrating Temperament, Development, and Psychodynamics." *Psychoanalytic Dialogues* 1 (4): 481–524.

Chasseguet-Smirgel, J. 1966. *Feminine Sexuality*. Ann Arbor: University of Michigan Press.

Chodorow, N.J. 1992. "Heterosexuality as a Compromise Formation: Reflections on the Psychoanalytic Theory of Sexual Development." *Psychoanalysis and Contemporary Thought* 15: 267–304.

Davidson, A.I. 1987. "How to Do the History of Psychoanalysis: A Reading of Freud's 'Three Essays on the Theory of Sexuality.'" In Francoise Meltzer. *The Trial(s) of Psychoanalysis*. Chicago: The University of Chicago Press

Dimen, M. 1991. "Deconstructing Difference: Gender, Splitting, and Transitional Space." *Psychoanalytic Dialogues* 1 (3): 335–52.

Fairbairn, W.R.D. 1941. "A Revised Psychopathology of the Psychoses and Psychoneurosis." In *Psychoanalytic Studies of the Personality*. New York: Routledge, 1952.

———. 1944. "Endopsychic Structure Considered in Terms of Object Relations." In *Psychoanalytic Studies of the Personality*. New York: Routledge, 1952.

———. 1946. "The Treatment and Rehabilitation of Sexual Offenders." In *Psychoanalytic Studies of the Personality*. New York: Routledge, 1952.

Fast, I. 1984. *Gender Identity: A Differentiation Model*. Hillsdale, NJ: The Analytic Press.

Ferenczi, S. 1914. "The Nosology of Male Homosexuality." In *Sex and Psychoanalysis*. Boston: Gorham Press.

Foucault, M. 1978. *The History of Sexuality. Volume I: An Introduction*. New York: Random House.

Freud, S. 1905. "Three Essays on the Theory of Sexuality." *Standard Edition* 7: 125–243. London: Hogarth Press, 1957.

———. 1911. "Psycho-Analytic Notes on an Autobiographical Account of A Case of Paranoia." *Standard Edition* 12: 9–82.

———. 1917. "Mourning and Melancholia." *Standard Edition* 14: 243–258.

———. 1923a. "The Ego and the Id." *Standard Edition* 19: 19–27.

———. 1923b. "Ego and the Super Ego (Ego Ideal)." *Standard Edition* 19: 28–39.

———. 1933. "Dissection of the Personality." *Standard Edition* 22: 57–80.

———. 1940. "An Outline of Psychoanalysis." *Standard Edition* 23: 144–207.

Friedman, R. 1988. *Male Homosexuality: A Contemporary Psychoanalytic Perspective*. New Haven: Yale University Press.

Glover, E. 1939. *Psycho-Analysis: A Handbook for Medical Practitioners and Students of Comparative Psychology*. New York: Staples Press.

Goldner, V. 1991. "Toward a Critical Relational Theory of Gender." *Psychoanalytic Dialogues* 1 (3): 249–72.

Grotstein, J.S. 1985. *Splitting and Projective Identification*. New York: Aronson.

Harris, A. 1991. "Gender as Contradiction." *Psychoanalytic Dialogues* 1 (2): 197–224.

Isay, R. 1989. *Being Homosexual: Gay Men and Their Development*. New York: Farrar Straus Giroux.

Kaftal, E. 1991. "On Intimacy between Men." *Psychoanalytic Dialogues* 1 (3): 305–328.

Kernberg, O.F. 1988. "Between Conventionality and Aggression: The Boundaries of Passion." In *Passionate Attachments: Thinking About Love*, ed. by W. Gaylin and E. Person. New York: Free Press.

Klein, M. 1932. *The Psychoanalysis of Children*. London: Hogarth Press.

Lewes, K. 1988. *The Psychoanalytic Theory of Male Homosexuality*. New York: Simon and Schuster.

Loewald, H.W. 1962. "Internalization, Separation, Mourning and the Superego." In *Papers on Psychoanalysis*. New Haven: Yale University Press, 1980.

Mitchell, S. 1981. "The Origins and Nature of The 'Object' in the Theories of Klein and Fairbairn." *Contemporary Psychoanalysis* 17 (3): 374–97.

———. 1988. *Relational Concepts in Psychoanalysis: An Integration*. Cambridge: Harvard University Press.

———. 1992. "Commentaries on Trope and Stolorow's 'Defense Analysis in Self Psychology.'" *Psychoanalytic Dialogues* 2 (4): 455–465.

O'Connor, N. and Ryan, J. 1993. *Wild Desires & Mistaken Identities*. New York: Columbia University Press.

Plant, R. 1988. *The Pink Triangle: The Nazi War Against Homosexuals*. New York: Henry Holt.

Segal, H. 1952. *Introduction to the Work of Melanie Klein*. New York: Basic Books.

Schafer, R. 1992. *Retelling a Life: Narration and Dialogue in Psychoanalysis*. New York: Basic Books.

Socarides, C. 1988. *The Pre Oedipal Origin and Psychoanalytic Therapy of Sexual Perversions*. Madison, CT: International Universities Press.

Stern, D. 1985. *The Interpersonal World of the Infant*. New York: Basic Books.

Trop, J.L. and Stolorow, R.D. 1992. "Defense Analysis in Self Psychology: A Developmental View." *Psychoanalytic Dialogues* 2 (4): 427–442.

3

Countertransference Obscurity in the Psychoanalytic Treatment of Homosexual Patients[1]

Martin Stephen Frommer

NOTABLY MISSING FROM PSYCHOANALYTIC literature is a consideration of the analyst's countertransference in the treatment of patients who are homosexual. This absence is particularly conspicuous given not only the highly charged nature of same-sex desire in the culture at large but also the more recent focus in psychological literature on homophobia as a significant cultural response to homosexual love and the cause of widespread anti-homosexual violence. It should follow then that psychoanalysts would have a good deal to say about countertransference experience with homosexual patients, but this has not proven to be the case.

This omission was recognized more than a decade ago. Kwawer, in 1980, documented the almost total absence in psychoanalytic literature of any consideration of the role of countertransference in working with men who are homosexual:

> For the most part male homosexuals have captured the lion's share of psychoanalytic attention, while the analyst's stance toward diagnosis and treatment is not discussed at all as a countertransference issue. Against the background of rapidly changing social and professional attitudes toward homosexuality, and in light of burgeoning interest in countertransference among psychoanalysts, the absence of any discussion of countertransference in the treatment of homosexuals is considered significant. (78–79)

While Kwawer pointed out this lack of attention to countertransference vis-à-vis homosexuality, he did not offer much in the way of suggesting a potential approach to the issue, and little interest in approaching this topic has been evident in psychoanalytic literature since. Why is this so?

While this lack of discussion may very well reflect a resistance on the part of analysts to fully engage their emotional experience regarding their homosexual patients and grapple with countertransference phenomena that may include homophobic feelings and reactions, this explanation by itself resolves the situation too easily and avoids the complexity that exists in the relationship between homosexuality and psychoanalysis. Countertransference resistance undoubtedly contributes to the absence of a consideration of the analyst's feelings in relation to same-sex desire, but such countertransference remains obscure for reasons not fully accounted for by countertransference resistance or denial. A search for a more complete explanation requires that we consider the evolution of psychoanalytic attitudes toward same-sex desire, and identify those obstacles, both emotional and conceptual, that may actually interfere with the analyst's recognition of countertransference.

Historical Perspective

The history of the relationship between homosexuality and psychoanalysis and the enmity and defensiveness that has existed between them is the result of theory building which has never recognized its own subjectivity. This has contributed to the oppression of homosexual men and women in that pathologizing theories about homosexuality have influenced not only cultural attitudes but the lives of gay men and women who sought psychoanalytic treatment during a time when homosexuality was something to be cured and sexual orientation was something to be changed. The consequence for countertransference recognition during this time is now clear: clinical depictions of homosexual patients and the theories constructed about them served to obscure countertransference feelings in the analyst because the homosexual patient became objectified. While Freud (1905) stated emphatically that "psychoanalytic research is most decidedly opposed to any attempt at separating off homosexuals from the rest of mankind as a group of special character," later, influential analysts characterized homosexuals in judgmental and denigrating ways. Bergler (1956), for example, wrote, "I have no bias against homosexuality [but] homosexuals are essentially disagreeable people, regardless of their pleasant or unpleasant manner . . . [which contains] a mixture of superciliousness, false aggression and whimpering. . . . [They are] subservient when confronted with a stronger person, merciless when in power, unscrupulous about trampling on a weaker person. The only language their unconscious understands is brute force" (28–29). Socarides (1968) depicted homosexual men as essentially maintaining a psychic organization that was borderline in character, never having entered the oedipal stage and therefore lacking a true differentiation of self and other. "Homosexuality," he wrote, "is filled with aggression, destruction and self-deceit. It is a masquerade of life . . . [involving] only destruction, mutual defeat, exploitation of the partner and the self" (8).

Lewes (1988) chronicles the efforts within psychoanalysis to define homosexuality as a disease as well as the clinical formulations which guided technique. These objectifying and denigrating depictions of patients who were homosexual foreclosed any consideration of the analyst's countertransference through masking the analyst's subjective feelings toward them. The analyst's emotional experience became rationalized. In its place stood theory, generated from a positivist conviction, without any acknowledgement that theoretical constructions and the perceptions that shape them emanate from the analyst's own subjectivity. Negative thoughts or feelings in response to the patient were viewed as expectable, objective reactions needing to be managed. Theory in this context served to obscure the analyst's recognition of subjective countertransference because the theory already explained and justified the analyst's experience. This is not an infrequent relationship between theory and countertransference awareness: our theoretical commitments determine not only the meanings we give to our countertransference and the uses we make of it, they also influence our awareness of countertransference in the first place and are therefore decisive for the whole course of treatment.

The conviction that homosexuality is pathological resulted in treatment techniques which attempted to change, with little success, the sexual orientation of homosexual patients. More enlightened analysts challenged this treatment goal, questioning the disease model it emanated from, the rare and debatable heterosexual adjustments achieved, and more generally, the very use of analytic technique in attempts to manipulate sexual orientation. While this point of view is certainly still represented within the analytic community, it no longer has the strong hold it once had.

More recent analytic approaches toward homosexuality have advocated a neutral stance, that is, the exploration of the patient's homosexual orientation within what is thought to be an analytically neutral technique using inquiry as a major tool. Here the analyst is encouraged not to take sides for or against the patient's homosexuality, but to inquire neutrally into its meaning and place in the patient's interpersonal and intrapsychic life. In short, on the face of it, psychoanalytic attitudes toward same-sex desire have undergone a shift, and in this regard homosexuality holds a perhaps unique position within the discourse of psychoanalysis: once considered pathology, it now assumes a tentative status within the realm of normal variation, warranting no particular psychoanalytic consideration or technique.

This point of view has been articulated in psychoanalytic literature by Mitchell (1981). He criticizes those analytic positions that presume the inevitable pathology of homosexuality as well as what he calls the "directive-suggestive" treatment approach which advises the analyst to depart from the traditional analytic position of neutrality by actively discouraging homosexual behavior and encouraging heterosexual behavior.

On the face of it, Mitchell's position addresses those problems inherent in homophobic directive-suggestive treatment approaches. The concept of neutrality invoked by him reflects a less blatantly biased stance on the part of the analyst and should be viewed as an improvement over more harsh and judgmental analytic attitudes toward the patient's homosexuality. One might think that a de-pathologized view of homosexuality would naturally result in a neutral stance, but it is a mistake to assume, however, that the analyst operates from a position of emotional neutrality regarding the patient's homosexuality merely because s/he adopts a technically neutral stance toward it.

Recent concepts of intersubjectivity which have reshaped traditional thinking about transference and countertransference suggest that whether or not the analyst behaves as if he were neutral, the patient is nonetheless influenced by the intersubjectivity of all the analyst's feelings, whether or not they enter the treatment through overt verbal communication. This important shift in psychoanalytic thinking has been characterized by the growing acceptance of countertransference experience and reactions as both inevitable and potentially useful aspects of the personal involvement between analyst and patient. Mitchell's suggestion of a neutral stance toward the patient's homosexuality bypasses the issue of the analyst's countertransference. As in other instances where neutrality is advocated in psychoanalytic technique, such a suggestion speaks more to what is apparent than real. At best, it addresses the surface of the analytic encounter and is reductionistic and dangerous to the patient when the subtleties of the analyst's countertransference experience are not acknowledged and understood. While a shift away from the directive-suggestive treatment approach coupled with a less overt characterization of homosexuality as pathological has tended to characterize the most recent generation of analytic writing about homosexuality there has still not been a corresponding increase in psychoanalysts' interest in or appreciation of the powerful countertransference potential of same-sex desire and its possible treatment manifestations and impact on gay patients.

Trop and Stolorow's (1992) clinical discussion of their patient, Alan, demonstrates the way in which unrecognized countertransference regarding homosexuality may infuse the treatment, even when there is an intersubjective focus. Alan seeks treatment because he is deeply depressed and does not know if he is homosexual or heterosexual. Trop and Stolorow give an account of the treatment in which the analyst provides repeated verbal endorsement and encouragement for the patient's heterosexual behaviors. Homosexual fantasies and urges are viewed as defensive in nature, counteracting internal feelings of danger and self-loathing when Alan is unable to comply with a woman's wishes. When Alan states that the analyst's enthusiasm about his dating women feels pressuring—that the analyst has an agenda for him—the analyst decides to back off but never explores in the treatment or in his discussion of it the possibility that this is so. When the patient feels discouraged and believes his dreams indicate he is homosexual, the analyst never inquires into Alan's dread about this possibility, the guilt he feels about his homosexual encounters, or the fact that they are mostly anonymous.

Throughout the treatment and in their discussion, Alan's homosexual longings are viewed as a means of restoring his sense of self as worthy and desirable. Repeatedly, Alan's homosexual behavior is equated with defensive, compensatory, self-reparative maneuvers while his heterosexual behavior is viewed as a nondefensive, healthy, striving. Alan comes to agree. The fact that sexuality, both homosexual and heterosexual, may be used for a variety of cohesive functions is never brought to light. How Alan uses his sexuality is separate from the questions he brings into treatment concerning his sexual identity, but this distinction is never made.

On one occasion, when Alan experiences intense excitement and orgasm when fellated by a man, he apprehensively discloses this event in treatment, saying that he knows the analyst would never find such activity exciting and must feel sickened by even imagining it. Trop and Stolorow report that "the analyst then interpreted Alan's belief that he was required to feel only what the analyst would feel, and that the analyst would not tolerate any sexual feelings that were different from his own" (Trop and Stolorow, 433). Alan is said to feel relieved knowing that if he were homosexual, the analyst would not abandon him.

The use of the word "tolerate" is of interest here. Clearly, if we learn anything about this patient from the treatment summarized, it is that Alan longs for admiration and approval from the analyst. We know from the outset how much this man sacrifices his own sense of self in an effort to get approval and ward off rejection. How comforting to learn that his homosexuality will in fact be tolerated and that his analyst will not abandon him! What if the analyst had asked Alan how he knew that the analyst would feel sickened by fellatio in a homosexual context? What about it would sicken him? Alan is never helped to explore his homosexual experience or his internalized homophobia in an open-ended way.

The authors suggest that Alan responded favorably to the series of interpretations offered regarding his homosexual behavior, and in the eight years following this line of interpretation Alan has not engaged in "overt homosexual activity." The authors at this juncture speak of overt sexual activity as if the genitalia of the person with whom one has sex defines the nature of one's erotic fantasy life. Moreover, sexuality in this article is viewed as monolithic and categorical. There is no allowance for the possibility that Alan's sexuality is fluid, i.e., both homosexual and heterosexual, serving multiple sexual needs and objectives.

This treatment illustrates well how the analyst's countertransference determines the inquiry and interpretive commentary about the patient's homosexuality in ways that can hinder the exploration of the patient's own experience, reinforce homophobic attitudes, and ultimately function much like those directive-suggestive treatment approaches which Mitchell seeks to replace with the recommendation of a neutral stance.

How can we best understand the countertransference phenomena reflected in this clinical case material? If a broad conceptualization of countertransference is used to refer to the analyst's total response to his/her patient, what attitudes, thoughts, and feelings are Trop and Stolorow unconscious of which result in the countertransferentially contaminated treatment described above?

The analyst's verbal endorsement and encouragement of Alan's heterosexual behaviors, his view of Alan's homosexual fantasy and behavior as thoroughly defensive in nature, and his lack of awareness and seeming interest in what caused his patient to feel pressured all may be understood as a manifestation of a specific type of countertransference attitude regarding homosexuality which consists of an unrecognized heterosexist bias on the part of the analyst in confronting homosexual experience. By "heterosexist bias," I am addressing two related phenomena: (1) the valuing of heterosexuality as superior and more natural or normal than other forms of human sexuality, and (2) the regarding of the world through a male heterosexual point of view that does not take into account the existence and legitimacy of other subjectivities (Green and Herek 1994). Schwartz (1992), in responding to Trop and Stolorow's case material, uses the term "heterophilia" to refer to the overvaluing of intimate relations between different-sexed partners and illustrates how heterophilic analysts may not directly disparage their patients' homosexual experiences, yet may indirectly communicate this ideology in the treatment. The idea that there is a heterosexist bias present in the way many therapists view homosexuality and respond to their homosexual patients is not new, but this subject has not been taken up within psychoanalysis until quite recently. (See Blechner 1993; Lesser 1993; Schwartz 1993; and Kaftal 1994.)

As the above clinical material indicates, countertransference phenomena in responses to homosexual experience need not emanate only from feelings which are identifiably homophobic—i.e., based upon anxiety and fear of same-sex desire. This is an important distinction in discussing the problem of countertransference recognition in work with homosexual patients: Heterosexist bias can operate in psychoanalytic practice independently from what is thought of as homophobia, and the analyst need not demonstrate particularly homophobic attitudes in order for his/her introspection about homosexual patients to be heterosexually biased and therefore ultimately anti-homosexual. Those analysts who do not perceive themselves to be homophobic may view the absence of a countertransference literature regarding homosexuality as reasonable. They may consider the issue of countertransference in response to homosexual patients to be overblown, or based on paranoid concerns which are a holdover from an earlier period in the history of the relationship between homosexuality and psychoanalysis. They are not aware that their responses to patients may be countertransferentially contaminated by heterosexist bias.

My concern here is with the existence of a heterosexual bias embedded in the analyst's way of thinking and responding to a gay patient, even when the analyst does not consider homosexuality as inherently pathological.

There is a need to make clear the various ways in which heterosexist bias may be embedded in the analyst's thinking, feeling, and theorizing about same-sex desire and the ways this bias manifests itself in the analyst's responses to homosexual patients. In attempting to describe the nature of analytic subjectivities which reflect heterosexist bias, it is important to recognize that the analyst's subjectivity regarding same-sex desire is influenced by the gender pairings of the psychoanalytic dyad in question, since gender issues loom large in countertransference regarding homosexuality. In this discussion, I will focus primarily on the psychoanalytic dyad in which the analyst is male and heterosexual and the patient is male and homosexual. This is not to suggest that countertransference reflecting heterosexist bias does not occur in other dyadic configurations, including those in which the analyst shares the patient's sexual orientation, or is female. The male psychoanalytic dyad in which the analyst is heterosexual is, however, perhaps most prone to the subjectivity I wish to consider here. In fact, gay male patients sometimes choose female or gay male analysts in an attempt to remove themselves from the male gender matrix of experience most often governed by heterosexual bias.

Unrecognized heterosexist bias obscures the analyst's awareness of countertransference in confronting homosexual experience, much like those circumstances in which the analyst's internalization of pathologizing theory forecloses a consideration of his/her subjective feelings toward homosexual patients. The analyst's introspection is shaped and limited by his/her theoretical commitments and biases. Kaftal (1994) makes a similar point when he suggests that heterosexual analysts come up against conceptual obstacles in confronting same-sex desire which are not generally available to them in the form of countertransference experience. We can only know our countertransference if we are not embedded in our bias.

The sources of the analyst's bias are both broadly cultural and specifically psychoanalytic. Cultural attitudes mandate that certain fixed relationships between biological sex, gender, and sexual orientation be maintained. Gender classifications based upon sexual dimorphism reflect a rigid binary. Our culture dictates what is appropriately masculine and feminine. Gender styles which deviate from the norms are often met with raised eyebrows, disapproval, and hostility. Gender on the face of it is "felt" to determine sexual object choice, and our conceptions of healthy masculinity and femininity seem to depend upon the preservation of these relationships. Gay men are problems for straight men because they are thought to be feminine. Accordingly, in our male-dominated culture, women are conceived of as the "opposite sex," the most extreme form of otherness, and thus a man who is "feminine" is considered shameful. As psychoanalysts we bring our gendered selves, and all that implies, to the process of understanding the other. Our gendered and gendering selves lead the way to and often guide the assumptions we make about the other and how their sexuality inhabits their psyches in ways different from ours. Whatever it means for a man to sexually desire and love another man, currently, our culture has infused same-sex desire with meanings that have the potential to evoke powerful countertransference reaction. Presently homosexual desire goes to the core of a man's socially constructed self and therefore puts one's total self on the line.

Traditional psychoanalytic theory, specifically oedipal theory, has served to reinforce and promote these cultural attitudes and stereotypes. While not originating as a specific bias against homosexuality per se, the way in which oedipal theory constructs the relationship between biological sex, gender, and sexual orientation serves to rationalize and perpetuate the analyst's heterosexist bias in facing homosexual experience.

Heterosexist Bias and the Analyst's Theory

Most analysts operate with some theory concerning the origins of their patient's homosexual orientation. The analyst's theory is often an amalgam of psychoanalytic assumptions about homosexuality internalized by the analyst, coupled with his or her own personal beliefs, attitudes, and feelings about same-sex desire. This theory shapes how the analyst listens to his homosexual patients and guides his responses to them, whether the theory is clearly formulated in the analyst's mind or only dimly perceived. When the analyst feels uncomfortable in response to homoerotic material which triggers anxiety, countertransference anxiety is readily dealt with by formulating interpretations to explain the meaning of the patient's homosexual feelings. For example, the analyst can explain the patient's passive longings or desire to be sexually penetrated as a defense against assuming the aggressive male role. Given the training of analysts and the disease model metapsychologies still taught to them, there are ready-made formulations for thinking about the patient's homosexuality which one can fall back on when feeling anxious. Theory, unfortunately, is often put to this use in analytic work. Here, interpretations of meaning, which involve the therapist's value system, are used to define what the patient is up to, and help distance the analyst from his own anxiety.

But the analyst's theory about same-sex desire shapes his approach to his homosexual patients even when countertransference anxiety is not at issue.

Take, for example, a recent clinical paper on the subject of homosexuality (Varga 1994) which begins by acknowledging the current climate of sensitization to prejudicial attitudes toward homosexuality. The author states that in both his theoretical and clinical thinking, his goal is to define the dynamics involved in "normal, healthy homosexuality," and to help homosexual patients move toward that healthy pattern. The author then discusses two different paradigms of Freudian theory and relates them in a particular fashion. One he characterizes as the basis for what he calls normal healthy homosexuality, while the other organizes his understanding of what he regards as pathology. Pathological homosexuality is said to be characterized by a narcissistic relatedness which in turn is rooted in a homosexual man's identification with a narcissistic sado-masochistic mother. Healthy homosexuality is said to be characterized by the primacy of a negative oedipal resolution in which "superego identification with the opposite-sex parent establishes a contra sex ego ideal, thus binding heterosexual libido, and leaving homosexual attraction to the same-sex parent intact." In these depictions of both healthy and pathological homosexuality, primary identifications with the maternal figure are at the heart of the homosexual's psychic organization.

Thus one aspect of a heterosexist bias that is embedded in this theory of origins is revealed by a classification system that attempts to delineate healthy or normal homosexuality from pathological homosexuality. Yet what we label as disturbed object relatedness in a heterosexual context does not get spoken of as pathological heterosexuality; the sexual orientation itself is never implicated. In fact, the phrase "pathological heterosexuality" has the ring of an oxymoron.

The conceptualization of the oedipal narrative used here and derived from traditional psychoanalytic theory reflects a heterosexist bias. In it, gender is theorized to be the central organizing principle of sexual orientation. As Lesser (1993a) points out, it is a discourse that is narrowly constructed from a male, heterosexual vantage point by analysts who were all male and, presumably, heterosexual, and then modified to fit all other possibilities. The negative oedipal theory is constructed on the premise that a primary female identification is the basis for the homosexual's sense of self and ego ideal. The same criticisms that have been voiced by women regarding both oedipal theory and concepts of penis envy, female masochism, and narcissism as the basis for a feminine identification, can be evoked here. Until quite recently there has been no gay analytic voice that is experience-near, like the voices of feminist psychoanalysts, to counter the theoretical assumptions that have been offered as fact. Theorizing about homosexuality exclusively from a heterosexual perspective is probably as limiting as theorizing about female sexuality exclusively from a male perspective.

What makes oedipal theory heterosexist is the way in which it conceptualizes the nature and process of identification. Oedipal theory mirrors and further reifies the masculine/feminine binary. In this way, psychoanalysis in general and the oedipus complex in particular has related to socially constructed ideas regarding masculinity and femininity as if they were a true reflection of the nature of human beings. As Corbett (1993) points out, psychoanalysts have repeatedly attempted to locate homosexuals within a theory of gender that rests on essential distinctions between what is considered to be masculine and what is considered to be feminine. Male homosexuality has been regarded as feminine, in large part because of the assumptions of the oedipal complex and the presence of what can be referred to as cross-sex identifications. Butler (1990) has described how cross-sex identifications have often been the basis for pathologizing attitudes in psychoanalysis. Traditional analytic theory has tended to reinforce the polarization of binary thinking that carves up gender into discrete categories of masculine and feminine and forecloses an adequate description of the dynamic processes and interrelationships which characterize identifications.

What are the clinical consequences of viewing homosexual men through oedipal theory which characterizes them as primarily female identified? One obvious consequence is that the conceptual constraints of this theory so guide the analyst's thinking that his appreciation of material that does not fit this frame is ultimately limited. Reports of clinical material emphasize a problematic underlying maternal identification, as do all theories which pathologize homosexuality, and de-emphasize the patient's co-existing identifications. The analyst winds up indirectly confirming for the patient that his homosexuality indicates that he is in fact less masculine or more feminine because the analyst believes this. This in turn reinforces the heterosexist bias in both members of the dyad. What gets lost is the fact that we are all filled with multiple identifications, both same- and cross-sexed, that these identifications are not static, but shift and overlap within ourselves, and that problematic identifications within a given sexual orientation do not implicate the sexual orientation as problematic. This reality calls into question the primacy of any one set of gender attributes for any individual. (See Butler 1990 for an elaboration of this position.)

Another clinical consequence of oedipal theory is that this formulation promotes a heightened sense of otherness in the relatedness between the heterosexual analyst and his homosexual patient, where the male-identified heterosexual analyst is safely boundaried from the female-identified homosexual patient. Isay (1989) makes the point that countertransference problems with gay patients are often triggered by the identification of feminine or female-related attributes in the context of maleness—the fear and hatred of what is perceived as feminine in other men and in oneself. Male analysts are not immune to anxiety and shame about the passive, feminine aspects of their character (this anxiety is, in fact, a necessary ingredient of analytic work) and may feel most comfortable when they are clearly differentiated from their gay patients. This may produce what Kaftal (1994) has described as a treatment dyad between straight analyst and gay patient which appears static, and which is characterized by both a profound respect for each other's boundaries and a lack of mutual affect: the heterosexual analyst appears to respect the fact of his patient's same-sex desire, but fails to inquire deeply into it. The patient, either sensing a lack of invitation to reveal the nuance of his own personal narrative, both sexually and otherwise, or anxious about the possibility of engendering in the analyst less than positive feelings, may feel safer maintaining a more boundaried, distant relatedness. This emotional configuration may reflect a comfortable compromise for both the analyst and the patient. Both may wish to avoid the anxiety associated with acknowledging that the patient's sexual orientation is of some emotional consequence between the two of them, affecting their relatedness in subtle yet significant ways.

Whether or not there is truly some essential difference between homosexual and heterosexual men, the socio-cultural consequences of this distinction strongly influences the dialectic between the two groups. This influence is present in the psychoanalytic dialogue between heterosexual analyst and homosexual patient and is an aspect of the intersubjectivity, whether or not it is acknowledged in the treatment setting. This subjectivity includes the relative status of each man in the culture at large, based upon membership in either a privileged or a stigmatized group. Issues of power, privilege, pathology, superiority/inferiority, male gender adequacy, the dread of being viewed as feminine by another male, the stigma of being gay, may all be part of the picture. The well-meaning analyst concerned with his or her less-than-affirmative feelings toward his patient's homosexuality may adopt a "politically correct" pseudo-affirming stance as a way of putting a cap on his/her countertransference. when these issues are present but not acknowledged in the relatedness between analyst and patient, they ultimately create emotional gridlock.

Perhaps the most damaging clinical consequence of heterosexist bias in the analysis of gay men is that the analyst may fail to recognize that a major function of the psychoanalytic endeavor with patients who are homosexual must include an examination and deconstruction of the social context—the culture's contribution to both the analyst and the patient's internalized heterosexist bias and homophobia. The social context of the homosexual patient has essentially been ignored by psychoanalytic theory, and this continues to be the case in much current practice today. When this occurs, the analyst fails to adequately address the issue of shame which is often present in the formation of a sexual identity that is experienced as homosexual.

The analyst's own heterosexist bias—the equation of the patient's homosexuality with something less masculine, more feminine, less developed, and therefore less good than the analyst's heterosexuality—and the analyst's difficulty in identifying and extricating himself from this bias, places him at a loss in knowing how to help the patient with the very same attitudes and feelings which both patient and analyst have introjected.

Homosexuality and Shame

A development task for all individuals concerns the formation of a positive identity along gender lines. This issue of identity, posed by the question, "Am I an adequate representative of my gender?" is a recurrent one throughout the life cycle. Gender roles, defined by historical and cultural norms, are rigidly integrated by children who by the age of three are cognitively and emotionally preoccupied with gender-role behavior. Children, like adults, are often painfully rejecting of peers who threaten the prescribed norm. Though gay men vary as to when they first recall feeling attracted to other males, many can date feelings which, in retrospective, are clearly understood as homoerotic to preschool and elementary school years. For example, a patient recalls at the age of five being held on his adolescent male neighbor's lap and feeling a physical vibration of excitement, an intense desire for bodily closeness, and a feeling of contentment he longed to re-experience. Soon he began to feel self conscious and ashamed when he felt his parents' discomfort with his behavior.

Recollections such as this one are not uncommon during the course of analysis with homosexual men, although they are often initially repressed or defended against. It is important to grasp the conjunction of the experiences of erotic feeling and shame illustrated in the example above. If male homosexuality emerges within a developmental matrix, and is coalesced by the end of preschool years like heterosexuality is presumed to be, then it must be acknowledged that homosexual adults who experienced homoerotic desire early and more or less exclusively are at first homosexual children. Homosexual children growing up in a society where gender role behaviors are rigidly defined and where gender is felt to dictate the gender of the love object often feel shame, humiliation, and self-hatred if their experience of gender does not conform to masculine gender role stereotypes as well as when their homoerotic feelings are sensed by themselves and others.

There is no other developmental circumstance that is fully comparable to the experience of the child who senses this difference but lacks the cognitive perspective to understand it and the emotional support to cope with it. Racial minorities, for example, who grow up in a mainstream culture that is hostile to them certainly experience prejudice outside their immediate family or community, but they still have others with whom to identify concerning their race. Their culture provides role models and potential sources for positive mirroring. The nature of their difference is labeled for them early on.

The homosexual male child is most often an alien within his family. Most of the time his parents and relatives are heterosexual, as are most of the peer groups available to him. He often adopts the identity of an outsider even before he can label the nature of his difference. When he is able to define this difference for himself in terms of homosexual desire, there is often a fuller emergence of the "outsider syndrome" and the feeling of not belonging: there is a secret that can be shared with no one, and he needs to behave in ways that mask it in order to avoid the pain of humiliation and contempt from parents, family, and peers. These feelings become interlaced with the conscious awareness of erotic attraction and sexual longing.

What happens to an individual's sense of self when sexual orientation becomes a defining feature can only be understood in a cultural context. One's self experience as a homosexual, heterosexual, or bisexual is determined in large part by the social meanings of those labels and the way in which those meanings get woven into one's sense of self. In fact, the actual experience of homosexual love is formed by the discourse in which it is discovered. Whether or not there really is some essential distinction to be made by dividing individuals into categories of heterosexual and homosexual, the cultural reality of these categories is unquestionable. The emotional, interpersonal, and social consequences of these categories of self-representation need to form the basis of any discussion about them.

While gay men may have homosexual narratives which reflect their own unique developmental experiences of growing up gay, it is crucial to realize that they have also internalized a prescriptive heterosexual narrative. The gay man, then, knows well a version of the analyst's heterosexual narrative because he has introjected it as all men do. He knows what he is supposed to think, feel, and how he is supposed to behave because all men are socialized to be heterosexual. This internalized heterosexual narrative coexists with the gay man's experience of same-sex desire. It is the collision between these two narratives that produces the sometimes repressed and encapsulated shame and self-hatred that can characterize a gay man's relationship to himself and interfere with his ability to form sexually intimate and loving relationships with other men. This shame and self-hatred, when it is present, emanates from the disparity between a gay man's self experience and the heterosexist bias that also operates within him.

How is a gay patient's shame and self-hatred to be addressed within the analytic setting? Little if no attention has been given to the analyst's role in helping patients who are homosexual achieve a more positive sense of self, and it is not coincidental that this omission parallels the absence of any consideration of countertransference in relation to same-sex desire. Elsewhere (Frommer 1994), I have described and illustrated some clinical aspects of analytic work with homosexual patients which attempts to focus the analytic inquiry on the developmental experience of the patient, without searching for a theoretical explanation to account for his homosexuality. The thesis of that argument is that when the analyst approaches the homosexual patient's orientation as natural and legitimate for him, the nature of the inquiry shifts markedly, as do the interpretations offered. What becomes primary is a fuller inquiry and reconstruction of childhood experience: the analyst acknowledges and labels for the patient the presence of his homosexual self in childhood and helps him identify, understand, and interpret the self-representations that were formed out of negative introjects and the object representations that were constructed in the context of a hostile and rejecting environment. The analyst focuses on the child's lonely attempts to negotiate a developmental experience in a homophobic setting and the emotional compromises and defenses that were formed in an effort to protect the self from injury.

In order for the analyst to make contact with the patient's child self and attend to, unmask, and analyze the critical dynamics involved in the child's developmental experience which can lead to shame and self-hate, the analyst must be able to consider fully the psychic consequences of growing up gay in a social context which stigmatizes the same-sex desire and marginalizes those individuals who do not preserve the culture's mandated relationships between biological sex, gender, and sexual orientation. In order to do this, he must first be able in his own mind to undo a prescriptive relationship between gender and sexuality. The emotional and conceptual obstacles which blind the analyst to his own countertransference often produce blind spots in the analysis. The analyst, then, fails to locate and inquire into derivatives of the patient's shame and help uncover the basis for it. This also prevents the analyst from engaging with the patient in a deconstruction of the relationships between gender and sexual orientation which have been internalized from the culture, and the ways in which the patient has been victimized by them. This aspect of analytic work ultimately entails the identifying and working through of introjects—something analysts do all the time. In this case, however, the analyst's ability to do this with the patient requires that he first be able to do this for himself.

It may be argued, from an interpersonalist position, that it is not incumbent upon the analyst or even useful for him to deconstruct his own subjectivity separately from the patient. Rather, the analyst need only create an analytic environment in which the patient feels invited to explore with the analyst how the analyst's subjectivity affects the patient. In other words, the analyst need not work through his own heterosexist bias, but merely facilitate with the patient a deconstruction of it as it exists in the psychoanalytic situation. While this point of view has its appeal, and may be a useful route for some analytic dyads, it presumes several conditions: the analyst must be able to truly facilitate this process, which in turn presupposes that he is emotionally and conceptually open to deconstructing his own subjectivity regarding gender and sexual orientation. To the extent that the analyst's prior emotional and theoretical commitments render him blind to his own subjectivity, any exploration of it in the psychoanalytic situation will have a strong "as if" quality. Moreover, the patient must be far enough along in his own relationship to his homosexuality that he is able to identify his own negative introjects as such, and hold his own in uncovering and confronting his analyst's heterosexist bias. This requires that the gay patient have already accomplished the bulk of the emotional and analytic work which I view as the task of the analysis.

Conclusion

In summary, this discussion has attempted to identify both the causes and consequences of countertransference obscurity in the psychoanalytic treatment of homosexual patients. Analysts must be able to recognize and grapple with their own subjectivity in response to same-sex desire if they expect to help their gay patients do the same. The degree to which any analyst—straight or gay—is able to intervene with a gay patient's shame, when it is present, is predicated on the degree to which the analyst has been able to extricate himself from the same internalized heterosexist bias that his patient has introjected. If the analyst is unable to do this for himself, all he may be able to do is commiserate with his patient's shame and self-hatred, but he is at a loss to help him move beyond it.

Note

1. Portions of this paper appeared in an article by the same author in *Psychoanalytic Dialogues*, 1994, 4 (2). Copyright 1994 by The Analytic Press.

References Cited

Bergler, E. 1956. *Homosexuality: Disease or Way of Life*. New York: Hill and Wang.

Blechner, M.J. 1993. Homophobia in Psychoanalytic Writing and Practice. *Psychoanalytic Dialogues* 3 (4): 627–37.

Butler, J. 1990. *Gender Trouble*. New York: Routledge.

Corbett, K. 1993. The Mystery of Homosexuality. *Psychoanalytic Psychology* 10 (3): 345–57.

Freud, S. 1905. *Three Essays on Sexuality*. Standard Edition 7: 125–243. London: Hogarth, 1957.

Frommer, M.S. 1994. Homosexuality and Psychoanalysis: Technical Considerations Revisited. *Psychoanalytic Dialogues* 4 (2): 215–33.

Green, B. and G. Herek. 1994. *Lesbian and Gay Psychology: Psychological Perspectives on Lesbian and Gay Issues* 1. California: Sage.

Isay, R.A. 1989. *Being Homosexual*. New York: Farrar Strauss Giroux.

Kaftal, E. 1994. Some Limitations of the Heterosexual Analyst's Introspection. Paper presented at the 14th Annual Division 39 Spring Meeting of the American Psychological Association, Washington, DC. April 14.

Kwawer, J. 1980. Transference and Countertransference in Homosexuality: Changing Psychoanalytic Views. *American Journal of Psychotherapy* 34: 72–80.

Lesser, R.C. 1993a. A Reconsideration of Homosexual Themes. *Psychoanalytic Dialogues* 3 (4): 639–41.

———. 1993b. The Bias that Dares Not Speak Its Name: Some Thoughts on Why Psychoanalysts Deny Their Anti-Homosexuality. Paper presented at NYU Postdoctoral Program Conference: Perspectives on Homosexuality: An Open Dialogue, New York, Dec. 4.

Lewes, K. 1988. *The Psychoanalytic Theory of Male Homosexuality*. New York: Simon and Schuster.

Mitchell, S. 1981. The Psychoanalytic Treatment of Homosexuality. Some Technical Considerations. *International Review of Psychoanalysis* 8: 63–80.

Schwartz, D. 1993. Heterophilia—The Love that Dare Not Speak its Aim. *Psychoanalytic Dialogues* 3 (4): 643–44.

Socarides, C. 1968. *The Overt Homosexual*. New York: Grune and Stratton.

Trop, J.L. and Stolorow, R.D. 1992. Defense Analysis in Self Psychology: A Developmental View. *Psychoanalytic Dialogues* 2 (4): 427–441.

Varga, M. 1994: The Reparative Motif in Male Homosexuality. Paper presented at the 14th Annual Division 39 Spring Meeting of the American Psychological Association, April 14, Washington, DC.

4

Objectivity as Masquerade[1]

Ronnie C. Lesser

AS PSYCHOANALYSTS WE ARE ALL used to reading clinical studies which are written as if the writer/analyst is presenting objective, irrefutable facts about patients. It is rare that we as readers consider the extent to which the writer/analyst has sifted through all the possible data for the "facts" she deems worthy of consideration—a process which reflects her own theory, personality, and values. Thinking of a case study as objective allows us to retain the belief that what goes on in psychoanalysis is reconstruction, and that the writer is merely recording that process. Dropping the guise of objectivity gives us quite another view: that the psychoanalytic process itself is one of construction (hopefully of co-construction), and that the case study is a reconstruction of one of the participants' view of it.

Consider the following short clinical vignette: Although J. has been involved sexually and emotionally with both men and women since I began treating him several years ago, the form these relationships have taken has varied. For the first few years his primary emotional and sexual involvements were with women, while he had sexual relations with men. Now, his primary emotional and sexual relationship is with a man, while he is also emotionally and sexually involved with a woman. There are a myriad of different ways I can interpret J.'s sexual style: he is compelled to be with both men and women due to a fear of foreclosing any possibility; he fears commitment and the self-definition that would come from it; his internalized homophobia (or, alternatively, his fear of women) makes it difficult for him to be comfortable with either sex; or his fear of feeling aggression and love toward one person is assuaged by his dividing his feelings between two people. While to some extent my interpretations resonate with J.'s experience, they also stem from my belief that there is something "defensive" about his sexual style. It is easy to overlook the extent to which what I view as "defensive" is tied to a normative model. I am reminded of how much I still anxiously hold on to a psychoanalytic narrative that I thought I had long ago relinquished. This narrative has always seemed analagous to being forced to choose a team for color war on the first day of camp. According to this storyline, one chooses a sexuality/gender team in the first few years of life. Playing on this team becomes such an ingrained, immutable, essential core of one's identity that one can never play on any other team again. The heterosexual team is the best one to play on, but even playing on the homosexual team is better than being one of those who doesn't choose any team. What is clear from my clinical work is that few people feel that they truly belong on one team, even though they feel compelled to act as if they do. Knowing that their performance differs from what they really feel causes many people confusion and anxiety, some of which they alleviate by constricting their affects, fantasies, and sexual behavior.

J. is less ambivalent about this narrative than am I: whenever I attempt to inquire about the meaning of his sexual style, he bristles and tells me that my questions reveal my values and perspective. "There are no questions that don't derive from models and your model values monogamy and a fixed, integrated sexual identity," he avers. Even though I know that J.'s ability to have his own point of view and not just accommodate to mine is a hard-won achievement, I find myself bristling. Since I think of myself as a radical social-constructionist who eschews notions of sexual identity as a fixed essence, I don't like having to think about my own conservatism or of how anxious it makes me to consider that what I had taken as a neutral question was really a mask for my own values and ideology. Considering this idea raises all sorts of other questions in my mind: Is there such a thing as neutral analytic curiosity? Would I have asked J. about the meaning behind his sexual style if I had seen it as one that freed him from constricting social convention, enriching both his sexual and emotional life? After all, his emotional and sexual palette has more colors in it than most, and there's no denying that he enjoys all of them. Would I have asked similar questions if J. had a fixed sexual identity, and wondered whether he was compelled to narrow his range in order to have a firm sense of himself?

Does my personal preference for a long-term monogamous, lesbian relationship make me envious of J.'s being able to have his cake and eat it too? Is my envy ameliorated if I take my own life circumstances as the standard, and derogate/pathologize anyone who is different? Does the fact that I chose to present the "facts" about J.'s sexual style early in this paper by describing the sex of his sexual partners reflect my view that desire is linked with the sex of the object, whereas J. might be attracted to people for reasons other than their sex? I think this case is a good example of the ways in which anxiety and indeterminacy both haunt and enrich the lives of all of us who are starting to bring postmodern and social constructionist ideas into our analytic work with patients.

No such anxiety and uncertainty afflicts psychoanalysts writing about homosexuality who have managed to adhere to a view that their ideas about sexuality are facts, objectively gleaned from reality. This objectivist stance was initiated by Freud and continues to be used by contemporary psychoanalysts who write about homosexuality. By taking their own views of "reality" as "objective" (much as I started to do in the case above before I reflected on it), psychoanalysts have been able to use "facts" to mask their own values, politics, and defensive and destructive purposes. The objectivist mask is a powerful one in our culture: who wants to disagree with experts who possess "scientific facts"? What I will do in this paper is argue that hidden beneath these "facts" lies a project infused with ideology, fraught with fear and hatred, and which serves defensive needs.

Freud set the stage for masking bias against homosexuals behind claims of objectivity when he stated in his 1920 paper, "Psychogenesis of A Case of Female Homosexuality":

> The position of affairs which I shall now proceed to lay bare is not a product of my inventive powers; it is based on such trustworthy analytic evidence that I can claim objective validity for it. It was in particular a series of dreams, interrelated and easy to interpret, that decided me in favour of its reality. (Freud 1920, 42)

Yet there was nothing "objective" about Freud's handling of the case: his anger at the eighteen-year-old patient for what he saw as her defiance and dismissiveness toward him led him to retaliate by not naming her in the paper (Harris 1991) and by terminating her treatment and sending her to a female analyst. Nor was there anything "objective" about Freud's interpretations. By viewing the patient through the lens of the positive oedipal complex, he concluded that her homosexuality was a defense against her love, disappointment, and anger at her father. Freud's interpretive strategy resulted in his putting both himself and the young woman's father first, overlooking the importance of the patient's relationship with her mother. Freud put men first in another way: by not being able to imagine the possibility that the woman could love another woman without first turning into a man. For Freud, sexual love between two women was love between a would-be man and a woman. For Freud's patient (and for all lesbians through the lens of subsequent psychoanalytic theory) there is no route away from heterosexuality: lesbian sex is viewed as an imitation of heterosexual sex by *un homme manqué*. Claiming objectivity allowed Freud to think of his interpretations as Truth, i.e., "a God's-eye view from nowhere," (Sampson 1994), masking the extent to which his own values, theory, personality, and privileged position as a man gave him an idiosyncratic lens for understanding his patient. This lens, as it turned out (and as I am convinced it has continued to turn out for many, if not a majority, of gay and lesbian analysands), was destructive to his patient.

An objectivist stance is also employed by Steiner, a contemporary psychoanalyst, in his claim that:

> The perverse solutions to these Oedipal facts of life are evident in the sexual perversions. The fact that a distinction between the sexes is essential to creative intercourse is denied by homosexuals, while that between the generations is ignored in paedophilia and child abuse. (Steiner 1993, 98)

Here Steiner reveals that he has managed to retreat from postmodern, hermeneutic, and social constructionist critiques to such an extent that he has maintained his belief that there is such a thing as a fact. He disavows the idea that what he calls facts are really interpretations, and that he prefers some more than others.

Another recent example of bias masquerading as objectivity is extracted from a debate which appeared in the journal *Psychoanalytic Dialogues* (1993). In an article about defense analysis, Trop and Stolorow presented the case of a man who was ambivalent about his sexuality, sleeping with both men and women. What was a source of pleasure for J. (the patient I presented earlier in this paper) was for this patient the source of conflict and suffering. From the outset of the report it was clear that the analyst considered the patient's homosexuality, which he termed an "enactment," to be pathological and his heterosexuality, mature. In addition, both analyst and patient colluded in the belief that the patient needed to make a choice; bisexuality would not be tolerated. What also seemed apparent was that the analyst's negative attitudes about homosexuality were communicated to the patient, who ended up not only sleeping exclusively with women, but having exclusively heterosexual fantasies by the end of treatment. Not surprisingly, the analyst took this as an indication of a successful treatment. When Blechner, Schwartz, and I (1993) responded to Trop and Stolorow's article by pointing to the analyst's prejudice and the extent to which we believed it had biased the treatment, Trop and Stolorow protested that they were innocent of anti-homosexuality, stressing that it was important for analysts not to succumb to pressure from a political group such as ourselves. They closed by citing a passage from Kohut which reminds analysts that they should always listen to the patient, because the patient is always right. This is used as evidence that they had indeed listened to the patient, who wanted to be heterosexual, while we had imposed our political agendas on the case.

I want to call attention to two narrative devices which Trop and Stolorow—and, as we saw earlier, Freud—appeal to in their comments in order to invalidate our views. The first, "The Myth of the Objective Analyst," is used by Trop and Stolorow in their insistence that there is such a phenomenon as objective listening, and that they are practioners of it.[2] This myth would have us believe that analysts are blank screens, able to reflect their patient's words back to him or her without imposing their own beliefs and attitudes. The second device, "The Myth of the Objective Theory," is used by Trop and Stolorow when they label us "political," thus implying that they are "neutral." Here they assume that it is possible for any theoretical position to be apolitical or innocent (Flax 1992). By innocence I mean the objectivist conviction that our ideas and perceptions of patients, and the theories which shape them, reflect an objective reality and as such are uncontaminated by politics or values. My aim in pointing this out is not innocent: it is politically motivated. My intent is to demonstrate that psychoanalytic theory about homosexuality, and developmental theory in general, are similarly political and are based on the norms, values, fears, and defenses of theorists who have attempted to elevate their theories to the status of Truth. I follow Cushman in his assertion that

> the very act of claiming the high ground of an objective, positivist social science is a political act that obscures the cultural context (and the political uses) of its truth claims. The force with which a theory is claimed to be the product of an objective gathering of uncontaminated "facts" is the degree to which its political roots and potential uses are obscured. As Foucault (1988)

> taught, discourse is power, and with the advent of the modern Western state, the social sciences have become indispensible to the exercise of power. (Cushman 1991, 207)

"The Myth of the Objective Analyst" and "The Myth of the Objective Theory" are derived from ideas about knowledge which have a long history in Western thought. According to Flax (1990), the self-understanding of Western intellectuals includes the belief that it is possible to obtain innocent knowledge by using the proper scientific methods. Those who employ this method are thus guaranteed innocence in their pursuit of a Universal Truth. These claims rest on several assumptions, such as the belief that it is possible to separate truth from prejudice (and here the philosopher Richard Rorty [1993] would say that prejudice is merely the label we give to that with which we don't agree), that the scientific method works independently from and without distorting its subject or object, and that the scientific process is self-correcting (Flax 1990).

In psychoanalysis such notions as the view of the analyst as a blank screen, the admonition that we use evenly-hovering attention, the notion of the analyst being able to free herself of memory and desire, the belief that we can listen to data without imposing our metapsychology on it, all stem from myths of objectivity. Thinking of our work as "reconstructing" the past of our patients is also a derivative of these myths. As Schafer (1992) has pointed out, the idea of reconstruction obscures the extent to which the analyst's narrative is deeply implicated in the psychoanalytic process, making the process more constructive than reconstructive.

The masking of bias through claims of objectivity is not unique to Freud, Steiner, or Trop and Stolorow. Rather, it is endemic to psychology's agenda, since one of its major goals has been to find the "foundational laws of a universal, transhistorical human nature" (Cushman 1991). In removing the individual from her embeddedness in a social and historical matrix, psychologists claim to present Truth that emanates from a privileged objective source (i.e. themselves), thereby exempting it from challenge and removing it from history and politics (Cushman 1991). Postmodern philosophy attempts to show us that speaker and listener cannot be separated from each other: we can not tease reality apart from our categories of knowing. While Western accounts of knowledge have traditionally linked it to an eternal truth, knowledge is now being seen as embedded within social systems (Flax 1992). Since knowledge is not prior to social organization, knowledge is inseparable from politics. Claiming to have an objective theory is a political claim that obscures the cultural context in which truth claims are derived (Cushman 1991). It is to such claims of objectivism that analysts such as Trop and Stolorow resort when stating that they are not anti-homosexual: they're merely neutral observers of homosexual patients who just happen to exhibit symptoms of pathology. Yet, our theories, prejudices, feelings, cultural beliefs, and attitudes about homosexuality shape how we listen: there is no homosexual patient, in this sense, but a patient seen through the eyes of an analyst who enters the relationship believing either that homosexuality is a symptom of pathology, or an alternate way of loving. Since anti-homosexuality is ubiquitous both within our culture and within psychoanalytic theory, it is impossible for any analyst to be unaffected by it (Mitchell 1993; Schwartz 1993). Psychoanalysts who deny their anti-homosexuality cannot evaluate and control the extent to which their views and treatment of gay and lesbian patients are biased and destructive.

I have argued that psychoanalysts have hidden their anti-homosexuality behind claims of objectivity. I will now consider why anti-homosexuality has been tolerated and/or accepted by a majority of psychoanalysts.

In attempting to explain why the United States has not intervened to stop the atrocities being committed in Bosnia, Rorty (1993) considers that this inaction is based on our ability to hate and dehumanize people whom we view as not like us. Thus, the most violent, negligent acts can be rationalized ("that's how things have always been in the Balkans") and tolerated. According to Rorty, people see themselves as a particularly good sort of human being who is defined by clear opposition to a particularly bad sort. What is critical to their sense of who they are is that they are not someone they define as other: a queer, a woman, an untouchable, etc. They thus contrast themselves, the paradigm members of the species, the real humans, with them, the primitive, perverted, or deformed examples of humanity. Rorty describes three strategies which are used to deny others human status, in order to buttress the view of one's own group as paradigmatically human.

The first strategy is to say that the other group is like animals. For example, Thomas Jefferson could have slaves and not think of himself as violating human rights because he was certain that the consciousness of African-Americans, like that of animals, "participates more of sensation than of reflection." The second strategy is to use "man" as a synonym of "human." Thus to be not male is to be non-human. The third strategy is to make a distinction between adults and children and to classify certain types of people as childlike—thus men have said that women are like children and needn't be educated or have access to power; and whites in the United States have said that African-American males are like children and thus can be addressed as "boy."

Psychoanalytic theory uses all three strategies in constructing "the homosexual." The animal-human distinction is used in classifying homosexuals as perverts, driven by uncontrollable impulses which resist being changed into symptoms. This metaphor likens perverts to untamed animals who are not in control of their impulses and contrasts them with "civilized," non-perverted human beings. As long as gay men and lesbians are seen as animal-like, bias and hatred against us can be tolerated and enjoyed.

The second strategy is used to stigmatize gay men because it is believed that they identify with women. Psychoanalytic theory has traditionally stigmatized both women, and men who are identified with women, since being male is considered the paradigm for being human. In addition, traditional psychoanalytic theory pathologizes cross-gender identifications in both men and women. In the psychoanalytic schema, identification and desire are essentially opposed: if one is male one desires women and if one is female one desires men. O'Connor and Ryan (1993) have discussed the way in which psychoanalysis has maintained and reproduced a culturally mandated split between identification and desire. Here the mandate is: one cannot love and be the same sex at the same time. The binary opposition between identification and desire buttresses the normative structure of heterosexuality. As Butler has expressed it:

> The institution of a compulsory and naturalized heterosexuality requires and regulates gender as a binary relation in which the masculine term is differentiated from a feminine term, and this differentiation is accomplished through the practices of heterosexual desire. (Butler 1990, 22–23)

The third strategy, the child-adult distinction, is commonly utilized by psychoanalytic theorists to derogate homosexuals and others who do not conform to cultural norms. Here again we meet bias masquerading as objectivity since developmental stage theorists speak and write as if they are innocently describing universal truths, rather than prescribing local, historical configurations.

Consider, for example, the notion that psychosexual development culminates in an end state of heterosexuality. This is not an innocent description of biology, but an elevation of a particular configuration of human relationships within contemporary Western societies to the level of

Universality. The word "homosexual" was coined in 1892, the word "heterosexual" eight years later (Halperin 1990). While there were obviously always homosexual and heterosexual acts, what was new was the idea of homosexual and heterosexual persons. The idea that one's sexuality reflects an essential truth about one's personality (Foucault 1978), that there are two discrete sexes (Laqueur 1990), or that transgenerational sex is inappropriate are all constructs which are specific to modern Western societies (see Schoenberg in this volume for a more in-depth look at the historical and cultural embeddedness of these concepts). The psychoanalytic choice of heterosexuality as the telos of development is political in that it purports that a local configuration of social life is an essential truth.

The outcome of elevating heterosexuality to the status of telos is that gay men and lesbians are barred from access to the Oedipal Stage. As homosexuals, we don't reach the Oedipal Stage because the Oedipal story is so narrowly constructed that it leaves out anyone who fails to conform to its vision of how adult life should be lived. Indeed, homosexuals can't enter the Oedipal Stage because of the way it is conceptualized, yet this is obscured by theories which state that the reason lies within us. Thus, these theories state that we fail to reach it, or fall back from it, and are thus always *pre*: pre-oedipal, pre-genital, pre-law, or pre-symbolic (Fuss 1993). To be labelled *pre* is not a question of semantics; in Rorty's (1993) terms, it is a judgment of inferiority, of childlike, sub-human status. These designations both reproduce and buttress cultural ideology about homosexuality. As long as gay men and lesbians are viewed as a primitive, sub-human group, psychoanalysts will tolerate and welcome theories which espouse anti-homosexual beliefs and practices.

The imposition of values and politics onto teleological concepts of development is not limited to heterosexuality, but also underlies our ideas about rational thought, the importance of having integrated, coherent selves and gender identities, maturity, separation-individuation, etc. The use of hierarchical stage models reifies this type of practice. It lends itself to the view that those people who don't develop values, relationships, capabilities, sexualities, forms of thought, and gender identities which we approve of are primitive and sub-human. In this context, an anecdote from cross-cultural research comes to mind: When Liberian tribesmen were asked to group pictures of furniture, utensils, and food, they grouped them by function; that is, the knife and fork and apple were placed together with the table and chair. The researchers were surprised to find that the subjects weren't grouping the items in terms of abstract categories (e.g., furniture, utensils, food), and kept trying to reframe the questions in order to elicit abstract thought. For example, they asked, How would a wise man group these items? The subjects persisted in grouping the objects functionally. Finally, the researchers, who were reluctant to believe that the subjects were not formal operational, asked, "How would a foolish man group these pictures?" The subjects then responded by grouping the pictures abstractly (Cole and Cole 1989).

Thinking of anyone as primitive, whether that someone is in a nonindustrialized country, a woman, a homosexual, or a member of a minority group, is to hold up one's way of being human as the paradigmatic version, and to classify other versions as sub-human. Psychoanalytic theories have reified cultural beliefs and values about the best ways to be human to the point that they are elevated to positions of Truth.

When it comes to homosexuality, such reification also serves to protect theorists from noticing how precarious and arbitrary are the boundaries between homosexuality and heterosexuality. Theorists who write and speak about homosexuality seem to want to say: "We heterosexuals don't think about sex all the time, aren't driven to repeat it all the time, like you. Our sexuality doesn't contain destructive components and defenses against it, our masculinity isn't fragmented or precarious, we don't identify with men if we're women, or women if we're men, and if our sexuality contains elements of perversion, they're only momentary, *en route* to procreative sex." Such rigid dichotomization is a symptom of a sexuality that needs to bolster its identity by comparing itself to what it is not, because it is afraid of all that it, in fact, is (Butler 1993). While psychoanalysts are familiar with this type of defensive strategy, termed projective identification, they are not familiar with the extent to which they themselves utilize it in both building theory and thinking about their patients.

Freud spoke to the futility involved in separating homosexuality and heterosexuality in a footnote he added in 1915 to *The Three Essays on Sexuality*. He stated:

> Psychoanalytic research is decidedly opposed to any attempt at separating off homosexuals from the rest of mankind as a group of a special character. . . . By studying sexual excitations other than those that are manifestly displayed, it has found that all human beings are capable of making a homosexual object-choice and have in fact made one in their unconscious. . . . We must loosen the bond between instinct and object that exists in our thoughts as

> it's probable that the sexual instinct to begin with is independent of its objects. (Freud 1905, 11)

Freud also suggested that the question of why people become heterosexual has no easy answer in biology, and merits a psychological explanation.

With these radical words, which foreshadowed contemporary post-modern and social constructivist critiques, Freud spoke to the malleability of human sexuality and its dissociability from biology and nature. Unfortunately, later in the same essay Freud revealed his deep ambivalence with this premise, when he spoke of heterosexual intercourse as the "normal" sexual aim (which should be gotten to at a rapid pace), connected passivity with femininity and activity with masculinity, and laid the groundwork for a normative theory of sexuality that was biased against both homosexuals and women.[3] We might speculate that one reason Freud proceeded in the direction of reproducing cultural biases against homosexuals is that he suffered from the anxiety of seeing "all that is solid melt into air," in Karl Marx's evocative words. Perhaps Freud was threatened by his insights into the constructed nature of sexuality, the idea of a sexuality unmoored from essentialist underpinnings in biology. American psychoanalysts seem to be more frightened of this aspect of Freud's theory than Freud himself, since they jumped on the bandwagon of his most conservative views about homosexuality and then extended them. Consider the ease with which psychoanalytic writing about lesbians has assumed lesbian pathology (Horney 1924; McDougall 1980; Siegel 1988), done away with bisexuality and the negative Oedipal stage (concepts which are central to some degree of tolerance of homosexuality), and dichotomized homosexuality and heterosexuality. In this way American psychoanalysts have attempted to preserve institutionalized heterosexuality and its prerequisites: feminine women and masculine men. If men are men and women are women and homosexuals are homosexuals and heterosexuals are heterosexuals, then we are all defined by what we are not, a clarity gained by the defensive negation of attributes we might in fact all share.

Butler (in Schwartz 1993) elaborates further on the defensive aspects of these dichotomies by positing that gender is acquired through repudiating homosexual attachments. Part of the process through which girls become girls and boys become boys is by being subject to a prohibition against homosexuality (i.e. taking the same-sexed parent as an object of desire). The prohibited object is then internalized in the ego as a melancholic identification. Heterosexual identity is founded on the melancholic incorporation of the homosexual love it disavows.

> Heterosexual melancholy [is] the melancholy by which a masculine gender is formed from the refusal to grieve the masculine as a possibility of love; a feminine gender is formed . . . through the incorporative fantasy by which the feminine is excluded as a possible object of love, an exclusion never grieved, but "preserved" through the heightening of feminine identification itself. (Butler, in Schwartz 1993)

Those who are given the right to define, describe, understand, and heal—the psychoanalytic community—are in a powerful prescriptive position. They determine definitions of health and pathology, proper and improper behavior, and the appropriate objects and practices of love and hate (Cushman 1991). I have attempted to show that definitions of sexuality are never objective, that they're always derived from the political ideology, defensive needs, and destructive feelings of theorists. Psychoanalysts who espouse views of homosexuality as perverted, disordered, or pre-oedipal have for too long been able to cloak their political agendas in objectivity and innocence, pathologizing or politicizing their critics. This masquerade has proceeded through the legitimacy and power afforded those who claim they are taking the high road of objectivity.

Psychoanalysis has done immeasurable and irreparable harm to gay and lesbian patients and analysts. Psychoanalysis as a profession has a responsibility to reexamine its commitment to pathologizing homosexuality; reexamine the defensive idea that anti-homosexuality is confined to a small minority of analysts; analyze the political, destructive, and defensive purposes anti-homosexuality has served; and assess the damage it has done to gay and lesbian patients. Most importantly, psychoanalysis must ensure that it make itself a safe place for gay and lesbian patients and analysts to be.

Notes

1. The title of this article is a play on Joan Riviere's "Womanliness as Masquerade." I have chosen this title in order to acknowledge Riviere's early recognition of the socially constructed nature of gender and sexuality.
2. Spence has discussed a similar idea as "The Myth of the Innocent Analyst," (1987).
3. Harris makes similar points in her essay, "Gender as Contradiction," (1991).

References Cited

Blechner, M. 1993. Homophobia in Psychoanalytic Writing and Practice. *Psychoanalytic Dialogues* 3 (4): 627–637.

Butler, J. 1990. *Gender Trouble*. New York: Routledge.

———. 1993. *Bodies That Matter; On the Discursive Limits of Sex*. New York: Routledge.

Cole, M and Cole. 1989. *The Development of Children*. New York: Scientific American Books.

Cushman, Philip. 1991. Ideology Obscured. *American Psychologist* 46 (3): 206–220.

Flax, J. 1990. *Thinking Fragments: Psychoanalysis, Feminism, and Postmodernism in the Contemporary West*. Berkeley: University of California.

———. 1992. The End of Innocence. In *Feminists Theorize the Political*, ed. by J. Butler and J. Scott. New York: Routledge.

Foucault, M. 1978. *The History of Sexuality, Volume I: An Introduction*, trans. Robert Hurley. New York: Random House.

———. 1988. The Political Technologies of Individuals. *Technologies of the Self: A seminar with Michel Foucault*, ed. by L. Martin, M. Gutman, and P. Hutton. Amherst: University of Massachusetts Press.

Freud, S. 1915. *Three Essays on the Theory of Sexuality*. New York: Basic Books.

———. 1920. Psychogenesis of a Case of Female Homosexuality. In S. Freud, *Sexuality and the Psychology of Love*. New York: Collier Books.

Fuss, D. 1993. Freud's Fallen Women. *The Yale Journal of Criticism* 6 (1): 1–23.

Halperin, D. 1990. Sex Before Sexuality: Pederasty, Politics, and Power in Classical Athens. In *Hidden from History: Proclaiming the Gay and Lesbian Past*, ed. M. Duberman, M. Vicinus, and G. Chauncey. New York: Meridian.

Harris, A. 1991. Gender as Contradiction. *Psychoanalytic Dialogues* 1 (2): 197–223.

Horney, K. 1924. On the Genesis of the Castration Complex in Women. *International Journal of Psychoanalysis* 5: 50–65.

Laqueur, T. 1990. *Making Sex*. Cambridge: Harvard University Press. 1990.

Lesser, R. 1993. A Reconsideration of Homosexual Themes. *Psychoanalytic Dialogues* 3 (4): 639–641.

Marx, K. 1888. "Speech at the Anniversary of the People's Paper," in *The Marx-Engel Reader*, 2nd edition, ed. by R. Tucker. New York: Norton, 475–476.

McDougall, J. 1980. *Plea for a Measure of Abnormality*. New York: International Universities Press.

Mitchell, S. 1993. Introduction to Commentaries on "Defense Analysis in Self Psychology." *Psychoanalytic Dialogues* 3 (4): 623–625.

O'Connor, N. and Ryan, J. 1993. *Wild Desires and Mistaken Identities*. New York: Columbia University Press.

Riviere, J. 1929. Womanliness as Masquerade. *International Journal of Psycho-analysis* 10: 303–313.

Rorty, R. 1993. Human Rights, Rationality, and Sentimentality. *Yale Review* 81 (4) (October): 1–20.

Sampson, E. 1993. *Celebrating the Other*. Boulder: Westview Press.

Schafer, R. 1992. *Retelling a Life*. New York: Basic Books.

Schwartz, A. 1993. Summary of a Section III Symposium Paper: "Refused Identifications, Melancholy Genders," by Judith Butler. *Women and Psycho-Analysis* 1 (2) (Summer).

Schwartz, D. 1993. Heterophilia—The Love That Dare Not Speak Its Aim. *Psychoanalytic Dialogues* 3 (4): 643–651.

Siegal, E. 1988. *Female Homosexuality: Choice Without Volition*. Hillsdale, NJ: Analytic Press.

Spence, Donald. 1987. *The Freudian Metaphor*. New York: W.W. Norton.

Steiner, J. 1993. *Psychic Retreats*. London: Routledge.

Trop, J. and Stolorow, R. 1992. Defense Analysis in Self Psychology. *Psychoanalytic Dialogues* 2 (4): 427–442.

———. 1993. Reply to Blechner, Lesser, and Schwartz. Psychoanalytic Dialogues 3 (4): 653–656.

5

Psychoanalysis and Women's Experiences of "Coming Out"

The Necessity of Becoming a "Bee-Charmer"

Maggie Magee and Diana C. Miller

WHEN A WOMAN SAYS TO HERSELF and to others that she wants, or has, a primary relationship with another woman, she is faced with the immediate acquisition and management of a new, and devalued, social and psychological identity. "Coming out," identifying as homosexual to self and others, is an intrapsychic and interpersonal process through which identity is both *created and revealed*. Coming out is always accompanied by anxiety and by wishes and impulses to hide as well as to reveal. Although coming out has been a primary subject of gay and lesbian literature (e.g., Weeks 1977; Bell and Weinberg 1978; Stanley and Wolfe 1980; Hart and Richardson 1981; de Monteflores 1986; Herdt 1989) and gay and lesbian therapists have addressed the psychological dimensions, developmental tasks, and stages of the acquisition of gay or lesbian identity (Cass 1979, 1984; Coleman 1982; Stein and Cohen 1984; Hanley-Hackenbruck 1988; Garnets and Kimmel 1991), little psychoanalytic attention has been paid to coming-out issues (Gershman 1983; Friedman 1988; Morgenthaler 1988; Isay 1989). This paper discusses coming out issues for women through an examination of papers by Freud (1920) and Khan (1964) and Fannie Flagg's novel *Fried Green Tomatoes at the Whistle Stop Cafe* (1987).

In "The psychogenesis of a case of homosexuality in a woman" (1920), Freud reflects on the universal human tendency to keep hidden from ourselves our own desires. "It would seem that the information received by our consciousness about our erotic life is especially liable to be incomplete, full of gaps, or falsified" (167). Impressed as he was by the forces of repression as well as by the amazing energies produced by loosening such countercathexes, Freud might have appreciated Adrienne Rich's (1980) description of the moment in which she "came out" to herself and filled a "gap" in her consciousness about her erotic life.

> I keep thinking about power. The intuitive flash of power that "coming-out" can give: I have an indestructible memory of walking along a particular block in New York City, the hour after I had acknowledged to myself that I loved a woman, feeling invincible. For the first time in my life I experienced sexuality as clarifying my mind instead of hazing it over; that passion, once named, flung a long, imperative beam of light into my future. I knew my life was decisively and forever different; and that change felt to me like power. (xii)

Rich uses a simple, powerful word for the nature of her attraction: "to name our love for women as love." Psychoanalysis has no concept of psychologically mature, healthy primary love between two women. Historically it has used names other than "love" to describe such attraction, including, a deviation or regression of libidinal energies arising as a defense against oedipal (Freud 1920; Fenichel 1945) or psychotic (McDougall 1970) anxieties; an identification with the father (Jones 1927; McDougall 1980, 1989); a reflection of masochistic pre-oedipal (Deutsch 1932; Socarides 1978) or narcissistic (Siegel 1988) object relations. (For reviews of this literature, see Magee and Miller 1992; O'Connor and Ryan 1993.) From these perspectives, coming out is seen as an impulsive *acting-out* of internal conflicts or deficits and/or as a *resistance* to working out these conflicts or deficits in the transference.

Others suggest that since sexuality is a "private matter," coming out is socially inappropriate and provocative. Elaine Siegel acknowledges "the homophobic attitude of much of our society and many mental health professionals," but sees no necessity for personal coming-out statements (1990, 449). But coming out is not simply a statement made to combat discrimination, nor is it usually a disclosure of private sexual experiences. Most frequently coming out involves choices about how to handle moments of *ordinary, daily* conversation. Even less than other social markers such as gender or "race" (whose supposedly "identifying characteristics" are thought to be discernible), that which is currently called "sexual orientation" is not self-evident. The invisibility of homosexuality forces choices about secrecy or disclosure in all social interactions that go beyond the superficial. A woman must decide whether to reveal; when and how to reveal; how to weigh the consequences of the disclosure; how much time and energy to allocate to deal with the responses in self and other set off by the disclosure; or, if deciding not to disclose, how to manage relationships with family members, friends, and work colleagues while keeping such significant information hidden. Unless an unmarried woman specifically reveals her lesbian relationship, she is assumed to be a single, heterosexual woman. This heterosexual assumption leads to interpersonal confusions and deceptions. But revealing a lesbian identity or relationship can turn an ordinary conversational moment into something extra-ordinary.

Consider, for example, such a simple matter as two women, perhaps casual work acquaintances, discussing vacations at lunch. A woman in a lesbian relationship may avoid having lunch with her colleagues because even in such a simple conversation she must face the issue of *whether to come out or not*. If she attempts to hide her relationship by suggesting that she vacations alone, rather than achieving any protection of her privacy, she may in fact draw more attention to herself and her situation. Her lunch companion may offer invitations for sharing vacation trips or may offer to fix her up with someone. If she identifies her lesbian partner who accompanies her on vacations as a "friend," she hides her primary significant relationship and is still assumed, therefore, to be a single, available, heterosexual woman. She must decide in these moments how much she wishes to establish an authentic friendship with this lunch acquaintance. How much does she wish to give the acquaintance honest information about her life or at least limit how much she deceives her? In myriad, daily, casual conversational moments such as these a woman in a lesbian relationship who keeps silent is doing more than remaining private. At the very least she is keeping a secret; often the secret involves telling a lie.

A married woman may choose not to socialize with work colleagues, and certainly may have private matters, sexual and otherwise, she does not discuss even with close friends. But a married woman does not attempt to hide from family, friends, and colleagues all signs and hints of *having* a primary marital relationship, and she does not identify her husband as her "friend." It is these circumstances, and their accompanying anxieties and conflicts, which distinguish lesbian patients from heterosexual women patients (Eisenbud 1982), not any special quality, quantity, or variety of preoedipal disturbance, narcissistic developmental arrest, oedipal anxieties, or self-disorder—all of which, of course, may also be present. Therefore, for a lesbian it is not possible, as Siegel would suggest, that sexual orientation is "a given that one does not much think about if one's adaptation is, indeed, healthy" (1990, 449). Such "not-thinking" is a psychological luxury unavailable to lesbian women. It may be understandable, therefore, why so many women find that openly acknowledging their lesbian relationship casts Rich's "beam of light into the future," and why their willingness to face the challenges of such acknowledgment releases in many the sense of power that Rich experienced. But at the same time, enormous damage to family ties, friendships, employment, professional advancement, and group membership may result from such disclosure. Such rejections are more difficult for those already psychologically vulnerable, including adolescents. A woman's abilities to develop a positive female self-image, to find and maintain a satisfying relationship, to disclose her lesbian identity and introduce her lesbian partner, and to manage the social and psychological consequences of such disclosures are capacities which in other circumstances psychoanalysts would call "ego strengths."

In Fannie Flagg's novel *Fried Green Tomatoes at the Whistle Stop Cafe*, Idgie Threadgoode has such ego strengths. Idgie is a "bee-charmer," a woman able to get honey from the hive without being stung by the bees. "Bee-charmer" is an apt name for a woman able to move toward love amidst her culture's stinging names for same-sex desire, able to affirm in herself feelings and behaviors which legal, religious, and psychological institutions define as evidence of socially disruptive behavior, sinful character, disturbed or arrested development, perverse sexuality, and disordered femininity.

Flagg describes the scene in which Idgie gets her name.

> Idgie, who was barefoot, started walking over to the big oak tree and halfway there, turned to see if Ruth was watching. When she got about ten feet from the tree, she made sure again that Ruth was still watching. Then she did the most amazing thing. She very slowly tiptoed up to it, humming very softly, and stuck her hand with the jar in it, right in the hole in the middle of the oak.
>
> All of a sudden, Ruth heard a sound like a buzz saw, and the sky went black as hordes of angry bees swarmed out of the hole.
>
> In seconds, Idgie was covered from head to foot with thousands of bees. Idgie just stood there, and in a minute, carefully pulled her hand out of the tree and started walking slowly back toward Ruth, still humming. By the time she had gotten back, almost all the bees had flown away and . . . Idgie [was] standing there, grinning from ear to ear, with a jar of wild honey.

> She held it up, offering the jar to Ruth. "Here you are, Madame, this is for you. . . . I never did it for anybody else before. Now nobody in the whole world knows I can do that but you. I just wanted for us to have a secret together, that's all."
>
> Ruth took her hand and smiled down at her. "My Idgie's a bee charmer."
>
> "Is that what I am?"
>
> "That's what you are. I've heard there were people who could do it, but I'd never seen one before today."
>
> "Is it bad?"
>
> "Nooo. It's wonderful. Don't you know that?"
>
> "Naw, I thought it was crazy or something?"
>
> "No,—it's a wonderful thing to be."
>
> Ruth leaned down and whispered in her ear, "You're an old bee charmer, Idgie Threadgoode, that's what you are." (85–87)

Idgie's courageously sticking her hand right into the hole in the middle of the oak and coming out with honey which she offers to Ruth is a powerful image of the psychological and social situation that must be mastered by the woman who reaches for sexual love or intimate relationship with another woman. She must find her way through a swarm of confusing, dangerous, and frightening social identities: "developmentally arrested" and "masculine" being two of the many stinging names psychoanalysis has used for such a woman. She must convince the anxious residents of the human hive that she is one of them, not an intruder to be feared and attacked.

Flagg sets her novel in the American South of the 1920s and '30s, a context in which it is easy to imagine social prejudice and religious intolerance against female homosexuality. But the film made from Flagg's novel reveals the difficulty 1991 America has portraying a woman who is "normal" and "feminine" and who wants to make her life with another woman. The film clearly shows that "tomboy" Idgie has a crush on "feminine" Ruth. But, unlike the reader of the novel, the viewer of the film never understands that Ruth's love is as early, total, and absorbing as Idgie's. Ruth's early love is censored in the movie version.

What names should be given to the relationship of Idgie and Ruth? Although the film contains no explicitly sexual scene, Ruth and Idgie are more than good friends. Both have loved Buddy and mourned his death. They raise Ruth's son together. They care for, and are taken care of by, their black workers and the tramps and homeless families of the Great American Depression. Idgie and Ruth, economically independent operators of the cafe, provide the nurturing center for the Whistle Stop community. These independent women become female role models for Evelyn Couch as she deals with menopause and marriage to Ed in the 1980s. But because it does not explicitly state that the women are *lesbian*, the film leaves unchallenged the many images of disordered femininity associated with lesbian women. The viewer may wonder if trouser-wearing Idgie is a "latent" lesbian, but nothing in the film prompts the viewer to consider that in the "normal," "feminine," pretty, soft-spoken, maternal Ruth one can also see a lesbian woman in love. The film illustrates the conflict inherent in the coming out process. Unless Ruth and Idgie are explicitly named lesbian, a heterosexual assumption is possible. But *if* the relationship were explicitly named lesbian, many viewers would no longer comfortably identify with Ruth and Idgie. The film leaves Idgie and Ruth partially closeted, thus allowing them to keep their position as admirable feminine role models.

A capacity for "bee-charming" is also essential in those who offer psychoanalytic treatment to lesbian patients. Analysts must be able to accompany their patients on their explorations of same-sex attractions and relationships. Anxieties and conceptual confusions about homosexuality will arise within the treatment, mix within the swarm of *other* anxieties and confusions, and threaten to confound both analyst and patient. We will give examples from two analytic attempts to get honey from the hive.

Coming Out in Vienna in 1920

Freud (1920) has provided a vivid description of a real-life contemporary of the fictional Idgie and Ruth, an adolescent "coming out" in middle-class Vienna in 1920. He describes scenes and situations still common in American families seventy years later. Throughout Freud's paper his language demonstrates how central to coming out are conflicts about *openness vs. guardedness* and *honesty vs. deception*.

> There were two details of her behavior, in apparent contrast with each other, that most especially vexed her parents. On the one hand, she did not scruple to appear in the most frequented streets in the company of her undesirable friend, being thus quite neglectful of her own reputation; while, on the other hand, she disdained no means of deception, no excuses and no lies that would make meetings with her possible and cover them. She thus showed herself too open in one respect and full of deceitfulness in the other. (148)

The 18-year-old patient tells her parents that she is in love with an older woman from a family of high social standing who lives outside the social conventions. At first the girl's mother becomes her daughter's confidante in the love affair. Her father is vehemently opposed to his daughter's interest in the woman.

The girl precipitates a crisis. She walks in a park with the woman at a time and in a place where she knows her father will see them. When the father sees his daughter with the woman, he turns angrily away. The woman, upon learning that the man who has just passed them in anger is the girl's father, tells the girl that they can no longer be together. Feeling rejected by both her father and her beloved, the girl throws herself into the approach of an oncoming tram. After this suicide attempt, she stays home in bed for six months. Her parents do not bring her for treatment during this time. It is only when she has recovered from her depression, and resumed her public courtship of the woman, that her parents, concerned about the family's social disgrace, take action. The father brings his daughter to Freud for treatment.

Such a story would be familiar to contemporary therapists: a homosexual attraction to an older or perhaps unsuitable person, depression, impulsive behaviors including suicide attempts, family crisis, and disruption. How is a therapist to understand the girl and her feelings? Why, with friends her own age of both sexes available, does she pursue an older, unavailable woman? What is the meaning of her forcing a crisis with her father? Does she want his approval for her love, or is she unconsciously provoking his help to end the relationship? Does she provoke a crisis because she is too insecure to withstand her father's disapproval? Is she an insecure adolescent uncertain about her own choices and unable to trust her own desires and feelings? Is she in anxious flight from heterosexual relationships, in anxious flight from sexuality? Is she so frightened and confused by her attraction to a woman that she creates a confusing, dangerous, and dramatic muddle? These are the "bee-charming" issues that face an analytic therapist of such a patient.

Shortly after treatment begins the patient brings a series of dreams. Curiously, Freud does not give us the content of any of these dreams, nor any of the patient's associations. One might even suggest that he *hides* the dreams. He simply asserts that they "could be easily translated with certainty. . . . They anticipated the cure of the inversion through the treatment, expressed her joy over the prospects in life that would then be opened before her, confessed her longing for a man's love and for children." (165). Freud sees a "contradiction between [these dreams] and the girl's utterances in waking life." He decides the contradiction is so great that the dreams are "false and hypocritical, and that she intended to deceive me just as she habitually deceived her father. I was right; after I had made this clear, this kind of dream ceased" (165). Convinced of the patient's desire to deceive him, Freud breaks off the treatment and advises her parents that if they want to continue treatment, it should be undertaken with a woman analyst.

What happened in this truncated and abortive therapeutic exchange? The patient tells first her parents and then her analyst that she is in love with a woman. Her analyst first reports that "she did not try to deceive me by saying she felt any urgent need to be freed from her homosexuality. On the contrary she could not conceive of any other way of being in love" (153). Yet she brings her analyst dreams about "her longing for a man's love and the love of children." Are such dreams contradictions, hypocritical, and false? If a woman dreams of a man's love and the love of children is she therefore either deceiving her analyst or not homosexual?

Compare Freud's approach to the sexuality of this 18-year-old patient with his thinking about sexuality in the case of Dora (1905a). In Dora, Freud also discovered a complexity of desire, finding what he called "two currents" in Dora's emotional life. Yet instead of seeing these as evidence of deception and hypocrisy, he used the contradictory currents in Dora to illustrate his belief that "thoughts in the unconscious live very comfortably side by side, and even contraries get on together without disputes—a state of things which persists often enough even in the conscious" (61). Freud saw Dora, as he did the 18-year-old patient of 1920, as a woman motivated by revenge against men. But in a later footnote he added new thoughts about Dora's motivations, namely that "her homosexual (gynaecophilic) love for Frau K was the strongest unconscious current in her mental life. . . . Before I had learnt the importance of the homosexual current of feeling in psychoneurotics, I was often brought to a standstill in the treatment of my cases or found myself in complete complexity" (120).

But in 1920, in spite of Freud's having learned the importance of the "homosexual current of feeling," treatment again came to a standstill. Although feminists and others (Bernheimer and Kahane 1985) have critically discussed transference and countertransference issues in the case of Dora and have questioned whether penis envy and revenge are sufficient to explain Dora's behavior toward Freud, until recently little attention has been given to the motivations of the nameless 1920 patient or to the transference and countertransference issues affecting that treatment.[1] Silva (1975) criticized Freud for telling the patient that she was homosexual. For Silva the patient's dreams (which we do not know) and the absence of genital sexual behavior between her and the other woman indicate that she is not homosexual but "an adolescent who finds herself in that transitory stage so common to young people of both sexes, who feel a conscious repulsion to everything sexual, due to a repression of their natural sexual longings" (359).

Freud is sure his patient is homosexual; Silva is sure she is a confused, heterosexual adolescent. Emphasizing the multidimensional and paradoxical aspect of gender, Harris (1991) suggests that the patient's love is "a heterosexual object choice in which a fictive 'boy' chooses a mother to idealize and save from an oedipal father" (209). What did Freud's patient want? What identifications were revealed, and what identities created, when she declared her love for another woman?

To appreciate Freud's patient's situation, one must understand the particular historical context in which she lived which shaped her ideas about love, sexuality, and women's relationships. Historically, women's relationships with one another had always been, of necessity, secondary to or preliminary to their relationships with men. As long as women were socially and economically dependent on either their fathers or their husbands, their feelings towards one another could be powerfully and publicly expressed in writing, in gesture, in tokens of loving exchange. When in late nineteenth century America and Europe some women began to have economic and social independence, they were able, as women had never been before, to establish primary, permanent relationships with one another. Faderman (1981) argues that the work of sexologists such as Westphal and his disciples, Krafft-Ebing and Havelock Ellis, and the work of Freud were instrumental in changing how such women understood their passionate feelings for one another. Freud's 1920 paper is a primary document of the translation of women's exercise of new social options into psychological attributes and sexual characteristics. Many women who envisioned same-sex relationships and longed for the opportunity to enjoy them did not, however, use the language of *sexual desire* to describe what they wanted. Often they spoke in language such as that with which, in 1836, Charlotte Brontë wrote to Ellen Nussey: "Ellen, I wish I could live with you always. I begin to cling to you more fondly than I ever did. If we had a cottage and a competency of our own I do think we might love until Death without being dependent on any third person for happiness" (Foster 1956, 130).

Some women, such as the fictional Ruth and Idgie, who had acquired that independence of "cottage and competency," either through access to education or through inheritance of economic resources, formed primary relationships sometimes known as "Boston marriages." Many such Boston marriages were enduring and productive, but feminist historians suggest they may not have been founded on genital sexuality (Smith-Rosenberg 1975; Faderman 1981). Biographers of women such as social activists Jane Adams and Mary Rozet Smith, president of Mount Holyoke College, Miss Marks and her companion, Miss Woolley (Cook 1979), and of Anna Freud (Young-Bruehl 1988) face the problem of naming: what to call relationships in which women live together sharing cottage and competency for forty or fifty years, raise children together, establish and run institutions together, and share their lives in sickness and health until parted by death. To name these relationships "homosexual" might be seen as an insult to the subject of the biography, or at least may give the subject a name she did not call herself (Katz 1983; Rupp 1989). But to leave these relationships unnamed or to call them "friendships" because of the absence of, or de-emphasis on, genital sexual behavior renders invisible important elements of female intimacy and replicates the historical devaluing and denial of female desire.

To understand Freud's patient, one must also understand that in 1920, as today, psychoanalysts, scientists, and homosexual activists were debating the nature of homosexuality. Freud's frustrating dialogue with the 18-year-old took place against the backdrop of Germany's flourishing, and predominantly male, homosexual civil rights movement, active in Germany from 1897 to 1933, when it was destroyed by the Nazis. Freud supported the political aims of this movement, including the abolishment of paragraph 175 of the German Penal Code which declared homosexuality a criminal act. In 1928 he contributed to the 60th birthday celebration of one of the leading homosexual activists and sexologists, Magnus Hirschfeld (Lewes 1988). But he disagreed with the sexual theories of the movement, specifically with Hirschfeld's formulations about homosexuality and with the literature from Hirschfeld's Institute for Sexual Research which proposed that homosexuals were a "third" or "intermediate" sex and that homosexuality was, like left-handedness, constitutional. He particularly disagreed with Hirschfeld's view that a male homosexual was "a feminine brain in a male body." Freud (1905b) wished to distinguish physical sexual characteristics from what he called "mental qualities" (142). A primary motivation of Freud at this time seems to have been to rescue homosexual *men* from being seen as having *feminine* mental qualities.

> It is only in the inverted woman that character-inversion of this kind can be looked for with any regularity. In men the most complete mental masculinity can be combined with inversion. (142)

Freud's therapeutic zealousness in the 1920 case arose from his belief that in this young woman he had a case that would prove the *psychoanalytic* theory of homosexuality—and disprove the theories of both *sexologists* and of *homosexual activists*. To this end, therefore, he stresses that his patient was a "beautiful and clever girl, of a family of good standing"; in other words, a patient in which there is no hint of congenital family disturbance, physical masculinity, nor "third sex" hermaphroditism. Freud calls the courting behavior of his young patient "masculine."

> That is to say, she displayed the humility and the sublime overvaluation of the sexual object so characteristic of the male lover, the renunciation of all narcissistic satisfaction, and the preference for being the lover rather than the beloved. She had thus not only chosen a feminine love-object, but had also developed a masculine attitude towards that object. (1920, 154)

As further evidence of what he calls her "masculinity complex," he says she "was in fact a feminist; she felt it to be unjust that girls should not enjoy the same freedom as boys, and rebelled against the lot of woman in general" (169). The object of her attentions was, significantly, an older woman who apparently enjoyed a considerable degree of economic and social independence.

The new names ("sexual," "homosexual," "masculine") given by sexologists and psychoanalysts for relationships once seen as quintessentially feminine may have contributed to the parents' preoccupations with their daughter's *openness*; ten years before they might not have minded a daughter's public display of affection toward another woman. At the same time, what Freud sees as the girl's guardedness makes him impatient. He sees as willfully deceptive her refusal to acknowledge to him, or to herself, what he knows must motivate her: *sexual* attraction to women motivated by revenge against men. But the theory of female homosexuality that Freud articulated failed to resonate with his patient's experience.

> Once when I expounded to her a specially important part of the theory, one touching her nearly, she reported in an inimitable tone, "How very interesting," as though she were a *grande dame* being taken over a museum and glancing through her *lorgnon* at objects to which she was completely indifferent. (163)

The developing transference Freud felt so acutely was perhaps more complicated than a vengeful deception. The patient may have been testing Freud in both the maternal and paternal transferences: "Are you, like my parents, primarily interested in my being who you want me to be, for your purposes?"

Freud's acknowledged interest in this case was not in clinical treatment but in the opportunity to present a case of homosexuality in women "in which it was possible to trace its origin and development in the mind with complete certainty and almost without a gap" (147). Freud filled any "gap" of uncertainty by declaring that a woman attracted to a woman "forsw[ore] her womanhood and sought another goal for her libido. . . . She changed into a man and took her mother in place of her father as the object of her love" (157, 158). Although he summarizes various factors contributing to the patient's homosexuality, including an original infantile fixation on her mother and the advantages for the girl of "retiring" from heterosexual pursuits in favor of her envious mother, Freud emphasizes her deception of, and revenge against, men. For Freud the patient's homosexuality was the product of her turning against the love of men when she could not have her real desire—her father's penis or his baby. The patient's dreams, therefore, "of a man's love and the love of children" were indeed contradictions, not necessarily of the patient's desires, but of Freud's ideas about homosexuality in women. Freud gives no indication that he is aware that any anxieties might attend the acceptance of a psychological identity of "forsworn womanhood."

Lesbian Relationships

Did Freud's patient ever find her way to other, more available women? She certainly received no help in understanding why she was attracted to that particular woman. And with a few notable exceptions (Lachmann 1975; Mitchell 1978; Eisenbud 1986; Sanville 1991), published psychoanalytic case descriptions do not show lesbian relationships established or improved due to psychoanalytic treatment. For some analysts this needs no explanation since these would not be seen as favorable treatment outcomes. Some would explain the absence of descriptions of improved lesbian relations as due to the level of disturbance characteristic of homosexual women. Since we do not see women who have lesbian identity or relationships as having clinical disturbances that distinguish them from heterosexual women, we explain the absence of such descriptions through the use of other factors.

The first is the analyst's personal comfort with, and theoretical support for, homosexual relationships. When the analyst does not have such theoretical support, certain clinical results may follow. First, the anxieties, defenses, and object relations issues that prevent the establishment of sound lesbian relationships will not be analyzed. They will simply be assumed to be manifestations of the pathology thought characteristic of homosexuality or of the disturbances assumed to make homosexual relations defensively necessary. The analyst will assume that when the narcissistic deficits or separation anxiety or oedipal conflicts are better resolved, the patient will be freer to have relationships with men, rather than assume that when such issues are better resolved, the patient becomes psychically freer to follow her attraction and find more satisfying objects, which *may* remain women. Second, unless the analyst is theoretically comfortable with homosexual relationships, the analyst may have difficulty seeing *any* lesbian relationship, no matter of what quality, as evidence of therapeutic progress or positive change and will not in clinical reports describe such relationships in positive terms. Some patients have painfully discovered at the end of their analyses that their analysts, who had throughout the analysis seemed to indicate acceptance of their homosexuality, expressed disappointment when the treatment ends "prematurely," i.e., without the woman establishing a relationship with a man.

We suspect that a second reason for the lack of descriptions of improvement in the relationships of lesbian patients in analytic treatment is that many analytic therapists whose patients' lesbian relationships *do* improve have kept silent about their work and have not published such cases. We do not share Mitchell's sanguine assumption:

> Most psychoanalysts approach homosexual material produced by their patients as they would any other experiences of their patients—simply as material to be inquired into and analyzed. Such analysts are not likely to write about psychoanalytic approaches to treating homosexuality, since they would tend to feel that homosexuality does not pose particularly distinctive or unique features in terms of analytic work. (Mitchell 1981, 63).

We find it difficult to believe that most analysts have escaped the anxiety-based ideas about homosexuality so prevalent in psychoanalytic theory and in the general culture. We do not think that many analysts whose patients' lesbian relationships improve neglect to report this development because they find it such an unremarkable occurrence. On the contrary, we believe that such analysts may be in the same position as their lesbian patients—ambivalent about whether to reveal or to hide, fearing that if they do come out, their work will, at best, not be appreciated and, at worst, attacked.

We believe that a publication closet exists for analysts who treat lesbian women. "Coming out" always has risks, but some periods in the history of psychoanalysis have been more accepting of homosexuality than others (Lewes 1988) and more tolerant of analytic work with those in "overt" homosexual relationships. Freud and Deutsch (1932), for example, published their cases in an analytic climate more tolerant than that in which M. Masud Khan (1964) described his work with a college student. Freud is impatient with his 18-year-old because she is disinterested in exploring the sexual aspects of her attraction. Deutsch's patient feels comfortable enough when she meets her ex-analyst on the street to tell her she has found uninhibited sexual pleasure with a woman, and Deutsch feels comfortable enough to report this development. But in 1964 Khan worries about how he and his patient will be seen if he describes his patient's excited sexual pleasure. As Khan begins to describe the patient's sexual relationship, which he calls "the homosexual episode" and the "focal symbiosis," he stops. Khan interrupts his description of the lesbian sexual relationship with an eight-page report of his attempts to *prevent* such sexual behavior through interpretation and with a description of his anxiety as the patient, in spite of his interpretations, pursued her course.

Khan reports that the patient had avoided homosexual experience previously because she feared "being trapped" (256). He stresses his concern about her sexual "acting out" and repeatedly declares that he knows the "ego-enhancing" effects of the lesbian relationship could only be achieved because *the patient was in analysis during that relationship with a male analyst.* Under these conditions he decides to "let her work her way out" in the analysis. Khan interprets his patient's anxiety about vaginal penetration by her woman partner as evidence that she was "not a true homosexual pervert but passed through a phase of homosexual perversion en route to health and a true integration of her femininity" (256). If a woman patient reported anxiety about vaginal penetration with a man, would Khan have interpreted her feelings as evidence that she was not a "true" heterosexual, or would he have suggested that she examine her fears or conflicts about penetration? The patient's fears of being "trapped" in a homosexual relationship also could not be explored since to Khan, apparently, such fears were "realistic," and therefore needed no examination.

But Khan's report is unique in psychoanalytic literature because it conveys the anxiety in both patient and analyst when inhibitions against homosexuality are lifted. Every lesbian patient's anxieties about her homosexual attraction will have become interwoven with her other conflicts and fears, and, as in any analytic treatment, these overdetermined longings, fears, and defenses will be consciously conveyed as well as unconsciously projected to the analyst, who must be familiar enough with his or her own anxieties about homosexuality to help the patient untangle her issues. If this process is defensively aborted, analysts may conclude that "psychotic" or "primitive" processes, "fragile" psychic structure (McDougall 1980), or "negative therapeutic reactions" (Quinodoz 1989) are characteristic of lesbian patients. Khan fears his patient will have "a breakdown." It is to his credit that he could tolerate the anxiety raised in him by his patient's one homosexual "episode." But if her longing to have "a life of one's own" (259) had included a permanent lesbian relationship, her anxieties about such longings must have gone unexamined.

Khan's concern that his "permitting" the lesbian relationship would be criticized by analytic colleagues may seem idiosyncratic, excessive, or dated. But thirty years later Limentani's comments on the case in Khan's obituary (1992) suggest that Khan's fears had foundation: "Her acting out of homosexual impulses with a friend (a novel experience) was precipitated by the patient's incapacity to tolerate frustration, and on reading the report it is easy to form the impression that the analyst did little to prevent it" (158). Limentani conveys the discomfort and disapproval some feel toward analytic work in which "homosexual impulses" are not "prevented" from seeking expression. As an analyst he would apparently have found some way to "prevent" such impulses. Because anxieties about homosexuality are so great, patients may consciously and unconsciously provoke policing or superego responses and prohibitions from their analysts (Mitchell 1981) Limentani's comments suggest that he would be an analyst at risk for making such countertransference-based policing responses.

Lesbian women do not wish to be seen as having "forsworn" their "womanhood," nor as loving women because they are bent upon revenge against men, nor as having no desire for "a man's love and the love of children." Freud's patient resisted his attempts to persuade her to accept his definitions of her desires. But these views and others equally critical still pervade many psychoanalytic descriptions of women attracted to women, contribute to the anxieties of coming out, and effect clinical work with lesbian patients.

Notes

1. Psychoanalytic discussions of this case include: Silva, J. (1975); Harris, A. (1991); Appignanesi, L. and Forrester, J. (1992); Magid, B. (1993).

   Discussions of the case by lesbian therapists or lesbian theorists making use of psychoanalytic theory include: Klaich, D. (1979); Faderman, L. (1981); Downing, C. (1989); Merck, M. (1993); Laureti, T. (1994).

References Cited

Bell, A., and Weinberg, M. 1978. *Homosexualities: A Study of Diversity Among Men and Women*. New York: Simon & Schuster.

Bernheimer, C., and Kahane, C., eds. 1985. *In Dora's Case*. London: Virago Press.

Cass, V.C. 1979. Homosexual identity formation: A theoretical model. *J. Homosexual* 4 (3): 219–235.

———. 1984. Homosexual identity: A concept in need of definition. *J. Homosexual* 10 (5): 105–126.

Coleman, E. 1982. Developmental stages of the coming out process. In *Homosexuality and Psychotherapy: A Practitioner's Handbook of Affirmative Models*, ed. by J. Gonsiorek. New York: Haworth, pp. 31–45.

Cook, B. 1979. The historical denial of lesbianism. *Radical History Review* 20: 60–65.

de Monteflores, C. 1986. Notes on the management of difference. In *Contemporary Perspectives on Psychotherapy with Lesbians and Gay Men*, ed. by T. Stein and C. Cohen. New York: Plenum Press, pp. 73–101.

Deutsch, H. 1932. On female homosexuality. In *The Psychoanalytic Reader*, ed. by R. Fliess. Madison, CT: International University Press, 1948.

Downing, C. 1989. *Myths and Mysteries of Same-Sex Love*.New York: Continuum.

Eisenbud, R. J. 1982. Early and later determinants of lesbian choice. *The Psychoanal Review* 69 (1): 85–109.

———. 1986. Lesbian choice: transferences to theory. In *Psychoanalysis and Women: Contemporary Reappraisals*, ed. by J. Alpert. Hillsdale, NJ: The Analytic Press.

Faderman, L. 1981. *Surpassing the Love of Men: Romantic Friendship and Love between Women from the Renaissance to the Present*. New York: Morrow.

Fenichel, O. 1945. *The Psychoanalytic Theory of Neurosis*. New York: Norton.

Flagg, F. 1987. *Fried Green Tomatoes at the Whistle Stop Cafe*. New York: McGraw-Hill.

Foster, J. 1956. *Sex Variant Women in Literature*. Naiad Press, 1985 paperback edition.

Freud, S. 1905a. A fragment of an analysis of a case of hysteria. *Standard Edition* 7: 7–122, London: Hogarth, 1955.

———. 1905b. Three essays on the theory of sexuality. *Standard Edition* 7: 135–231. London: Hogarth, 1951.

———. 1920. The psychogenesis of a case of homosexuality in a woman. *Standard Edition* 18: 145–172. London: Hogarth, 1957.

Friedman, R.C. 1988. *Male Homosexuality: A Contemporary Psychoanalytic Perspective*. New Haven: Yale University Press.

Garnets, L. and Kimmel, D. 1991. Lesbian and gay male dimensions in the psychological study of human diversity. In *Psychological Perspective on Human Diversity in America*, ed. by J. Goodchilds. Washington, DC: American Psychological Association.

Gershman, H. 1983. The stress of coming out. *Am. J. Psychoanal.* 43 (2): 129–138.

Hanley-Hackenbruck, P. 1988. Psychotherapy and the "coming out" process. *J. Gay and Lesbian Psychother.* 1 (1): 21–39.

Harris, A. 1991. Gender as contradiction. *Psychoanal. Dialog.* 1: 197–224.

Hart, J., and Richardson, D. 1981. *The Theory and Practice of Homosexuality*. London: Routledge.

Herdt, G. 1989. Introduction: Gay and lesbian youth, emergent identities, and cultural scenes at home and abroad. In *Adolescence and Homosexuality*, ed. by G. Herdt. New York: Haworth.

Isay, R. A. 1989. *Being Homosexual: Gay Men and Their Development*. New York: Avon.

Jones, E. 1927. The early development of female sexuality. *Int. J. Psychoanal.* 8: 459–472.

Katz, J. 1983. *Gay/Lesbian Almanac*. New York: Harper & Row.

Khan, M. 1964. The role of infantile sexuality and early object-relations in female homosexuality. In *Alienation in Perversions*, ed. by M. Khan. New York: International Universities Press, 1979.

Klaich, D. 1979. *Woman + Woman: Attitudes Toward Lesbianism*. New York: Morrow Quill.

Lachmann, F. 1975. Homosexuality: some diagnostic perspectives and dynamic considerations. *Am. J. Psychother.* 29 (2): 254–260.

Lauretis, T. 1994. *The Practice of Love: Lesbian Sexuality and Perverse Desire*. Bloomington and Indianapolis: Indiana University Press.

Lewes, K. 1988. *The Psychoanalytic Theory of Male Homosexuality*. New York: Simon and Schuster.

Limentani, A. 1992. Obituary: M. Masud R. Khan. *Int. J. Psychoanal.* 73: 155–159.

Magee, M. and Miller, D. 1992. "She forswore her womanhood": psychoanalytic views of female homosexuality. *Clin. Social Wk. J.* 20: 67–87.

McDougall, J. 1970. Homosexuality in women. In *Female Sexuality*, ed. by J. Chasseguet-Smirgel, et al. Ann Arbor: Michigan University Press.

———. 1980. *Plea for a Measure of Abnormality*. New York: International Universities Press.

———. 1989. The dead father: On early psychic trauma and its relation to disturbance in sexual identity and in creative activity. *Int. J. Psychoanal.* 70: 205–219.

Merck, M. 1993. The train of thought in Freud's "Case of Homosexuality in a Woman." In *Perversions: Deviant Readings*. New York: Routledge.

Mitchell, S. 1978. Psychodynamics, homosexuality, and the question of pathology. *Psychiatry* 41: 254–263.

———. 1981. The psychoanalytic treatment of homosexuality: Some technical considerations. *Int. Rev. Psychoanal.* 8: 63–80.

Morgenthaler, F. 1988. *Homosexuality, Heterosexuality, Perversion*. Hillsdale, NJ: Analytic Press.

O'Connor, N. and Ryan, J. 1993. *Wild Desires and Mistaken Identities*. New York: Columbia University Press.

Quinodoz, J-M. 1989. Female homosexual patients in psychoanalysis. *Int. J. Psychoanal.* 70: 55–63.

Rich, A. 1980. Foreword, in *The Coming-Out Stories*, ed. by P. Stanley and S. Wolfe. Watertown, MA: Persephone Press.

Rupp, L. 1989. "Imagine my surprise": Women's relationships in mid-twentieth century America. In *Hidden from History: Reclaiming the Gay and Lesbian Past*, ed. by M. Duberman, M. Vicinus, G. Chauncey. New York: New American Library.

Sanville, J. 1991. *The Playground of Psychoanalytic Psychotherapy*. Hillsdale, NJ: Analytic Press.

Siegel, E. 1988. *Female Homosexuality: Choice Without Volition*. Hillsdale, NJ: Analytic Press.

———. 1990. Review of Richard C. Friedman's *Male Homosexuality: A Contemporary Psychoanalytic Perspective*. *Psychoanal. Rev.* 77 (3): 447–450.

Silva, J. 1975. Two cases of female homosexuality: A critical study of Sigmund Freud and Helene Deutsch. *Contemp. Psychoanal.* 11 (3): 357–376.

Smith-Rosenberg, C. 1975. The female world of love and ritual: Relations between women in nineteenth-century America. *Signs: Journal of Women In Culture and Society* 1 (1): 1–30.

Socarides, C. 1978. *Homosexuality*. New York: Aronson.

Stanley, P., and Wolfe, S., eds. 1980. *The Coming Out Stories*. Watertown, MA: Persephone Press.

Stein, T. and Cohen, J. 1984. Psychotherapy with gay men and lesbians: an examination of homophobia, coming out and identity. In *Innovations in Psychotherapy with Homosexuals*, ed. by E. Hetrick and T. Stein. Washington, DC: American Psychiatric Press.

Young-Bruehl, E. 1988. *Anna Freud: A Biography*. New York: Summit Books.

Weeks, Jeffrey. 1977. *Coming Out: Homosexual Politics in Britain, from the Nineteenth Century to the Present*. London: Quartet Books.

6

Current Psychoanalytic Discourses on Sexuality

Tripping Over the Body

David Schwartz

A CENTRAL PART OF THE CONTEMPORARY colloquial discourse on sexuality is a system for describing the putative stabilities in individuals' erotic desires. This system asserts that most people's "sexual orientation," as it has recently come to be called, can be classified as being one of a limited number of specific types. Thus, if we say that someone is heterosexual, we are locating him or her within this currently taken-for-granted system of sexual identity and implicitly subscribing to various assumptions which that system entails. Some of these assumptions are (1) that the designation of three sexual orientations is a reasonably complete description of the sexual universe, i.e., most every adult is either homosexual, heterosexual, or lately, bisexual, (2) that the most salient way we can classify a person's psychoerotic system is with respect to the *gender* of the object he or she eroticizes (as opposed to, for example, what activities or body parts he or she engages), and (3) that these three categories of sexual orientation each represent something about a person which is in some sense *real, fundamental, stable, and ineluctable*, meaning, in effect, that we seek objects as dictated by our sexual orientation and not that we establish a psychoerotic pattern suited to current conditions which include what objects are available and what situational pressures are present.

From the point of view of *popular* culture, the current tripartite sexual orientation system executes certain functions quite well: It offers a parsimonious way of referring to erotic life which is immediately understood. Further, the postulate of three mutually exclusive categories rules out certain anxiety-producing possibilities. For example, men who have organized their self-esteem around conventional notions of masculinity may more easily sequester their passive same-sex wishes if they speak and think in a framework which reassures them that such wishes only *really* exist in homosexuals or bisexuals. Perceived defects in the self can more easily be exceptionalized, deemphasized, or simply repressed when there seems to be a real other to whom the defects may be attached. The queer/other comes in handy when the "normal" self is threatened.

Needless to say, this colloquial discourse does not reflect basic psychoanalytic principles. A *psychoanalytic* description of a person's psychoerotics need not emphasize the category of sexual orientation at all and would necessarily stress a great deal else. After all, it has been a cornerstone of all psychoanalytic theories that beneath the surface of conscious self-definitions and projected reifications are unconscious processes which contradict or deviate sharply from whom we think we are, how we superficially seem, and how we construe our own motivations. Most psychoanalytic models of the mind have retained some idea of an unconscious primary process, a vision of the human who sustains contradictions, who perpetually awaits the fulfillment of impossible wishes, daily and nightly rewriting an idiosyncratic and changing script. To believe in the reality of three given sexual orientations, each wedded principally to gender and stable over time, rather than to consider these orientations words only, and very reductive words at that, would be to reject a great deal which has become fundamental to clinical psychoanalysisis since the *Wolfman* (Freud 1918). While everyday language may speak as though human sexuality were thus neatly compartmentalized and restrained, in principle, psychoanalysts would regard these compartments as the proverbial tips of a very juicy iceberg.

The sexual orientation discourse of psychoanalysis is most observable in psychoanalytic literature when same-sex desire is the primary topic of a given work. This is not to say that this discourse is seldom influential in psychoanalytic writing in general; only that its presence is not obvious in papers that do not focus on sexual life in some particular way. In what follows I will stress papers which touch directly on the subject of same-sex desire.

Recent psychoanalytic writing dealing with same-sex desire can be organized into roughly three camps. The first is exemplified by writers such as Charles Socarides (1978), and more recently, Jeffrey Trop and Robert Stolorow (1992). Theirs is a pathologizing and otherwise disparaging view of same-sex desire. These writers subscribe to a very colloquial view of sexual desire. In a recent case presentation, Trop and Stolorow (1992) write that the patient entered treatment wondering whether or not he was homosexual; they then show how the analyst *matched* the literal-mindedness of the patient, as they happily report that Alan was helped to see that, on the contrary, he was heterosexual. The case report culminates ten years later, with no small amount of implicit self-congratulations, with Alan "engaged to be married" to a woman and claiming to have stopped having sex with men. The reification of sexual orientation by analysts of this persuasion has consequences which are clearly seen in their approach to psychoanalytic technique: insofar as the patient identifies sexuality as problematic, they abandon the psychoanalytic principles of neutrality and non-directiveness, replacing them with the practice of directly advancing their notion of "natural" development. Trop and Stolorow implicitly, and Socarides explicitly, describe how they use empathic interventions to remove what they see as obstacles to heterosexual adjustment, which they position as emerging spontaneously when good analytic work is done.[1]

A more recent development in psychoanalytic theorizing about sexual desire is exemplified by the writings of Richard Friedman (1988). He declares that in adulthood sexual orientation is a cohesive "psychobiological" structure, the consolidation of which is "irreversible." Friedman, writing about men only, argues that sexual orientation develops in conjunction with gender identity, which he also sees as a "psychobiological" structure, analogous to a part of neuroanatomy. According to Friedman, there are, for the most part, two sexual orientations, which develop as follows: Heterosexuality develops in conjunction with "normal" gender identity, and homosexuality develops as a consequence of "gender identity disturbance," which Friedman also labels "unmasculinity." The theory asserts that after the spawning of a sexual orientation by either normal or pathological gender identity, sexual orientation consolidates independently of gender identity and becomes "irreversible." Therefore, Friedman argues, for a homosexual patient, no psychoanalytic intervention intended to uncover an underlying heterosexuality should be attempted. It won't be there because the development of homosexuality is in effect a replacement, quite literally, of the heterosexual orientation that might have developed. It is as if the spot in the brain where sexual orientation resides can only be taken up by one sexual orientation, which itself is permanent. Furthermore, and quite consistent with his theory of sexuality, Friedman insists that in people who are consciously *heterosexual*, psychoanalysis will reveal no unconscious homosexuality, for there is no such thing. He therefore counsels against any clinical intervention intended to modify the sexual orientation of a patient.

Further clinical implications of his theorizing can be drawn from his description of a gay non-patient colleague of his, which Friedman furnishes as part of an effort to portray the "normal" development of gay men. In this description, "Tim" emerges as an emotionally limited individual who maintains no intimate relationships with people of either gender, and who disguises himself in the world as a "bachelor." Friedman ignores these telling details of Tim's situation. He neither recognizes them as indicators of psychopathology, nor refers to them as shortcomings of any kind. Thus, while he finds no reason to analyze same-sex desire as a symptom, his description of a putatively well-adjusted gay man gives the clear impression of someone with a defective personality. This, too, is consistent with his theory of the development of sexual orientation: The sexual preferences of gay men are the result of a psychobiological disturbance; although that disturbance (of gender) may be overcome, men who have experienced it will show its stigmata in their adult emotional and interpersonal lives. We should not judge them by the same standards as heterosexuals who benefited from normal gender identity development. One can imagine how assumptions such as these might influence the level of expectation and implicit respect an analyst would convey to a gay patient.

What about Friedman's treatment of *heterosexual* men in light of his theoretical assumptions about sexuality? I suspect that under the influence of Friedman's theoretical assumptions, an analyst would be very *unlikely* to discover, or even be interested in, the role of any same-sex yearnings in the life of a patient who describes himself as heterosexual. Of course many heterosexual men would be only too happy to have an analyst who offered such an abbreviated treatment, thus limiting the extent of stressful intrapsychic and interpersonal exploration. It would seem, then, that to be consistent with Friedman's theory of same-sex desire, some basic psychoanalytic theory must be abandoned. Friedman, in fact, does specifically grant the need to abandon some aspects of psychoanalytic theory, in particular the traditional assumption of the mobility of object choice in adults, referred to in the classical literature as the mobility of libidinal cathexis.

The third and newest arrivals to the contested site of psychoanalytic writing about sexual orientation include analysts such as Kenneth Lewes (1988),

Richard Isay (1991), Kenneth Corbett (1993), and Stephen Frommer (1994). Their work is part of a new and concerted effort (mostly on the part of gay and lesbian analysts, though Mitchell [1978, 1981] and Kwawer [1980] come to mind as exceptions) to remedy the traditional disparagement of same-sex desire in psychoanalytic writing and practice. If my remarks on the writings of some gay analysts betray my disagreements with them, I hope no one will be misled into imagining that I underestimate the chasm of difference between their work and that of Socarides and Trop and Stolorow. The writings of this latter group are part of a destructive chapter in the history of psychoanalysis which began in the 1930s with writers such as Bergler (1944), and goes on today with Socarides, Trop and Stolorow, Joseph Nicolosi, and others. Analysts such as Isay, Corbett, Lewes, Schaffner, Blechner, Lesser, and Frommer are synthesizing a powerful antidote to that noxious work. With that in mind, permit me to describe some aspects of this new psychoanalytic discourse on sexuality.

Of this group of writers, Isay, Lewes, and Corbett have the most in common with one another with respect to theory. They position their theory of male same-sex desire squarely within the framework of Freudian developmental theory. Their revision of post-Freudian writing on this subject is accomplished with admirable parsimony: By simply insisting that the vicissitudes of the young boy's erotic attraction to his father may occupy as important and benignly determinative a position in his growth as that of the boy's attraction to his mother, Isay and Lewes, in particular, show how Freudian *developmental* theory inevitably predicts the maturing of at least some men who preferentially eroticize men. Isay and Lewes simply took Freud's postulations of constitutional bisexuality and the negative oedipal complex (1905 and 1923, respectively) quite seriously. Some boys, for various imaginable reasons, make the father a predominant erotic focus. Family dynamics play a role in fashioning and modulating the degree of conflict which the boy will experience with respect to this and, therefore, what weight other erotic trends might have. Thus they reject the proposition that such boys would be seen only under conditions of disturbance or trauma.

In a recent paper, Corbett (1993) has tried to refine this position a bit further: he points out that psychoanalytic writers have often claimed that gay men's eroticization of passivity and receptivity represents feminine identifications which are in turn accompanied by concomitant distortions of body image—"I have no penis," "my anus is a vagina," etc. Using a combination of clinical material and descriptions of gay male sex, Corbett argues that there is no evidence for invoking feminine identification as a way to explain passive homoeroticism. He goes a step further to assert his larger point, which is that gay men tend to experience a gender difference which is neither femininity nor culturally given masculinity, but, in Corbett's language, a different *kind* of masculinity. In this way Corbett elaborates Isay and Lewes's work: not only is it possible for a boy to pursue eroticization of his father and still come out psychologically normal, but neither need he necessarily show any "gender pathology."

Thus, for these gay writers there is more than one healthy sexual orientation. Homosexuality is no less natural, basic, or enduringly real a sexual orientation than is heterosexuality. It emerges in psychosexual development on a par with heterosexuality.

Of this group, Isay (1991) has had the most to say about psychoanalytic technique. His contribution can be summarized and generalized as follows: Psychoanalysis with individuals suffering societal ostracism because of their sexual orientation should include direct affirmation of the validity of their psychoerotic systems, including, when it is deemed helpful, self-disclosures about the analyst's sexuality. Moreover, Isay implicitly argues that the oppressed position of gay men and lesbians in contemporary society may require that their treatments include a greater degree of validation for their sexual desires than is usual in psychoanalysis. In effect Isay is saying that our culture adds a resistance which the analyst is in a position to help the patient overcome. Beyond this, Isay believes that psychoanalysis should be conducted no differently with gay men and lesbians than with anyone else.

Let me reiterate: There are large and real differences among the three theoretical camps. They include differences in etiological theories of same-sex desire, differences in what relationships analysts see between psychopathology and erotic preferences, if any, and differences in what technical recommendations analysts make when same-sex desire is a significant part of a patient's psychology. Furthermore, such differences loom even larger at the present historical moment, a moment when psychoanalytic theory and psychoanalytic institutions are being challenged to reexamine their ideas about sexuality and abandon rotted prejudicial structures. Gay and lesbian analysts and others concerned with advancing an agenda of diversity and tolerance can easily become preoccupied with the urgency of discrediting the unfounded and patently biased theories and practices present in some psychoanalytic work.

In such a time and climate, the gay-affirming writing of someone like Isay can be very appealing. He tracks a "normal" developmental path for gay men, lending a classical voice to the chorus of those yearning both for inclusion and for support in their belief in the normality of a "real" gay identity. The here-and-now value of such theoretical amendments, in contrast to the numbing perseverations of homophobes, heterophiles, and biologizers, can be exhilarating enough to distract us from the fact that some of the theoretical moves on the part of Isay and others are part and parcel of the very discourse which has tended to undermine the liberatory potential of psychoanalysis. Let me explain further.

All three perspectives—Socarides, et al., Friedman, and the gay analysts—reify and endorse sexual stability and implicitly devalue erotic flexibility and mobility. They might tend to call such elements of erotic indeterminacy a type of "confusion" or, pejoratively, a "lack of boundaries." More concretely, none of these writers makes room in their theories for an individual who might be better off without imagining that he or she needs a sexual "orientation" at all. A male patient of mine, married to a woman, but whose sexual fantasy life includes a wish to be ravished by the Dallas Cowboys, would be less anxious if he didn't feel pressured to be an uncomplicated heterosexual. Certainly his marriage would be less conflicted. The claim that erotic stability exists and, even more improbably, that it is a hallmark of health and virtue is seriously problematic in two ways. First, any theory of eroticism which normalizes same-sex desire or any other psychoerotic system by declaring it a naturally stable form, a sexual "identity," is false. Given Kinsey's data, all that we know of the flexibility of human sexual practices through anthropological and historical research, as well as the numerous midlife conversions we are all familiar with, is it not untenable to postulate a natural stability in human sexual patterns? Second, endorsing alleged sexual stability sets up an evaluative hierarchy, a class system of sexual virtue much like the one which has been and is still used to disparage same-sex desire. What does it gain society to have same-sex desire accepted as canonical, as the basis of a stable sexual identity, if this is achieved at the expense of locating, publicizing, and punishing some other "perverse" sets of desires? I am thinking here of attacks on transvestism and pornography. Freud's inclusion of a pervasive *instability* in his theory of human motivation has been of enormous value in encouraging respect for the complexities of minds and lives which are other to one's own. The minimization of this respect in the form of reifying sexual identities threatens us with serious intellectual and moral losses.[2]

All three discourses also have this in common: they fail to dislodge gender from its position as the central organizer of eroticism. They theorize the human as necessarily absorbed with gender in his or her erotic practices; the gendered body of your object of desire defines your sexual nature and gives you a sexual identity. That an enriching erotic preference could be constructed irrespective of gender, perhaps in relation to shared interests or sexual practices for which gender is not pertinent, has no place in these discourses.

In truth, we do not yet have positive or even neutral words for what I am describing. When psychoanalysis refers to sexuality without gender, it uses the word "fetish," a loaded term to say the least, but oddly one whose history may offer some substantiation for my claim here. Freud (1927) argued that the fetish is a substitute for the phallic mother (or perhaps we should say the breasted father), i.e., the sexual object who is not limited by gender, though I am sure this is not the way he would have it. What Freud called the wish to deny castration, we may reasonably translate as the longing for an ungendered eros. Thus, he was aware of human wishes to unsex, degender, and unlimit erotic experience, wishes which have been allowed to drift into the backwater of contemporary psychoanalytic theorizing about sex, even in the work of gay analysts. Let us say that all human sexual practice is fetish, each one defending against wishes to transgress and falsely claiming that without *it* there can be no real arousal. The sexual orientation fetish, including the fetish of heterosexuality as well as the fetishes more commonly referred to, can function to deny deep wishes to escape gender and its arbitrary restrictions. In the models of sexuality which I have reviewed thus far, there is no place for such wishes. Corbett (1993), as I mentioned earlier, attempts to rectify the old psychoanalytic claim that passive-receptive desires in gay men are the result of feminine identifications; a central part of his argument hinges on clinical material which indicates that during anal receptive sex, gay men have erections and feel masculine, implying that the absence of erection or of felt masculinity are *the* false assumptions of the old theories. Why worry about men having feminine identifications? Perhaps men of various sexual persuasions would have better sex, as well as better lives, if they were *encouraged* to seek and enjoy so-called feminine experiences, whether or not openly and consciously so. There is no need to sanitize such expansive desires by insisting that they, too, are masculine. If a given man can enhance his sexual pleasure by simply engaging the idea that for tonight his anatomy has been magically transformed, *he* has something to teach. It is only necessary to exclude such an eroticism if we have the idea that the way gender has worked in our culture ought to be preserved—an uncompelling idea, to say the least.

Thus far, I have in effect argued that to have a theory of sexual desire which is consistent with the liberatory intent of psychoanalytic principles, we must definitively sever ties to essentialist thinking about sex: This means not accepting any reification of the concept of sexual orientation, nor accepting any idealization of the idea or practice of sexual stability. Furthermore, it would entail displacing a reified notion of gender from its position of primacy in the theorization of sexual desire; we must give up the idea that our culture's preoccupation with putting the anatomy (principally the genitalia) of the object in the foreground is "natural" or built in to "normal" psychological functioning.

How do I think we can do all this, or in other words what am I for? The answer to *this* question hinges on how the reification of the concept of sexual orientation, the idealization of sexual stability, and the central positioning of gender in sexual identity theory are all to be understood. The prevailing view of sexual *pleasure* in psychoanalytic theory is consistent with that of mass culture and of most other discourses: it is that the erotic is fundamentally physiological. Orgasm is the *sine qua non*; the body of the other, its physical condition, touching it, looking at it, having it touch you, are all considered to be the defining features of erotic pleasure. Even the gender of one's erotic object is defined in terms of its anatomic genitals, as opposed to the other indicators of gender status, such as receptivity, aggressivity, etc.

I probably need to point out that none of the claims that sexual pleasure hinges on a bodily interaction turns out to be true. The extraordinary economic success of telephone sex certainly testifies to this. In theorizing erotic pleasure as necessarily physiological, we have deprived ourselves of a great deal of erotic pleasure, for the most part by inhibiting and disparaging various non-physiological eroticisms. What exactly these non-physiological pleasures may be, I will have some trouble saying, since the restriction of sexual pleasure to bodily contact has entailed restricting the vocabulary for describing it to a physiological vocabulary; but I will try.

The playful use of domination and submission is one erotic pleasure that has been marginalized and otherwise restricted within this physiologistic discourse. The eroticization of environments[3] has similarly been limited. It may be worth noting that gay men and lesbians have been at the forefront of efforts to reclaim these erotic realms, dogged by moralists much of the way. The eroticization of political rebelliousness, innovation, and novelty have been explored within very narrow limits.[4]

To finish the statement of my hypothesis: The enactment of the physiologistic theory of sexual pleasure, itself a classic fetish, has led to significant deprivation and conflict. We cope with this by obsessively dwelling on the transcultural and transhistorical claim that eroticism resides essentially in the gendered body. Clearly I see this as one fetish, a theory fetish, which does need treatment. And the correct treatment for a societal neurosis of this sort, is to deconstruct the unsupported defensive claims of the physiological ideology, including its irrational beliefs in *true* sexual orientations, gender identities, and normative sexual practices; open the system to the denied pleasures; diminish the conflict and thereby reduce the need for the obsessive symptom. So what am I for? I am for reemphasizing the elasticity of the capacity to eroticize. In particular, our concept of the erotic must be untethered from physiological constraints (in gendered forms or not), and its limits should be imagined as perpetually shifting and unknown.

I want now to offer some clinical material which may help to concretize the technical implications of my argument. I offer clinical material as part of a presentation such as this one with serious reservations, principally because of the complex distortions they are prone to. Having said that, allow me to offer two brief examples. One comes from an individual therapy, and the other from a couples treatment.

In the individual case, a forty-year-old heterosexually married Asian man—I will call him "Sam"—tells me that early in his marriage he would tell his wife graphic stories of his sexual encounters with other men, usually strangers in improbable situations (such as an elevator operator *in* the elevator). Sam reported that his wife seemed to find these stories very erotically stimulating. However, he neglected to tell his wife that these stories were accounts of events which really had taken place; Sam had left this question vague. At some point he did indicate the truth of the stories to her. She became furious, claiming not to have known, thinking all along that they were only play, and now refusing to listen to such stories ever again. This marked the beginning of long period of increased distance in their marriage. In his treatment with me, I had to resist subtle pressures to either endorse or disparage Sam's same-sex eroticism. He, complementarily, had felt both guilt and a sense of superiority with respect to this aspect of his personality. I did endorse the vitality of which this eroticism seemed to be a part. Sam *did* get closer to his wife and simultaneously reported *no* decrease in his erotic interest in men. My admittedly *post hoc* formulation is that his increased flexibility with respect to his same-sex desire diminished his need to use this aspect of himself in a hostile way. With his various eroticisms coexisting peacefully, he was much more of a loving companion to his wife, and both profited.

Here is a capsule of a couples treatment with a less satisfying outcome. A heterosexual couple of New England patrician lineage, married for over twenty years with one child—I will call them John and Mary—told me that one of their problems was that John had a perversion: He felt most inclined to have sex with his wife, as well as to be loving toward her generally, after he received an enema. The couple embarrassedly explained that early in their marriage John would "manipulate" Mary into giving him an enema by complaining of constipation. At some point prior to coming to see me, Mary, with the encouragement of a therapist, refused to continue to do this, saying she felt degraded by it. John then became increasingly hostile toward her, and Mary became increasingly resolute in her rage toward him. The couple's child, whom they had treated with both physical and verbal brutality, was a lesbian. At the time of the termination of their work with me, Mary thanked me for helping her to "understand homosexuality better," by which I believe she meant accepting her daughter. I was unhappy to note that by my own standards, the couple's mutual belligerence had only abated to a small degree. My *post hoc* formulation of this case is that I did not do enough to increase their capacity to tolerate the unconventional eroticisms of their family. If perhaps John's love of enemas had not become labeled as "manipulative" and "degrading," channels to intimacy, now closed, could have been left open. I wondered if Mary's expression of gratitude to me for one kind of increased tolerance was not a cue as to the direction I might have gone in, from which I was blocked, principally by my own culturally rooted anxiety.

Notes

1. Mitchell (1981) has described this approach to technique at much greater length.
2. Some might argue that to speak of the "truth" of sexual *instability* one might be left as vulnerable to the charge of reification as to assert the existence of sexual stability. In response I would argue that in criticizing assertions of sexual stability I make no *prescription* for sexual conduct, either on an individual or a societal level. Rather I draw on historical and anthropological work to justify my claim of instability and vast variety in the sexual realm. At any rate, the only practices about which I do mean to prescribe are certain theorizations which do not reflect these data (see Boswell 1980; Herdt 1987; Greenberg 1988).

3. I am referring here to the usage of public sites for particular kinds of erotic activity. One such site, best known to the public, is the bathhouse, institutionalized by gay men.
4. There is one very important exception to this statement, which seems to have been forgotten. In the 1970s many women made the conscious choice to eroticize their own gender as part of an effort to alter and live apart from the system of sexism. From my point of view theirs were acts of creative, courageous, political eroticization, not the discovery of pre-existing dispositions.

References Cited

Bergler, E. 1944. Eight prerequisites for psychoanalytic treatment of homosexuality. *Psychoanalytic Review* 31: 253–286.

Boswell, J. 1980. *Christianity, Social Tolerance and Homosexuality*. Chicago and London: The University of Chicago Press.

Corbett, K. 1993. The mystery of homosexuality. *Psychoanal. Psychol.* 10: 345–357.

Freud, S. 1905. Three essays on the theory of sexuality. *Standard Edition* 7: 125–144. London: Hogarth Press.

———. 1918. From the history of an infantile neurosis. *Standard Edition* 17: 3–22.

———. 1923. The ego and the id. *Standard Edition* 19: 3–66.

———. 1927. Fetishism. *Standard Edition* 21: 149–159.

Friedman, R. 1988. *Male Homosexuality: A Contemporary Psychoanalytic Perspective*. New Haven: Yale University Press.

Frommer, M.S. 1994. Homosexuality and psychoanalysis: Technical considerations revisited. *Psychoanal. Dial.* 4: 215–233.

Greenberg, D. 1988. *The Construction of Homosexuality*. Chicago: The University of Chicago Press.

Herdt, G. 1987. *The Sambia: Ritual and Gender in New Guinea*. Berkeley: University of California Press.

Isay, R. 1991. The homosexual analyst. *Psychoanal. Study of the Child* 46: 199–216.

Kwawer, J. 1980. Transference and countertransference in homosexuality: Changing psychoanalytic views. *Am. J. Psyther.* 34: 72–80.

Lewes, K. 1988. *The Psychoanalytic Theory of Male Homosexuality*. New York: Simon and Schuster.

Mitchell, S. 1978. Psychodynamics, homosexuality and the question of pathology. *Psychiat.* 41: 254–263.

———. 1981. The psychoanalytic treatment of homosexuality: Some technical considerations. *Int. Rev. Psycho-Anal.* 8: 63–80.

Socarides, C. 1978. *Homosexuality*. New York: Aronson.

Trop, J. and Stolorow, R. 1992. Defense analysis in self-psychology: A developmental view. *Psychoanal. Dial.* 2: 427–442.

Part 2

Rethinking Sexuality

Theoretical Perspectives

7

On "Our Nature"

Prolegomenon to a Relational Theory of Sexuality

Muriel Dimen

Introduction: "My Mother Had the Face of an Angel."

IN MID-JULY OF 1993, a gay man told a television interviewer that he was glad of Dr. Dean Hamer's finding that, according to the *New York Times*, "one or several genes located on the bottom half of the ... X chromosome may play a role in predisposing some men toward homosexuality" (Angier 1993). The finding showed, said he, that there's nothing wrong with being gay. His actual words were, "I'm not gay because my parents did anything wrong."

This moving and extraordinary statement just about said it all. So I am going to use it as my text, deconstructing it in order to indicate a way of thinking about not only homosexuality but sexuality in general. The following remarks, made originally at the conference that gathered many of the papers in this volume, do not constitute an object-relational theory of sexuality; indeed, there is as yet no such thing.

Rather, this effort is a preliminary move: Putting homosexuality in "relational perspective," seeing it in the tension of one- and two-person psychologies, means relocating sexuality altogether on the intellectual map. To reposition sexuality thus is to engage ideas that thread through both scientific and popular thought, especially what I will call the Discourse of Nature, itself a technology of power, a cultural meditation on normality and morality that, by masquerading as the mirror of nature, effects social control. Explicating this discourse is a task whose scope exceeds this brief contribution. Here I can only suggest its dimensions: when it comes to a theory of sexuality, you can't have it all. If you want a psychoanalytic theory of desire, then you have to give up the Discourse of Nature.

Two sorts of "nature" show up in this Discourse. Let us return to the text: I think we all understand what this man is talking about. I don't mean that we all know what it's like to be gay, that our problems are the same, that we're all the same under the skin, between the sheets. But we do know what it feels like to believe that the way we are hurts our parents, that our "*nature*," as *The Crying Game* put it, shames them. You may recall a moment from another film, *The Elephant Man*, when the protagonist says, "My mother had the face of an angel." Choked with tears, he pauses, then goes on, "I was a great disappointment to her." If we didn't know what he felt like, we wouldn't choke up with him. We're familiar with the guilt, the shame and self-loathing, the helpless sorrow, the mourned or perhaps presently unmournable loss, the yearning and love. You don't have to be gay to have these feelings, and being gay does not mean you have to have them, but certainly some people feel these things because of being gay in our culture.

It's no wonder, then, that this man welcomed Hamer's news. His personal nature had been vindicated by Nature itself. He no longer had to blame his parents, and they no longer had to blame themselves. There was nothing for anyone to blame anyone else for. In the first reading of his words—I'll get back to the second in my conclusion—he was saying that he was gay not because his parents raised him wrong but because that's what he was by Nature, gay. There was no blame, no right, no wrong, just a natural fact. Just the facts, ma'am. No emotion.

But not just the facts. And lots of emotion. We all want biology on our side. It *means* something to find one's nature mirrored in what used to be called the facts of life, the facts of Nature. It's very personal, not to mention political. Biology with a capital B, the discipline that gives official standing to the Discourse of Nature, vindicates us. The great legalizer, it authorizes us. Studied, imagined, and in that way created by science (Fausto-Sterling 1986; Haraway 1989; Keller 1992), biology becomes Biology. The scientific discipline of biology serves as the abstract means to explicate, validate, regulate, and, thereby, also create the most private experiences of self.[1] Heterosexual people tend to be oblivious to this legitimation, just as white people usually don't note the color of their skin. It's what the New Left tagged "privilege"—skin privilege, gender privilege, class privilege. Here we are talking about sex privilege.

If You're Not Straight, You Must Be Crazy.

Heterosexuality's privilege has various charters. For the devout, it's Scripture. For the secular, including psychoanalysts, it's Darwinian evolutionary theory. Indeed, Darwinism has for intellectuals just about the same ethical and intellectual weight as religious doctrine has for believers. This parallel is no accident. In Western thought, the narrative of natural selection long ago supplanted the story of creation as the true account of the origins and fate of the human species (Lewontin 1991). To the victor went also the spoils: in late nineteenth-century secular life, evolutionary theory came to carry the intellectual and moral charge that had until then been the exclusive property of religion.

Psychoanalysis in turn borrows from this nearly scriptural authority. The classic psychoanalytic theory of sexuality, which is in point of fact the only theory of sex psychoanalysis has (Dimen 1995), leans on evolutionary theory for scientific support, appealing to it as discoverer, purveyor, and arbiter of truth (e.g., Freud 1913, 1 and passim; since examples are too numerous to cite, see Fliegel 1986, 13, 16, 26–28, for a summary critique; and Schafer 1977, 350). Darwinism validates the psychoanalytic sexuality of choice—heterosexuality—and thereby confirms the privilege given it by cultural convention, including psychoanalytic reasoning (e.g., Freud 1931, 228).

The sort of Darwinism on which Sigmund Freud relied has recently come into question. According to "strict adaptationism," as Stephen Jay Gould terms it, every behavior must have its reproductive consequences:

> The Darwinian tradition . . . reduces all large-scale evolutionary phenomena to extrapolated results of natural selection working at the level of individual organisms within populations (the "struggle for existence," as Darwin stated, or, in modern terms, "reproductive success"). (Gould 1987, 218)

In the newer view, not all behaviors are so evaluated; moreover, the individual is not the sole unit on which natural selection operates. Strict adaptationism, however, remains the model in everyone's mind when evolutionary theory comes up. Despite its scientific shortcomings (Gould 1981), despite, or because of, its service to moral ideals, cultural conventions of normality, and political forces (Haraway 1989: 320–22 and passim; Keller 1992,

113–43), it wears the badge of science and hence stands as a guarantor of objective and neutral truth.

Upon reflection, however, strict adaptationism turns out to be the scientific rationale for what David Schwartz has dubbed "heterophilia": the usually unarticulated, "overarching idealization" of heterosexuality that informs our culture and our theories of desire (1993, 648). Heterophilia finds its most concentrated, often strident expression in human sociobiology. This account of sex and gender, especially in its popular form, holds that all organisms have at their core the imperative to reproduce successfully. They are driven to leave as many of their genes behind as they can in order to win the competitive game of survival. Indeed, genes themselves are thought to compete (Dawkins 1976).[2]

Ruled by their particular biological reproductive roles, human males and human females live out this cutthroat core akin to animals but differently from each other. Since sperm, "little more than genes with a delivery system" (Gould 1987, 36), are bounteously produced with little investment of energy, men achieve their goal by impregnating as many women as frequently as they can, however they can—courtship, seduction, rape. Women, in the cost-benefit view permeating sociobiology (Keller 1992, 125; Haraway 1989, passim), gain from the more domestic virtue of prudence. Having invested more by creating nutrient-rich eggs and being about to invest more by using their bodies to bear and nurture their young, they secure their reproductive advantage by carefully selecting superior men to impregnate them.

This story of human procreation is created by political sleight of hand disguised as science. It conforms to the standard, though flawed, sociobiological way of reasoning: project patterns derived from human society onto non-human animals and then derive human behavior from the study of them (Fausto-Sterling 1986, 160–161; Lewontin, et al. 1984; Ross 1994, 253). In the case of sex, first study apes and monkeys, ducks and insects, next find there the direct link between sexuality and biological reproduction, and then call monogamy and sexual violence natural (see also Fausto-Sterling 1986, ch. 6 and 1993). Gould's sarcastic summary is not unfair: "The sociopolitical line of the pop argument now leaps from the page: males are aggressive, assertive, promiscuous, overbearing; females are coy, discriminating, loyal, caring—and these differences are adaptive, Darwinian, genetic, proper, good, inevitable, unchangeable." (Gould 1987, 36).

Heterosexuality is the behavioral hero in this story. Since the measure of any behavior is its contribution to species reproduction, heterosexuality, by matching penis to vagina, receives top marks.[3] Unsurprisingly, non-heterosexualities show up only exceptionally on the sociobiological map. When they do, it's to serve reproductive needs; see, for example, Daniel Kevles' example of homosexual pair-bonding of females among ring-billed gulls on the Channel Islands, deemed a survival strategy providing greater opportunity for both females to be impregnated by promiscuous males (cited by Gould 1987, 47). Homosexuality's usual absence is the clue to its value in this account: None. On these grounds, homosexuality might be argued to come and go like other traits lacking survival value; that is, randomly. However, in sociobiological eyes, if it's females' nature to nurture, and males' to predate, then females and males who have other inclinations at the core of their beings are maladaptive. It is not far to go to think that the maladaptive is unnatural, that is, abnormal, hence ill or bad, immoral, insane.

The story of Heterophilia constitutes the Discourse of Nature. Many disciplines participate in this Discourse, not only Biology, but psychoanalysis, marxist and other social theories, feminism, even anarchism (the anarchist Peter Kropotkin used cooperativeness in nature as partial justification for the political program he set forth in *Mutual Aid* [1972/1902]). If Nature is thought to be the bedrock of human nature, then it stands as a fount of truth, and everyone wants to locate their view of human society in it. As Ross puts it, however, "ideas that draw upon the authority of nature nearly always have their origin in ideas about society" (1994, 15). In the Discourse of Nature, the terms of biological "necessity," social normativity, and sanity are fungible, as psychoanalytic participation makes quite clear. Many times, for example, Freud links his understanding of sexuality to Darwinian narrative. In many other places and in many ways such linkage itself is also forged to moral precepts, assertions of social need, and models of mental health.

This fungibility of categories is evident in the literary structure of Freud's "Three Essays on the Theory of Sexuality" (1905). As its narrative progresses from broad to narrow, the requirements of procreation, the demands of culture, and the lineaments of sanity gradually come to imply and evoke one another (e.g., 229). Sexuality begins in polymorphousness. By the end, cultural stricture, psychic integrity, and reproductive survival speak in one voice. Sexual desire must conclude as the subordination of fore-pleasure to end-pleasure, in which (penile) discharge takes place in the correct (vaginal) receptacle. Freud may argue that "*neuroses are, so to say, the negative of perversion*" (1905, 165). He may tell us that we fall ill because we inhibit non-procreative desire. He may diagnose neurosis as the occupational hazard of civilization (1905, 231; 1930). But the conventional Darwinian story of sexual nature told by psychoanalysis is the story of cultural convention: Heterosexual and potentially procreative intercourse is foregone at the cost of moral and emotional normality. Or, if you're not straight, you must be crazy.

SNAFU: An Excursion into Psychoanalytic Contradictions

Ahh. Normality, that for which we all long, but believe, deep in our despairing hearts, that we will never attain. At last we're getting to the bottom of things. Normality is a torment equally of psyche, society, and, therefore, theory.[4] I have in mind here not only the Foucauldian critique (1980), according to which normality is constituted by knowledge, that is, by ideologies and regulating practices that activate and authorize patterns of domination. I have also in mind problems particular to psychoanalytic knowledge of sexuality, which routinely implies and entails developmental theory.

In my opinion, developmental theory customarily constitutes a theory of normality, of normal development. Put this another way. Many of you reading these words will have taken a course in "Abnormal Psychology." But have you ever taken a course in "Normal Psychology"? "No," you will say. But "Yes" you must answer, only it's gone under another name: Sometimes it's called "Personality Theory," most often it's called "Development." What these courses in the phenomenology of the normal teach is the process and steps of psychological, including sexual, growth and change.

To anticipate an objection: I am not suggesting we do away altogether with developmental theory. We require some way to think about change, if only because, along with death and taxes, it's one of the few certainties. Still, present theories of psychological development won't quite do. The problem is not exactly one of truth—the debatability of psychoanalytic truth (Mitchell 1988, 123–170) is intellectually desirable. The problem is more that of theory. Indeed, one of the juicy riddles psychologists and psychoanalysts have on their plate is how to theorize psychological change without imprisoning in normality the multiplicity of personal experience and the "multilinearity" (to borrow a term from anthropology [Steward 1955]) of psychological process (see O'Connor and Ryan 1994, 16).

You see, whenever I think of the word "normal" (and let me apologize right away for referring to an experience that may be familiar only to provincial New Yorkers), all I can visualize is one of those electronic signs on the Long Island Expressway. You know, you're driving home after a lovely weekend in the Hamptons or Fire Island when suddenly you see it, the sign that strikes dread in your heart, the sign that says, "Normal Traffic Conditions Ahead." NORMAL traffic conditions? On what traffic reporters fondly dub "The World's Longest Parking Lot?" I don't know about you, but whenever I see that sign, I think, "Oh God, please, no, anything but that." They say there are no atheists in a foxhole. I say, there are no atheists in the nightmare that constitutes normality on the Long Island Distressway.[5]

But wait a minute. Isn't that what normality is? A nightmare? Think of the classic World War II acronym, SNAFU. A military term, it evokes what psychoanalysts know truly defines the normal—the paradox, if you will, at normality's heart: "Situation Normal, All Fucked Up." Indeed, originally it is normality itself that makes the mess, at least according to *The Dictionary of American Slang* (Wentworth and Flexner 1967, 493):

> SNAFU. Original Army use c. 1940. The original Army connotation was that the situation was "fucked up" owing to an excess of Army rules and routine.[6]

Freud too believed, as is well known and I've stressed, that order creates disorder. It's just the refusal to recognize this fact that's pathologically destructive.[7] Not only inhibition and neurosis but "civilization and its discontents" was, finally, Freud's watchword. If, then, neurosis is normative in civilization, what other meanings inhere in the notion of "normal"?

To put it another way, if we subtract the normative from the normal, what's left over? The excess, it seems to me, consists in the regulatory force of the idea of the "normal," a notion central to the power of psychoanalysis as a political and social institution. "Normality" is a powerful force because it seems to designate what's only good and right, that is, what's natural. This naturalness is, however, an artifact created by a discursive process that projects "assumptions about nature back and forth between biology and society in a vicious rhetorical circle" (Ross 1994, 19). Spun round and round, the natural, the normal, and the moral become confused, one with the other, barely separable even upon inspection.

Normalizing is central to psychoanalytic prescriptivity, that is, to its way of participating in regulatory practice. Stephen Mitchell notes this prescriptivity in an account of psychoanalytic homophobia. He identifies "an omnipotent ideal that placed the analyst in the position of arbiter of the good life" (1993, 623). My only quibble is that he localizes this admirably described power to name the normal in a mere two decades, the 1960s and 1970s. In contrast, many accounts situate psychoanalysis among the most powerful twentieth-century institutions of social reproduction, whose job it is to re-create the status quo, i.e., "the normal," each generation and every day (Dimen 1992; Ehrenreich 1989; Kovel 1981).

Psychoanalytic thinking renders its own prescriptivity simultaneously normal, natural, and moral by creating a master narrative of human nature out of a particular sexual theory. Freud's compelling, universalizing story of human psyche, culture, and biology is a good example. In "Totem and Taboo," his prime text on desire as the hub of human history, he argues that psychoanalysis will be key to a synthetic theory of human nature: "The beginnings of religion, morals, society, and art converge in the Oedipus complex" (1913, 156). In a footnote, Freud first disclaims this centrality, saying he's just added one more factor. Then he goes on to insist that, even though people will resist this factor emotionally, it will have to be critical to the theory. Indeed, he himself is (perhaps genuinely) nonplussed: "It seems to me a most surprising discovery that the problems of social psychology, too, should prove soluble on the basis of one single concrete point—man's relation to his father" (1913, 157, n. 1). Gender critique aside—although patriarchy is in many ways the point here—to establish a totalizing theory resting on a single, elemental cause is, in post-Enlightenment Western thought, a claim to Truth.

As both marxists and postmodernists argue, however, claims to Truth are also claims on power. Take scientific notions of gender. Anne Fausto-Sterling (1986) argues that biological theories about differences between women and men serve power needs. Like Richard Lewontin, et al. (1984), she holds that systems of knowledge are created in the interest of ruling classes. A chapter begins:

> Jobs and education—that's what it's really all about. At the crux of the question "Who's smarter, men or women?" lie decisions about how to teach reading and mathematics, about whether boys and girls should attend separate schools, about job and career choices, and, as always, about money—how much employers will have to pay to whom and what salaries employees, both male and female, can command. (1986, 13)

If Fausto-Sterling and Lewontin, et al. hold that "knowledge is power," Michel Foucault proposes the converse. Seeing knowledge as produced rather than controlled, he gives equal time to the formulation, "power is knowledge" (1980; 1988). There is a will to knowledge constituted by a political economy of sex, immanent in which are strategies of power (1980, 12, 73). The state wants to ensure orderly behavior, not only to punish crimes *ex post facto*; its interest is in the internalization of social control. "The more peaceful (e.g., controlled) the population, the more the state's power is legitimated and assured" (Flax 1990, 208). Such social control, or domination, depends on creating truths, and therefore on the systems that produce them: "there can be no exercise of power except through the production of truth. These 'truths' reflect the 'facts of human nature' as revealed by biological and human sciences. These discourses tell us what it is to be human" (Flax 1990, 207).

Scholarly disciplines create a politically efficacious view of human life by claiming both to find its source in nature and thereby to demonstrate its truth, goodness, health, normality. Simultaneously forged are "[c]oncepts of deviancy, illness, maladjustment, and so forth," for they "are products of the same discourses that create the normal" (Flax 1990, 207).[8] Key to this socially-controlling view of human nature is sexuality. A plethora of disciplines—"demography, biology, medicine, psychiatry, psychology, ethics, pedagogy, and poltiical criticism"—produces the truth of human nature by creating "sexuality" (Foucault 1980, 33; 25–26). For example, demography emerged as a scientific discipline when, in the early eighteenth century, the category of population became for European states a social control problem distinct from questions about people as political actors. "At the heart of this economic and political problem of population was sex: it was necessary to analyze the birth rate, the age of marriage, the legitimate and illegitimate births, the precocity and frequency of sexual relations, the ways of making them fertile or sterile, the effects of unmarried life or of the prohibitions, the impact of contraceptive practices" (Foucault 1980, 25–26). The resulting analyses, by dividing and classifying, rendered some sexualities natural, others not. The unnatural became a particular dimension in the sexual domain, covering everything outside of marital sex (Foucault 1980, 39). This continuing production of new discourses on sex (of which the present contribution, let it be noted, is one), or what Foucault calls "scientia sexualis," permits "something called 'sexuality' to embody the truth of sex and its pleasures." This socially naturalized creation called sexuality is the correlate of the discursive practice of the scientia sexualis, which defines sex as being "by nature," vulnerable to pathology and therefore requiring therapy, containing meanings requiring decoding, situating concealed processes, a center for multiple and indeterminate causalities (Foucault 1980, 68).

In postmodernist perspective, the truth of the Natural is social and political, and as such subject to deconstruction. If, then, we look into the heterophiliac Discourse of Nature, we find that the natural is not self-evident, undifferentiated, eternal bedrock. If natural defines the normal, the normal seeks its validation as a moral category by claiming its natural origins. To put the matter even more complexly and therefore more accurately: if natural/unnatural is a key binary for evolutionary theory, then normal/abnormal, sane/mad, and healthy/unhealthy are key binaries for psychoanalysis. In turn, these dualisms interchange with the good/bad, the right/wrong, and the moral/immoral that anchor the system of cultural conventions we call morality. This entire set of binaries forms the matrix that confines psychoanalytic thought about sexuality, leading it along the straight and narrow to an unintended destination.

Desire and Evolution: On the Winding Road to Ambiguity

The lure of science to clinicians floundering in uncertainty is its claim to Truth and the quiescence of closure. I am recommending, however, that we not take the bait because we have an even more inviting, if disturbing, way to go. If we elaborate on these complexities, contingencies, and ambiguities, the seams in the Discourse of Nature begin to show and split. To recapitulate: if the survival of the biological species is the goal of reproduction, it's the biological organism that's usually taken as the main evolutionary product. If so, then the question that strict adaptationism insists we ask is also the question that, according to psychoanalysis, the incest prohibition excites: how is one of those products, those individual organisms, made? We want to see the primal scene up close. A theory, whether psychoanalytic or evolutionary, that starts from this (oedipal) question (and obsession) inevitably winds up naturalizing and normalizing heterosexuality.

Yet the mating game, which psychoanalysis, sociobiology, and popular culture commonly think of as embodying the natural, no longer holds much interest for other evolutionary theorists. If the psychoanalytic paradigm shift has moved thought up towards the social, biological thought has focused it down towards the microscopic. The sociobiology of human beings may be serving patriarchal stereotype dressed up as nuanced theory. But population biology cares little about the primal scene. Nor does it address sexuality in any way recognizable to psychoanalytic thought. In these molecular days, most biologists think about genes, not individuals; they study gene pools, not species (let alone social organizations like the nuclear family and its psychological complexes).[9] In the view of one strong critic, herself a biologist, mainstream biological thinking currently represents the essence of life as nothing more than a string of amino acids (Keller 1992, 96 and passim).

Contemporary biological theory, in other words, does not adequately describe the species that psychoanalysts, at least, want to understand, a species that is more than its genes.[10] What psychoanalysts want to know is what's either flattened out by sociobiology or of no interest to Biology or only recently present in the work of some Darwinian feminists (Anne Fausto-Sterling, personal communication): the complexities of desire and culture, the relational contingencies and meanings of mating and fertilization, and "all the ambiguities of the term reproduction as applied to organisms that neither make copies of themselves nor reproduce by themselves" (Keller 1992, 132). What's most interesting to us is what's most interesting about the human species: "Flexibility may well be the most important determinant of human consciousness; the direct programming of behavior has probably become maladaptive" (Gould 1977, 257).

It is an ethnographic truism that the human species requires more than its amino acids to reproduce, to put it with some irony. The nature of human nature is, as anthropologists like to say, cultural as well as biological, and therefore inherently various (Lévi-Strauss 1969/1949, 3–25). "We are, as Simone de Beauvoir said, *'l'être dont l'être est de n'être pas'*—the being whose essence lies in having no essence" (Gould 1977, 259). As three contemporary marxist biologists put it, "The only sensible thing to say about human nature is that it is 'in' that nature to construct its own history" (Lewontin, et al. 1984, 14). This construction is inevitably a social process. No human being survives as an isolate; put a baby down alone on a desert island and see what happens. As held by theories of cultural evolution (Steward 1955), not the individual organism, but the society or culture is the unit of survival.

That human beings are cultural and that cultures differ and change, these facts will surprise no reader of this volume. The question is what these commonplaces mean for psychoanalysis. René Spitz (1957) provided one answer: put a baby down in a crib and don't talk to it, he said, you'll see what happens—it dies of apathy. Winnicott, of course, supplied another: There's no such thing as a baby, he proclaimed rhetorically, to dramatize his point that the infant exists only in an environment mediated by the maternal object, only in a relational context (cited in Khan 1958, xxxvii). The human species is not only biological, not only cultural, it's also relational. We are as much part of the context as the context is part of us, even though the speaking subject I'm designating as "we" is also different from the linguistic, psychological, and social matrix of relations I'm calling "context." This relational context must be reproduced if the species is to survive. Now, what does this mean? Leaving aside the reproduction of social relations and institutions (which is culture's job and which, ultimately, must also be accounted for, but not within the confines of this essay [see Dimen 1992]), we might say what we're talking about is object relations and the desire drenching them.[11]

Yet once we admit desire into the Discourse of the Natural, the whole story of the natural normality of heterosexuality explodes. The idea that sexuality roots most importantly in evolutionary, reproductive requirements loses credibility and meaning. Desire, a concept whose elusiveness fills "Americans, pragmatists to the core," with dread (Levenson 1994, 692), can be most efficiently defined by what it is not: "Wants, needs, can be met. Desire is another kettle of fish entirely" (Levenson 1994, 692). Desire is about lack, absence, longing. Unlike need and demand, it is fundamentally unsatisfiable, a permanent, driving incompleteness. The yearning in which it manifests itself can be approximated in language but is, finally, unspeakable and therefore ambiguous (JMitchell and Rose 1982, 1–58).[12]

However intensely felt, desire becomes sensible only through culture. Claude Lévi-Strauss's characterization of the universality of the incest prohibition could apply as well to desire: "Culture has at all times and at all places filled this empty form, as a bubbling spring first fills the depressions surrounding its source" (1969/1949, 32). Jacques Lacan, in a certain sense, is correct to say that desire is unspecifiable in the absence of the symbolic order (Mitchell and Rose 1982). Where he goes wrong is when he falsely universalizes the patriarchal phallus as the metaphorical embodiment of the Law, that is, of culture (see Flax 1990, 104, on the denied literality of phallus-as-penis; see also A. Harris 1991, 204). To put it more humorously, desire is like invisible ink: it won't show up unless it gets wet. And what w(h)ets it is the coloring, flavoring, meanings of the cultural and historical institutions and discourses without which it could not be represented and in that sense would have no existence.

Most graphically, desire denotes what Freud calls "sexual impulses—in the ordinary sense of the word" (1905, 134), sexual desire as we vulgarly think of it, sex in all its concreteness, physicality, and excitement. Yet even before Freud, who understood sex as biological drive, anthropological researchers were teaching that no particular sexual desire is natural (Morgan 1870 in the United States and Tylor 1889 in England; indeed, cultural relativism and an appreciation of cross-cultural diversity reach far back in Western thought, to not only Montaigne but even Herodotus). Human organisms cannot and do not exist without cultural form, without social institutions, language, and so forth. Cultural forms, furthermore, vary, if not infinitely, then very, very widely. Since they do, human desire must be, as Margaret Mead put it, malleable (1928; Lévi-Strauss 1969/1949, 32). It must be ready for anything—which means it must also be ready for nothing in particular. It must be nonspecific or, what is the same thing, omnivorous. In any event, it can't keep kosher.

Is this a long way to say what Freud (1905) did in brief, that desire is polymorphously perverse? Not quite. The full force of his idea is unfelt unless the understanding of sexuality slips the leash. It's no longer enough just to point out Freud's obligation to Darwinism. And it is equally insufficient to argue that Nurture dominates Nature in the domain of sexuality (or, indeed, in any other domain; for example, intelligence). Sexual theory requires freedom from the determinism that psychoanalysis, like many other fields, has employed as an explanatory and rhetorical strategy. Determinism is part of what Jane Flax calls the "Enlightenment metanarrative" (1990, 30). In postmodernist view, it is a story of how human progress takes place through the application of reason to human life. This linear reckoning of cause and effect underlies all Western disciplines and knowledges, constructing their search for singular truths.

My argument for psychoanalysis, like Gould's for Darwinism (1987), is to give up all determinism.[13] It may seem, for example, that desire's cultural variability demonstrates its independence from Nature. Appearances, however, deceive. The argument that cross-cultural variation disproves biological determination won't quite wash. It's true, but it's not the whole truth. As told, it substitutes one determinism for another, making culture, not biology, the prime mover. In the determinist game, however, that which is closest to the physical wins. The culturalist strategy, used without critiquing determinism, leaves sexuality and desire as *tabulae rasae* to be inscribed according to culture's needs. Yet the creator of cultural needs is our old friend, Nature: in a culturally determinist model, the rigors of evolutionary survival dictate cultural needs (see, e.g., M. Harris 1989). Desire, once constituted, emerges, yet again, as Biology's unambiguous, undifferentiated, uniformed servant.

The quite different implications of polymorphous perversity are more appreciable in postmodernist perspective. Desire's prime quality is its ambiguity, of which its vaunted cultural malleability is a consequence. In introducing their definition of wish, J. LaPlanche and J.B. Pontalis say, "Any general theory of man [sic] is bound to contain ideas too fundamental to be circumscribed; this is no doubt true of desire in Freudian doctrine" (1973, 482). To render this experientially: The confusion we experience in trying to decode desire *is* the decoding. Desire is ambiguous. Sometimes it is focused and precise, sometimes it's elusive and inconclusive. Desire is discontinuous, shifting, it is what waits to be given definition within and between selves. Among the diverse meanings it has received, all situationally plausible, are the classic linkage to reproductive goals; the equally classic Freudian de-linking of drive, aim, and object; the Lacanian gap between the Imaginary and the Symbolic; and object-relational yearning for attachment.

Strict adaptationism is not, however, a theory of ambiguities. Rather, it theorizes linearities, irreversibilities, and dualisms. Orgasm, for example, is said to further species survival: "Anticipated sexual pleasure for *both* sexes is most likely an initiator (a stimulus of sorts) to begin mating behavior" (Small 1993, 148). Yet when desire emerges as an indeterminate end in itself, as, with its passions, impossibilities, and pain, it often is, a quantum leap has been taken, and the rest is (human, if not primate) history—and psychoanalysis. Biological determinism suits the Freud who wed desire to procreation, not the Freud who queried the abrogation of ambiguity in, say, the commonsense matching of masculinity to activity, femininity to passivity (see May, this volume). As such, much evolutionary theory skirts the twentieth-century paradigm shift from either/or to both/and—from positivism to uncertainty and relativity, empiricism to social constructionism and deconstructionism. Its logic instead cuts desire to fit cultural fashion. Like the "colonial imperialist paradigms" that saw "as 'natural' those expressions of black life which conformed to a pre-existing pattern or stereotype" (hooks 1990, 26), the Discourse of Nature creates nature in the image dear to the heart of a heterophiliac culture.

Conclusion: Between Instinct and Object

To put my argument at its strongest: We should sever the tie between psychoanalysis and the Discourse of Nature. We should forgo not only the classical grounding of sexuality in the requirements of evolutionary survival, but also the relatively recent relational idea that what's natural is not sex but attachment. As Thomas Domenici puts it (in this volume), where classical theory sees affective and interpersonal needs as "an overlay upon a more basic template of sexuality and aggression," object-relations theory reverses the matter, making sexuality the secondary precipitate of a desire for connection and intimacy.

If Freud missed something about relatedness, this naturalizing of attachment overlooks something about desire. "Excitement," Adam Phillips observes, "tends to turn up in object-relations theory as a defense against something reputedly more valuable. . . . The implication . . . is that freedom is freedom from bodily excitement. As though in states of desire the self was, as it were, complying with the tyranny of the body" (1988, 71). Object relations theory, by subordinating the erotic to relatedness, partakes of a certain puritanism that may be discerned in, for example, Winnicott's "distrust of, or dismay about, the nature of instinctual life" (Phillips 1988, 71). That psychoanalytic puritanism (an oxymoron, no?) is, itself, regulatory practice hardly needs demonstrating, but in any case will have to be argued elsewhere.

What I am suggesting and initiating is a deconstruction of psychoanalysis's use of Biology, its participation in the Discourse of Nature which is the foundation for its regulatory power. Psychoanalysis and the Discourse of Nature are historically mutually constitutive: the idea of Nature informs the theory of human nature which, in that vicious rhetorical circle, recreates a notion of givenness. Yet, as Ross (1994, 250) argues, nature lacks a common meaning, even as it seems to be common sense; everyone, from conservation biologists to sociobiologists, from economists and politicians to poets, means something different by it.

For psychoanalytic purposes, the idea of the Natural is not so much wrong as incoherent. It's certainly true that, given that the human species reproduces itself biologically through the union of spermatozoon and ovum, a penis and vagina that, you might say, want each other are critical for the propagation of species; as is, therefore, a psyche appropriately coded for a set of heterosexualizing institutions, like, marriage, parenting, and the family. However, this reproduction doesn't just happen; to borrow Beauvoir's pronouncement on women, heterosexuality is made, not born.

To take a dialectical view: That which potentiates reproductive heterosexuality also undoes it. Desire must flower for heterosexual—and procreative—activity to occur. If it does, however, then so do impulses and tendencies —polymorphous perversity—that may contradict procreative sex and the normative structures housing it. As Freud's thesis on the direct relation between neurosis and sexual inhibition suggests (1905), many psychological and cultural events must take place if one is to be turned on by people of only one sex, either one's own or the opposite. Being excited by the Other doesn't just happen. It requires a context, one potentiated by the one- and two-person work/practice/activity of relatedness.[14]

I recognize, at this point, a likely objection: At the very moment when homosexual desire seems to have received the same scientific imprimatur as heterosexuality, that is, when it's gotten a place at the genetic table of life,[15] I am arguing, "Oh, let's just forget about reactionary old Nature." The problem, however, is not nature, but the rhetorical (as well as material) use we make of it. As Ross persuasively puts it in regard to the Darwinian theory, "Competition, cooperation, or conflict—take your pick. Nature can be politically reassuring for any one who wants it to be" (1994, 19). Nature has been and is used both popularly and scientifically to condemn homosexuality. Recently the tide appears to have turned. Scientific theories, however, ebb and flow with public opinion. The Discourse of Nature, in other words, is not on the side of the angels, or, better, of those who are customarily demonized. Appealing to it is like carrying a loaded gun to fend off assailants: you're more likely to get shot than if you weren't packing, and, finally, it doesn't remove the cause of crime.

Of course, once we exit the familiar (should I say familial?) expressway to Nature, we travel an anxious byway, which brings me back to an alternative reading of this essay's initial text, a single, spoken sentence whose curious syntax sings a vital and necessary anxiety. One of the accomplishments of a normalizing theory of sexuality is that it provides landmarks in an otherwise open and sometimes seemingly endless sea of desire. Even its inherent pathologizing serves as a guide of sorts: if it pathologizes you, well, at least you know where you are, you've been wronged or you are wrong, but you do have an identity.

The television text with which I began, however, rejects all theory. It reads, if you remember, "I'm not gay because my parents did anything wrong." We have so far taken this to mean, "I'm gay not because my parents did anything wrong but because that's how I naturally and rightly am." On this understanding, we have interpreted its anxiety as related to the righteous emotional and moral demand placed on theory to exonerate children and parents from a psychologically and socially harmful, unfair blame. And we have seen that, in validating this demand, the text has recourse to the facts of Nature, taken to be morally unblameworthy, neutrally true, an explanation beyond explanation.

Still, if you consider the text's negation, the placement of the "not," then another meaning emerges. We've heard, "I'm gay *not because* my parents. . . ." But the actual sequence is, "I'm *not* gay because. . . ." The "not" refuses the predicate beginning "gay because." There is, says the text, no "gay because." There's only "gay." "Gay" neither wants nor needs explanation. Do we, the syntax asks, say "I'm heterosexual *because* . . . ." Don't we, only explain that which is, somehow, "different," which sticks out, calls attention to itself as unnatural? Explanations only harm, suggests the text; they pathologize, stigmatize, and delegitimize.

One reason, we can conclude, that there is to be no "gay because" is that homosexuality should be understood as natural, normal, just like heterosexuality which, as "the absent standard" (Sampson 1993) of psychological and political normality, neither wants nor needs nor receives explanation. Gay should receive the same privilege as straight, including what we might call "SNAFU privilege," the right to be fucked up without having your desire stigmatized because of it, or the right to have your sexual problems addressed without your sexual preference being pathologized. Like heterosexuality, gay identity should be the uncontested base of identity politics as well.

One can only agree. And yet. . . . It's not my job here to opinionate on identity politics, whose exigencies often require what Gayatri Chakravorty Spivak has termed, in regard to women, a "strategic essentialism" (Spivak and Rooney 1994), which in this case might mean using Darwinian theory as a claim to truth and power. It is more imperative that I address what I find troubling in this implicit refusal of explanation, which I think emerges from an anxiety born of ambiguity. For one thing, if we don't provide explanations, someone else will: you have to have a position to counter the hydra-headed forces of anti-homosexuality, misogyny, and so on. For another, refusing explanation refuses what we do know, that our experience and history have something to do with who we are, with—and I think we may still say this in the *Crying Game* sense—our own personal individual "nature."

To refuse explanation is to refuse the complexity of desire and the tangle of pain. Sex is not uncomplicated, to put it mildly. Its scariness is not always intrinsic to its excitement, and, in entailing as much unpleasure as pleasure, it doesn't always provide as much joy as it might. If we don't usually want to look a gift horse in the mouth and ask why we're having a good (sexual) time, we do tend to want to know why we're not. Absent explanation, there's no way to figure out what's wrong. Who/what causes sexual (and other psychic) pain? Sometimes the villain is the Other, sometimes it's us. Sometimes we blame our parents because of the pain sex brings us, but are mistaken to do so: The pain may come from social prejudice, or it may emanate from the grievous losses we all meet on life's trail. Sometimes, however, we are right to hold someone else to account: people make mistakes, and sometimes we even collude in those made by our parents.

How to understand these complications and ambiguities? There are a variety of routes. One is traditional, to posit binaries that eliminate ambiguity: the normal/evolutionary/heterosexual versus the pathological/unnatural/queer. But there are others: for example, Chodorow's recent argument from a classical position that all sex, including heterosexuality, should be interpreted as compromise formation (1992). I am proposing a third route, one formed in the main tension or, perhaps we may call it, paradox, in Freud's sexual theory. Recall this footnote to the "Three Essays":

> The most striking distinction between the erotic life of antiquity and our own no doubt lies in the fact that the ancients laid the stress upon the instinct itself, whereas we emphasize its object. The ancients glorified the instinct and were prepared on its account to honour even an inferior object; while we despise the instinctual activity in itself, and find excuses for it only in the merits of the object (1905, 149 n. 1)

This quote establishes two poles of a paradox: on the one hand, instinct, in Freud's problematic term, or as we might nondeterministically reformulate it, desire, and, on the other, object, or better, object-relation. Freud's theory of sexuality developed, I think, in the tension of this paradox. As time went on, his thought followed the pattern of the "Three Essays." Pulled by the discourse of the Natural to pathologize non-heterosexual desire, it succumbed increasingly to the object pole, making sense of sexual activity in terms of object-choice and forgetting desire.

We can resist the lure of Truth's closure. By entering the ambiguous, charged space between the poles of paradox, we can recoup what was best about Freud's de-linking of drive, aim, and object without subscribing to the normalizing Discourse of the Natural. Let us utilize the notion of paradox that relational theorists (e.g., Benjamin 1988; Ghent 1992), building on Winnicott, have been applying in a variety of domains, from clinical process to metapsychology to psychoanalytic feminism. Our guide could be Margo Rivera's dictum with regard to treating multiple personality disorder: "The problem," she says, "is not the multiplicity, but the dissociation" (1989). And then let us see what possibilities we encounter. Perhaps we can construe two parallel and paradoxical processes, one in which relationship governs the erotic and another in which erotism governs relationship. What about moving the body outside the discourse of Nature into questions of embodiment, of the meaning and representation of the body as experienced in relational context? The terms of our thought can encompass a necessary tension between the amorphous sea of desire and a developmental process that provides experiences of coherence, in which hetero-, homo-, and othersexuality are mutually constitutive, not a sequential and hierarchical binary (Butler 1995). By thinking this way, we could render sexual desire, like gender, an outcome of "acts of interpretation" (Harris 1991, 213). Perhaps then developmental process itself, even stages, might emerge as efforts of meaning, not givens.[16] Perhaps the shame and the blame, inhering so often in desire as to seem essential to it, could emerge as the constructions they are. In any event, the practice of paradoxical thinking suits the ambiguity of sex: it is a way to say that experiences of pleasure make of each sexual nature a creation; one emerging from prior constitution, to be sure, but always subject to the personal evolution that is, in any case, its lifelong project (Dimen 1982).

Notes

1. Postmodernist psychologists, influenced by Michel Foucault, have begun to describe the dialectical process whereby Biology creates Psychology. Philip Cushman (1991), for example, critiques Daniel Stern's theory of infant development (1985) for its naturalization of one particular version of self. Stern's manifest contribution is the idea that relatedness is psychologically hard-wired. It would appear, then, that his argument is more about culture than about nature. If, however, we ask who it is who's doing the relating, Cushman observes, we in fact find none other than the atomized Western self, situated by Stern's theory in a pre-linguistic, pre-symbolic Nature and thereby defined as originary.
2. Gould distinguishes several categories of Darwinist thought: classical; strict adaptationism; "good sociobiology," mostly about non-human animal behavior; and "bad sociobiology," that is, "pop sociobiology" or "cardboard" Darwinism (1987, 25–51; see also Lewontin, et al. 1984), which focuses on human beings. Others, e.g., the primatologist Haraway (1989), think there is no such thing as "good sociobiology."
3. A match that is, by the way, the founding trope of classical psychosexual theory; even, one might say, its ego-ideal.
4. Whether "normality" is an unavoidable and even necessary displeasure, which was Freud's contention, remains a matter too complicated to take up here.
5. David Bouchier, the radio commentator, journalist, humorist, and sociologist, said all this perhaps a little more concisely. He describes a suburban feeding ritual:

> "Come on over. We're having a barbecue." What other message can strike such gloom and despondency into the suburban soul? Perhaps only

> "Normal Traffic Conditions Ahead" has the same heart-chilling effect. (1994)

6. By the way, most dictionaries define it as "Situation Normal, All Fouled Up," a normalizing and, what may be the same thing, de-eroticizing gesture in itself (see, e.g., *The Random House Dictionary of the English Language* 1966, 1346).
7. Levenson renders Freud's idea in a contemporary vernacular: "Maybe, as Mel Brooks put it, 'Life stinks' and recognizing that is a prerequisite for living successfully" (1994, 706).
8. "Failure of disciplinary practices becomes the basis of 'experts' to ask for more resources and power to pursue and exercise their knowledge in the name of the public good" (Flax 1990, 208). Barbara and John Ehrenreich have called these experts the "professional-managerial class" (1979; Ehrenreich 1989), a class that came into being between 1870 and 1920 and whose work, ranging from law and medicine to middle management, from social work and psychotherapy to education, from academia to journalism, entails conceptualizing other people's work and lives (Ehrenreich 1989, 13). What a good way to describe the regulatory power of psychoanalysis.
9. Indeed, the reproduction of the species is in some sociobiological texts merely in service of the reproduction of the gene (Dawkins 1976).
10. This assertion would probably hold for most species; the difference is that human beings think and write about it.
11. To speak of object relations and desire is, in a sense, to speak two different languages whose compatibility requires some mechanism of mutual translation. I think about the problem thus: In relational perspective, the intrapsychic and the interpersonal are mutually constituted; from this already postmodernist angle, there's no chicken and egg, each is always already there. The intrapsychic comes into being and takes on its meaning and value in the charged, desiring field between persons, while, paradoxically, that field is realized through the inner worlds of the participants. And so our question about the evolution of the human species and what's natural in it entails a very specifically psychoanalytic discussion of object relations, of the internal representations of self and others as they are contextualized by emotion and value. Emotion and value inhere, in my view, in the desire in which object-relations are suspended. From a feminist perspective, Jaggar (1989) argues for the intermixture of emotional and social value: just as social values always carry an emotional charge, so emotions are always permeated with social values.
12. The debate on desire is intense and complex. According to Levenson (1994),

> one enters it, as one must, but with trepidation. In one-person terms, desire seems to spring full-blown in intrapsychic process, almost a species characteristic. In the linguistically-based Lacanian view, it emerges as a consequence of the failure of speech, of the gap between the Imaginary and the Symbolic. From a two-person vantage point, however, desire turns out to be oddly intersubjective.

In its sexual incarnation, desire is our "only instinct requiring the stimulation of another person," as Lévi-Strauss put it when, arguing with Freud, he characterizes the incest taboo as the beginning of social life in nature (1969/1949, 12). Even though Lacan insists that the maternal relation, in which desire first emerges, belongs in the non-symbolizable Imaginary, we pragmatist Americans might insist, as Levenson does, that "desire requires another person." Levenson goes on to remark on the "peculiar paradox built into this wish to find one's completion in the regard of the Other," one that involves Hegel's Master-Slave dialectic. To put this in more relational terms, desire is the symbolically represented and polysemic longings constituting both objects and the space between them. Benjamin (1988) elaborates on both the object-relational and gendered implications of this structure of desire.

13. In Gould's view, the natural world, constituted as strict Darwinism's purview, contains many ambiguities (1987, 13–14) that could be better appreciated by a view of "biological potentiality" (Gould 1977). He makes a plea for a non-determinist, Darwinian theory of contingency and interactivity capable of attending, without reductionism, to diversity, complexity, and ambiguity (1977; 1987).
14. It was to explain this by no means self-evident phenomenon that Freud wrote the "Three Essays" after all. That he there recapitulated cultural prejudices of homophobia and sexism, and that he created a one-person psychology compatible with the biological determinism to which he looked for confirmation and authorization, serves as fodder for a contemporary re-interpretation of sexuality.
15. I borrow from Bruce Bawer's fine title, *A Place at the Table*, in a context that he might, however, not appreciate.
16. As Adrienne Harris argues, to view sex, object choice, or gender as grounded in biology ("the real") disregards what's fundamental to "Freud's radical intervention in our understanding of personality. Biologically determined theories keep such experiences as gender and sexuality outside the system of meaning itself. To be meaningful, these experiences must be understood as symbolizable. Gender, then, and the relation of gender to love object can be understood only by acts of interpretation" (1991, 212–213).

References Cited

Angier, Natalie. 1993. *New York Times*, July 16: A1.

Aron, L. and A. Harris, eds. 1993. *The legacy of Sándor Ferenczi*. Hillsdale, NJ: The Analytic Press.

Barratt, B. 1993. *The postmodern impulse in psychoanalysis*. Baltimore: Johns Hopkins University Press.

Bawer, B. 1994. *A place at the table*. NY: Simon & Schuster.

Benjamin, J. 1988. *The bonds of love*. NY: Pantheon.

Bouchier, D. 1994. "Cooking on the barbecue is man's work." *New York Times*, Long Island edition, July 3, Section 13, p. 1.

Butler, J. 1990. *Gender trouble: Feminism and the subversion of identity*. NY: Routledge.

———. 1995. "Melancholy gender/refused identification." *Psychoanalytic Dialogues* 5 (2): 165–180.

Chodorow, Nancy. 1992. "Heterosexuality as compromise formation." *Psychoanalysis and Contemporary Thought* 15 (3): 267–304.

Cushman, P. 1991. "Ideology obscured: Political uses of the self in Daniel Stern's infant." *American Psychologist* 46: 206–219.

Dawkins, R. 1976. *The selfish gene*. Oxford: Oxford University Press.

Dimen, M. 1982. "Notes for the reconstruction of sexuality." *Social Text* 6: 22–31.

———. 1992. "Theorizing social reproduction: On the origins of decentered subjectivity." *Genders* 14: 98–125.

———. 1994. "Money, love and hate: Contradiction and paradox in psychoanalysis." *Psychoanalytic Dialogues* 4: 60–100.

———. 1995. "Introduction," Symposium on Sexuality/Sexualities. *Psychoanalytic Dialogues* 5 (2): 157–63.

Ehrenreich, B. 1989. *Fear of falling: The inner life of the middle class*. New York: Pantheon.

Ehrenreich, B. and J. Ehrenreich. (1979). "The professional-managerial class." In *Between labor and capital*, ed. by P. Walker. Boston: South End Press.

Fausto-Sterling, A. 1986. *Myths of gender: Biological theories of women and men*. NY: Basic Books.

———. 1993. "The five sexes: Why male and female are not enough." *The Sciences* (March/April): 20–24.

Flax, J. 1990. *Thinking fragments: Psychoanalysis, feminism, and postmodernism in the contemporary West*. Berkeley: University of California Press.

Fliegel, Z. 1986. "Women's development in analytic theory: Six decades of controversy." In *Psychoanalysis and women: Contemporary reappraisals*. Ed. by Judith L. Alpert Hillsdale, NJ: The Analytic Press, 3–32.

Foucault, M. 1965. *Madness and civilization: A history of insanity in the age of reason*. Trans. R. Howard. NY: Vintage.

———. 1975. *The birth of the clinic*. Trans. A. M. Sheridan Smith. NY: Vintage.

———. 1980. *The history of sexuality: Volume I*. Trans. R. Hurley. NY: Vintage.

———. 1988. "The political technologies of individuals." In *Technologies of the self: A seminar with Michel Foucault*. Ed. by L. Martin, H. Gutman and P. Hutton. Amherst: University of Massachusetts Press: 145–161.

Freud, S. 1905. "Three essays on the theory of sexuality." *Standard Edition* 7: 125–248. London: Hogarth, 1953

———. 1913. "Totem and Taboo." *SE* 13: 1–17, 125–155.

———. 1930. "Civilization and its discontents." *SE* 21: 59–148.

———. 1931. "Female sexuality." *SE* 21: 221–245.

Ghent, E. 1992. "Paradox and process." *Psychoanalytic Dialogues* 2: 135–59.

Gould, S.J. 1977. *Ever since Darwin*. NY: Norton.

———. 1981. *The mismeasure of man*. NY: Norton.

———. 1987. *An urchin in the storm: Essays about books and ideas*. NY: W.W. Norton.

Haraway, D. 1989. *Primate visions: Gender, race, and nature in the world of modern science*. NY: Routledge.

Harris, A. 1991. "Gender as contradiction." *Psychoanalytic Dialogues* 1 (2): 197–224.

Harris, M. 1989. *Our kind*. NY: Harper.

hooks, b. 1990. *Yearning: Race, gender, and cultural politics*. Boston: South End Press.

Jaggar, A. 1989. "Love and knowledge: Emotion and feminist epistemology." In *Gender/body/knowledge: Feminist reconstructions of being and knowing*. Ed. by A. Jaggar and S. Bordo. New Brunswick, NJ: Rutgers University Press: 145–171.

Keller, E. F. 1992. *Secrets of life, secrets of death: Essays on language, gender and science*. NY: Routledge.

Khan, M.R. 1958. "Introduction." In *Through paediatrics to psychoanalysis*, ed. by D.W. Winnicott. N.Y.: Basic Books.

Kovel, J. 1981. *The age of desire*. NY: Pantheon.

Kropotkin, P. 1972 [1902]. *Mutual Aid: A factor of evolution*. London: Penguin Press.

LaPlanche, J. and J.-B. Pontalis. 1973. *The language of psychoanalysis*. Trans. D. Nicholson-Smith. NY: Norton.

Levenson, E. 1994. "Beyond countertransference." *Contemporary Psychoanalysis* 30: 691–707.

Lévi-Strauss, C. 1969 [1949]. *The elementary structures of kinship*. London: Eyre and Spottiswode.

Lewontin, R. C. 1991. *Biology as ideology: The doctrine of DNA*. NY: Harper Perennial.

Lewontin, R.C., S. Rose, and L.J. Kamin. 1984. *Not in our genes: Biology, ideology, and human nature*. NY: Pantheon.

Mead, M. 1928. *Coming of age in Samoa*. NY: Dell.

Mitchell J. and J. Rose, eds. 1982. *Feminine sexuality: Jacques Lacan and the école freudienne*. Trans. by J. Rose. NY: Pantheon.

Mitchell, S.A. 1988. *Relational concepts in psychoanalysis: An integration*. Cambridge: Harvard University Press.

———. 1993. "Introduction [to commentaries on Trop and Stolorow]." *Psychoanalytic Dialogues* 3: 623–26.

Morgan, L.H. 1870. *Systems of consanguinity and affinity of the human family*. Washington: Smithsonian Institution.

O'Connor, N. and J. Ryan. 1994. *Wild desires and mistaken identities: Lesbianism and psychoanalysis*. NY: Columbia University Press.

Phillips, A. 1988. *Winnicott*. Cambridge: Harvard University Press.

Rivera, M. 1989. "Linking the psychological and the social: Feminism, poststructuralism, and multiple personality." *Dissociation* 2 (1): 24–31.

Ross, A. 1994. *The Chicago gangster theory of life: Nature's debt to society*. London: Verso.

Sampson, E. E. 1993. "Identity politics: Challenges to psychology's understanding." *American Psychologist* 48 (12): 1219–1230.

Schafer, R. 1977. "Problems in Freud's psychology of women." In *Female psychology: Contemporary psychoanalytic views*. Ed. by Harold Blum. NY: International Universities Press: 331–360.

Schwartz, D. 1993. "Heterophilia—The love that dare not speak its aim." *Psychoanalytic Dialogues* 3: 643–52.

Small, M.F. 1993. *Female choices: Sexual behavior of female primates*. Ithaca: Cornell University Press.

Spitz, R. 1957. *No and Yes*. NY: International Universities Press.

Spivak, G.C. and E. Rooney. 1994. "In a word. Interview." In *The esssential difference*. Ed. by N. Schor and E. Weed. Bloomington: Indiana University Press.

Stein, J., ed. 1966. *The Random House dictionary of the English language*. New York: Random House.

Stern, D. 1985. *The interpersonal world of the infant*. NY: Basic Books.

Steward, J. 1955. *The theory of multilineal evolution*. Bloomington: Indiana University Press.

Tylor, E.B. 1889. "On a method of investigating the development of institutions: Applied to laws of marriage and descent." *Journal of the Royal Anthropological Institute* 18: 245–69.

Wentworth, H. and S. Flexner, eds. 1967. *Dictionary of American slang*. NY: Thomas Y. Crowell Co.

8

Re-Reading Freud on Homosexuality

Robert May

SOMEONE WHO KNOWS PSYCHOANALYSIS as deeply respectful of individual complexity and as abstaining from prejudicial judgements, especially in the area of sexuality, may be surprised and taken aback to experience the mistrust and suspicion which even the word "psychoanalytic" evokes in gay and lesbian circles. Certainly that has been my experience at Amherst. In co-teaching a seminar on Freud and narrative I saw the struggle gay and lesbian students had in reading Freud as anything other than oppressive. And as a psychotherapist I have experienced the hostile projections with which some gay and lesbian students endow the mental health service.

Growing up with the repeated experience of homophobia, like the repeated experience of racism, certainly shapes one's consciousness and expectations. Those of us who work in liberal institutions or live in large urban centers may be a bit sheltered from this. We tend to exist midst people relatively aware of the unfairness of group prejudice. One does still hear at places like Amherst the opinion that homosexuality is, in that marvelously assuming term, "unnatural." Some students, at least in private, will voice this view and we currently have one faculty member who has taken that position publicly. But out there in the world things are more raw. One example, just because it is recent and vivid for me: along the railroad track in Montana, is the painted statement that "Humans Hate Filthy Queers." This is displayed amidst the usual visual and verbal obscenities that in the world of graffiti are considered good, manly (human) fun.

"Homophobia" seems an anemic term for this vicious mixture of hatred and fear. And we can only expect to see and hear more of this now that the so-called Christian right has lost Communism as an enemy and increasingly turns its moralistic attention to domestic matters.

It is tempting to see the mistrust of gay and lesbian people towards psychoanalysis simply as a generalization of their experience with the culture, or as part of the common disinclination to make any clear distinctions between psychiatry and psychoanalysis. When the *New Yorker*, in a piece on gays in the military (April 5, 1993), says that "it was not until the second World War that the military, influenced by psychoanalytic theory, which considered homosexuality an illness, began asking recruits if they were homosexual," it has almost certainly reversed the lines of influence. The military in this country has hardly been a bastion of psychoanalytic theory, whereas psychoanalysis was seeded in a psychiatric profession shaped and reshaped by the Second World War. But, alas, these explanations would also be evasions. The unfortunate fact is that American psychoanalysis has a particular history of stigmatizing homosexuality.

If one were to pick two books representative of mainstream American psychoanalysis's view of homosexuality from the late '50s through the early '70s, they would have to be those by Irving Bieber (1962) and Charles Socarides (1968). Both take the firm position that homosexuality is pathological. And both see themselves squarely in the tradition of Freud; although to take that position they must ignore Freud's repeated statements that homosexuality should not be seen in itself as neurotic or as an illness (see Abelove 1986; Lewes 1988). Bieber even maintains that his stance is a *sine qua non* of a psychoanalytic view: "all *psychoanalytic* theories assume that adult homosexuality is psychopathologic." (1962, 18). Bieber's group, members of the Society of Medical Psychoanalysts, pool analysts' judgements about their own patients and conclude that "at any age, homosexuality is a symptom of fear and inhibition of heterosexual expression" (1962, 305). Homosexuality is compared to an upper respiratory infection or a peptic ulcer: something that may happen regularly but is nonetheless decidedly unhealthy. And they go on to deny that latent homosexuality is inevitable in "well integrated heterosexuals," any more than "latent peptic ulcer" would be (1962, 305). Thus the idea of bisexuality, which Freud saw as crucial to his theory, is jettisoned in favor of a normative notion of health.

Socarides follows a similar line. He variously describes homosexuality as "a widespread emotional disorder" (1968, 3), a "disturbance" (4), and a "serious illness" (6) which it should be society's aim to prevent. Both Bieber and Socarides are fully confident that homosexuality can be cured by psychoanalytic treatment (for a critical assessment of this kind of "cure" see Isay 1989, chapter 8; Duberman 1991). Socarides's work is a particularly troubling example of vilification in the guise of diagnosis. As an example of the tone, here is the final paragraph of his introduction:

> The "solution" of homosexuality is always doomed to failure and even when used for utilitarian purposes, e.g., prestige, power, protection by a more powerful male, the accomplishment is short-lived. Homosexuality is based on the fear of the mother, the aggressive attack against the father, and is filled with aggression, destruction, and self-deceit. It is a masquerade of life in which certain psychic energies are neutralized and held in a somewhat quiescent state. However, the unconscious manifestations of hate, destructiveness, incest and fear are always threatening to break through. Instead of union, cooperation, solace, stimulation, enrichment, healthy challenge and fulfillment, there are only destruction, mutual defeat, exploitation of the partner and the self, oral-sadistic incorporation, aggressive onslaughts, attempts to alleviate anxiety and a pseudo-solution to the aggressive and libidinal urges which dominate and torment the individual. (1968, 8)

How did American orthodox psychoanalysis end up in this position? Henry Abelove, in his delightful and instructive piece "Freud, Male Homosexuality, and the Americans" (1986), attributes this development to that quality of American culture which so often worried Freud: its pervasive moralism. Isay (1989) cites the eagerness of immigrant analysts to become successes in America through conforming to American culture and mores. Another factor, it seems to me, is the way in which American psychoanalysis, at least in its mainstream, was predominantly a psychiatric profession. Both Bieber and Socarides write very much as physicians. This has at least two important consequences. First, the white coat of science is used to mask and legitimate value judgements. Bieber argues for the objectivity of his data (which after all consisted of analysts' opinions about their own patients) by referring to "well-trained psychiatrists with experience making value judgements based on clinical impressions and interpretations" (30). Socarides refers to his book as a "medical work" (4) and his tone throughout asserts his right to definitive knowledge. Thus moralism masquerades as medicine. The second influence of the medical frame is the tendency on the part of its practitioners to use psychoanalysis as a source of diagnostic labels. This approach sees Freud as providing a new classifying vocabulary. It pays exclusive attention to the content of Freud's theories and remains relatively oblivious to their structure or process. This is akin to, in the matter of dreams, caring only about "dream book" symbolism and ignoring what remains most useful to us: the process of interpretation and the syntax of the unconscious.

The particular assertion of the pathologic nature of homosexuality which characterized American orthodox psychoanalysis may also have to do with certain theoretical imperatives. American psychoanalysis remained centered in that derivative of the classical theory known as ego psychology. This meant a theory which continued to honor the Oedipus Complex, a model of development in which sexual object choice was crucial and cross-gender choice the model. To make this model more flexible and even-handed requires strenuous and often awkward effort (see Blos, 1985, on "allogender" and "isogender"). Theories which became more interested in so-called preoedipal matters, the British school for example, did not have to focus on homosexuality as pathology.

Reading Freud

Why bother reading Freud? I gather it is possible to be interested in psychoanalysis these days without reading Freud. Perhaps it is also possible to be a philosopher without reading Plato. Or rather, without *re*-reading: one can see these texts as mere history (as if history were *then* rather than now—a very unpsychoanalytic view). It seems to me that our founding texts are of more than sentimental or antiquarian interest. Psychoanalysis remains lively in part because Freud's writing is so full of complexity, layering, and contradiction that it not only allows but *requires* rereading from different points of view.

There are many interesting rereadings going on these days. I think, for instance, of Thomas Ogden's thoughtful elaboration of the Freudian subject as "created, sustained (and at the same time de-centered) through the dialectical interplay of consciousness and unconsciousness"(1992, 517). In the area of gender, Juliet Mitchell (1974), Jacqueline Rose (1989), and Elizabeth Young-Breuhl (1990) each trace the ways Freud fatally complicates the conventions of male and female, sometimes in a fashion that, as Mitchell puts it, appears to confirm convention but actually undermines it (Mitchell 49). Bersani (1986) traces the radical implications of the Freudian notion of sexuality as fluid, collapsing on itself, contradictory, and timeless. Bersani's appreciation of tension and paradox is shown in the way he describes his project: "I want to celebrate a certain type of failure in Freud's work. The word 'celebrate' is crucial: I will be arguing that the psychoanalytical authenticity of Freud's work *depends on* a process of theoretical collapse"(3).

The Freud who interests me, and whom I think is the redeeming Freud, is the Freud who is constantly doubling back to undercut distinctions, distinctions to which he himself has allegiance, or even has himself constructed. This self-destructing Freud is in tune with our contemporary sense of the instability of meaning, the limitations of binary positions, and the importance of noticing what's outside the frame. Freud's writing is not just about psychoanalysis. It *is* psychoanalysis in that it comes alive through diversions, layers, contradictions, and the continuing process of the collapse of one meaning followed by the re-emergence of a new yet familiar version. The psychoanalytic method is constantly being created in the writing.

What I want to do in this paper is consider the first of the *Three Essays on the Theory of Sexuality* (1905), the essay in which Freud sketches (and subsequently modifies over the next fifteen years) his basic notions about homosexuality. What I intend is a re-reading that will highlight the radicalism of Freud's thought. This will be a "discontented" reading in two senses. The Freud who I believe remains most persistently interesting and valuable is the Freud who could never be content with a given formulation and was constantly revising and undercutting. Mine is also a reading which tries to *dis*connect from *content* and to pay more attention to the structure and movement of the thought process.

The Question of Categories

Labels, diagnostic or otherwise, require stable categories. If we are going to sort people, we must have some way of telling one from another. Thus, for instance, all the demented legalities which characterize societies organized around racial distinctions. And thus the importance of homosexuality or gayness as a clarifying and complicating third term in gender studies.

The Freud of the media and the popular mind seems to be the Freud of oppressive, hierarchical labeling: Freud the misogynist who condemned women to be mere anatomy; Freud the homophobe who thought homosexuality should be cured; Freud the physician who thought psychoanalysis should be a medical specialty. Of course none of these Freuds bears close reading, but one hears of them all. How is it that psychoanalysis has come to be seen as an oppressive ideology which supports the current power arrangements in society? Duberman's characterization of Irving Bieber as "a central casting version of the portly, pompous psychiatrist, contentedly patronizing everyone" (1991, 268) reflects the anger which psychoanalysis has evoked in its "success." To be established, respected, socially empowered to judge others—this was the triumph of orthodox psychoanalysis in the 1950s. It became, then, an irresistible target for the righteous anger of the unwillingly diagnosed and of those who had good reason to feel excluded and demeaned: women, gays, even psychologists and social workers wanting admission to mainstream psychoanalytic institutes. The rise of biological psychiatry, the radical decline in society's willingness to pay for long-term psychotherapy, and ideological shifts in the culture all have combined to destroy the foundation of psychoanalysis' social power. It will be interesting to see if the anger against psychoanalysis decreases in turn.

But the problem is intellectual as well as social. We have to acknowledge that our psychoanalytic heritage regarding labeling is mixed. One of the fascinating tensions in Freud's writing involves on the one hand a host of implicit and taken-for-granted categories, deployed with a tone of certainty and *Knowing*, but on the other hand the repeated invention of concepts which turn out to be deeply subversive of those very same categories.[1]

To show how this goes, in relation to the question of homosexuality, I would like to reintroduce some pieces of the *Three Essays* (1905). In this work Freud wrestled, over a period of fifteen years, with the basic concepts of sexuality and gender. The text has the feel of an analytic session: twisting, turning, disjunctive, and laced with asides which run on in page-long footnotes and are layered like the cities of Troy. It is not an easy piece to read or to teach. The logic can seem elusive and the language archaic. From what we consider to be our current enlightened point of view, the essays can be read as an oppressive list of categories and distinctions, a parade of labels, a diagnostic side-show.

The essays *are* full of diagnostic terms and the underlying assumptions include "the descending scale from health to insanity" (15). To name just some of the major distinctions: normal versus perverse, heterosexual versus homosexual, innate versus acquired, male versus female, insane versus healthy, fetishism versus normal love, mental versus physical, sadism versus masochism, and active versus passive. To the modern nose the whole business reeks of hierarchies. Some seem implicit and tonal, such as the frequent references to classical, "high" culture (Greece, Goethe). There is also a pervasive tone of certainty and authority. For instance, we are told that "psychoanalysis has cleared up one of the remaining gaps in our understanding" (21n), that through psychoanalytic technique "it is possible to obtain the most accurate knowledge of the nature and origin of these formally unconscious psychical structures" (30), that "the unconscious mental life of all neurotics (without exception) shows" (32). As readers we have to resist taking this tone of imperial confidence as the whole story.

Freud begins the first essay with a challenge to convention: the popular view of sexuality as developing at puberty, involving an irresistible attraction to the opposite sex, and aimed at intercourse—these ideas "give a very false picture of the true situation" (1). Among other radical strokes, he severs the link between sexual object and sexual aim. At the same time, the structure and tone developed in the first few pages of the essay is that of classifying and categorizing. In outline form, with multiple subheadings, Freud gives us a taxonomy of "inversion." The language—"aberration," "inversion"—is bound to sound judgmental and stigmatizing to a contemporary reader. It is easy for the reader to feel that the omniscient classifier is rank-ordering people, setting them in descending order like bugs on pins.

But we should notice that the meaning of "aberration" and "inversion" are exactly what Freud declared in the first paragraph as his own intent: breaking rules, turning things upside down. This latent alliance with the invertors becomes overt when he suddenly undermines the whole project of classification: "Nevertheless, though the distinctions cannot be disputed, it is impossible to overlook the existence of numerous intermediate examples of every type, so that we are driven to conclude that we are dealing with a connected series" (4). Here we see a persistent and characteristic intellectual move in the *Three Essays*: Freud sets up categorical distinctions and then promptly undermines them.

Perversion

Before long we encounter the word which is a major obstacle to contemporary readers, especially those sensitive to gay issues. "Perversion," with its epithet "pervert," is a harsh and assaultive term to many. In seeing the term in the context of Freud's writing, it's important to notice that the vocabulary Freud is trying to free himself from centers around the label "degeneracy," a pseudo-neurological term used in his day to categorize (and stigmatize) homosexuality. Freud argues strenuously against the usefulness of calling people degenerate. For him the term perversion is a new and more neutral way of referring to certain sexual activities. But of course any word attached to something that makes people anxious undergoes a malevolent linguistic creep over the years and becomes sooner or later stigmatized (the terms "mental health" and "mental illness" would be a parallel example).

But even allowing for this, our uneasiness about the way the term perversion is used persists. Freud says that "perversions are sexual activities which either (a) extend, in an anatomical sense, beyond the regions of the body that are designed for sexual union, or (b) linger over the intermediate relations to the sexual object that should normally be traversed rapidly on the path toward the final sexual aim" (16). We can hear clearly the norms, the hierarchies here: bodies "designed" for a certain purpose and a path which should be speedily traversed—no loitering—towards a final aim. Heterosexual genitality is the goal: "One of the tasks implicit in object-choice is that it should find its way to the opposite sex" (95); "We were thus led to regard any established aberration from normal sexuality as an instance of developmental inhibition and infantilism" (97). This is perhaps progress in terms of being a less pejorative hierarchy, but certainly still a hierarchy.

Case closed? Hardly. We're just at the point where the fun begins. Leo Bersani asks: "To what extent does the Freudian text ruin the very notion of disciplines of knowledge at the very moment that it anxiously seeks to become one itself?" (1986, 5). As we reread, we notice how Freud undermines the categories he is deploying. The definition of perversion I read a moment ago is preceded by a sentence which runs, "Here, then, are factors which provide a point of contact between the perversions and normal sexual life and which can also serve as a basis for their classification" (16). There's the rub: contact. A scale, or a hierarchy, becomes a chain, made up of links. A "descending scale" means that all points potentially touch each other. At the end of the first essay, where Freud refers to the descending scale from health to insanity, he goes on to say "it must also be considered that an unbroken chain bridges the gap between the neuroses in all their manifestations and normality" (37). Here is the enlivening paradox: a binary distinction is bridged, and therefore subverted, by contact between any two adjacent links in the chain. There must then be a place where the distinction breaks down and we *can't* tell the difference.

Let us follow the vicissitudes in Freud's use of that dividing and divisive word "perversion." Section three of the first essay is titled "The Perversions In General." "It is natural," says Freud in broaching this, in his time, unnatural topic, "that medical men, who first studied perversions in outstanding examples and under special conditions, should have been inclined to regard them, like inversion, as indications of degeneracy or disease" (26). Freud then proceeds to demolish that distinction:

> No healthy person, it appears, can fail to make some addition that might be called perverse to the normal sexual aim; and the universality of this finding is of itself enough to show how inappropriate it is to use the word perversion as a term of reproach. In the sphere of sexual life we are brought up against peculiar and, indeed, insoluble difficulties as soon as we try to draw a sharp line to distinguish mere variations within the range of what is physiological from pathological symptoms. (26f)

Thus while using words like perverse, healthy, normal, as if they had clear meanings, what Freud *does* is erase the distinctions. And he comes close to what would be the accepted enlightened language today: in "variations" we have not *perversions* but simply *versions*.

At the same time, Freud's unease with totally blurring the line may be shown in the fact that he then proceeds, in a paragraph which again begins "nevertheless," to specify *some* perverse acts as beyond the pale. The next sentence swings us back again: "But even in such cases we should not be too ready to assume that people who act in this way will necessarily turn out to be insane or subject to great abnormalities of other kinds" (27). This uncomfortable intercourse between the normal and the perverse is then externalized by Freud's attributing the blurring of boundaries to the "domination of the most unruly of all the instincts" (27), which is to say a fluid and de-objectified sexuality which overflows boundaries.

In the following paragraph Freud tries for a new definition of what might be pathological in perversion and comes up with the criteria of exclusiveness and fixation. So we seem now to have a distinction between perversion which is normal, and perversion which is perverse. However, you will not be surprised to hear, Freud's linking urge cannot allow *this* distinction either to stand. He goes on to say that even the "repulsive" and "horrifying" perversions (coprophilia, necrophilia) are "the equivalent of an idealization of the instinct" (27), and he ends the section with a statement, exemplified by a quote from Goethe, which captures concisely the contradiction of hierarchy in a psychoanalytic way of thinking: "The highest and the lowest are always closest to each other in the sphere of sexuality" (27f).

As another example of this destabilizing process, let's look in more detail at an example of Freud's ambivalence about authority and certainty. We could pick an instance on almost any page, but a particularly intriguing one comes in a footnote which begins on page 10 and runs through most of the three following pages (visually one can't help thinking of the text as consciousness and the footnotes as something other, and in this instance unconsciousness clearly has the upper, or rather lower, hand). The footnote is added to the text in 1910. Freud starts boldly: "It is true that psychoanalysis has not yet produced a complete explanation of the origin of inversion; nevertheless, it has discovered the psychical mechanism of its development, and has made essential contributions to the statement of the problems involved" (10f). He goes on to assert that "In all the cases we have examined we have established the fact that . . ." and proceeds to the notion that "inverts" have been fixated on their mothers in childhood and thus identify with the woman and take their sexual object on a narcissistic basis. This is all very Knowing, and we have inherited a long subsequent history of the psychoanalytic pretense to a dynamic "explanation" of homosexuality. But even in this flush of imagined discovery Freud cannot let it rest. He proceeds to add another paragraph to the footnote, a paragraph which begins "It must, however, be borne in mind . . ." (a typical rhetorical gesture in this piece) and goes on to point out that only a single type of invert has been studied, people whose sexual activity is "stunted" (by societal censure), and that the problem of inversion is certainly more complex than this.

In 1915 another level is laid down in this footnote, beginning with the statement that "Psychoanalytic research is most decidedly opposed to any attempt at separating off homosexuals from the rest of mankind as a group of a special character" (11). This is of course precisely what Freud had seemed to be doing in the first section of the footnote. But now the distinction becomes instead a connection: "All human beings are capable of making a homosexual object choice and have in fact made one in their unconscious" (11). He goes on to say that psychoanalysis considers object choice to be independent of gender, restating here the notion of fluidity of attachments which makes his position in the *Three Essays* such a radical revision of our view of sexuality. Freud maintains that both so-called normal and so-called inverted types develop from one human ground. He then locates this state of equal-opportunity-in-object-choice as characteristic of childhood, of "primitive" states of society, and of early periods of history. So, having demolished the distinction which had been set up in the beginning of the footnote, Freud now is bringing in a *new* series of hierarchies: developmental, anthropological, and historical. It seems that the collapse of distinctions creates a vacuum into which something must rush.

Freud goes on to comment that *hetero*sexuality is as much a "problem that needs elucidating and [is] not a self-evident fact" (12). He then dismisses chemistry or constitution as the source of an answer and alludes to a multiplicity of determining factors. Doubt has entered in again. But once more he reverts to a statement that "in inverted types, a predominance of archaic constitutions and primitive psychical mechanisms is regularly to be found" (12). So we are back to constructing an hierarchical distinction, with the language of narcissistic object choice, the erotic significance of the anal zone, and the like. Then that swing creates its own tension, which bridges and blurs the distinction: "There is nothing to be gained, however, by separating the most extreme types of inversion from the rest on the basis of constitutional peculiarities of that kind. What we find as an apparently sufficient explanation of these types can be equally shown to be present, though less strongly, in the constitution of transitional types and of those whose manifest attitude is normal" (12). Here we see, again, the connected series, the "unbroken chain." He then goes on to say that although the end product may appear to be qualitatively distinct, analysis shows that the determinants are only different in degree.

In 1920 the final layer of this seemingly interminable footnote is laid down. Freud talks approvingly about Ferenczi's (1914) distinction between "subject homoerotic" and "object homoerotic" (essentially a distinction between identity and object choice). But at the end of this lengthy addition to the footnote, Freud concludes that "while granting the existence of these two types, we may add that there are many people in whom a certain quantity of subject homo-erotism is found in combination with a proportion of object homo-erotism" (13). So much for *that* distinction! Once again the line is blurred. This last layer of the footnote then moves into a long discussion about organic determinants, "puberty glands," and the like. We find ourselves in the grip of science and are given a testicle transplant. It would seem here that Freud is searching around once again for an anchor. Having undermined the easy points of reference and created a world full of blurring, connection, and linked opposites, he turns finally to biology as an anchor, the same way he turns to the positivistic illusion of history as an anchor in the case of the Wolf-Man (see May 1990). But even this future chemical certainty is undermined by the last sentence, in which Freud expresses his confidence that further research will produce direct confirmation of Fliess's notion of bisexuality (see Gay 1988, 154–156). Interestingly, this hope for certainty from biology is also the theme of last sentence in the book, the summary of the *Three Essays*. The trajectory of the footnote mirrors the trajectory of the whole work.

Conclusion

I believe that this rhetorical pattern, the posing and then merging of opposites, the repeated undoing of certainty, shows us something about psychoanalytic thinking that is more important than any particular content or set of categories. Freud is modeling a method for us when his urge to label is repeatedly undone by a subversive curiosity and a wish to violate common understanding by turning things on their head. Noticing this quality shows us the possibility, even the necessity, of saving Freud from the Freudians as far as the psychoanalytic approach to homosexuality is concerned. More broadly, I intend this piece as another argument, following on a reading of Freud's "Wolf-Man" (May 1990), for psychoanalysis as a process which exists through the repeated creation and then collapse of meaning. The psychoanalytic method constructs a space characterized by the posing and then merging of opposites, by the endless undoing of certainty. It is psychoanalysis's commitment to self-dissolving categories that saves it from the constant temptation simply to replace one set of inevitably moralistic labels with another, and that makes it a theory which can enliven the study of all sexualities.

Note

1. I mean here such concepts as unconsciousness, overdetermination, compromise formation, deferred action, and bisexuality. For further discussion of the destabilizing aspects of these ideas, see Mitchell (1974), Bersani (1986), May (1990), and Odgen (1992).

References Cited

Abelove, H. 1986. Freud, male homosexuality, and the Americans. *Dissent* Winter: 59–69.

Bersani, L. 1986. *The Freudian Body: Psychoanalysis and Art*. NY: Columbia Univ. Press.

Bieber, I., et al. 1962. *Homosexuality*. NY: Basic Books.

Blos, P. 1985. *Son and Father: Before and After the Oedipus Complex*. NY: The Free Press.

Duberman, M. 1991. *Cures: A Gay Man's Odyssey*. NY: Simon and Schuster.

Ferenczi, S. 1914. The nosology of male homosexuality (Homoerotism). *International Journal of Psychoanalysis* 2: 131–136.

Freud, S. 1905. *Three Essays on the Theory of Sexuality*. New York: Basic Books, 1962.

Gay, P. 1988. *Freud: A Life for Our Time*. NY: Norton.

Isay, R. 1989. *Being Homosexual: Gay Men and Their Development*. NY: Farrar, Straus, Giroux.

Lewes, K. 1988. *The Psychoanalytic Theory of Male Homosexuality*. NY: Simon and Schuster.

May, R. 1990. The idea of history in psychoanalysis: Freud and the "Wolf-Man." *Psychoanalytic Psychology* 7 (2): 163–183.

Mitchell, J. 1974. *Psychoanalysis and Feminism*. NY: Random House.

Ogden, T. 1992. The dialectically constituted/decentered subject of psychoanalysis. I. The Freudian subject. *International Journal of Psycho-Analysis* 73: 517–526.

Rose, J. 1989. Where does the misery come from? Psychoanalysis, feminism and the event. In *Feminism and Psychoanalysis*. Ed. by F. Feldstein and J. Roof. Ithaca: Cornell Univ. Press.

Socarides, C. 1968. *The Overt Homosexual*. NY: Grune and Stratton.

Young-Breuhl, E. 1990. *Freud on Women: A Reader*. NY: Norton.

9

Passionate Differences

Lesbianism, Post-Modernism, and Psychoanalysis

Noreen O'Connor

> I am feeling numb, dragging through the grey days, it's all worthless.
>
> The pain is killing me, there is no let up.
>
> I'm so lonely I could die.
>
> People scare me—I know when women see me they want to murder me.
>
> The only relief is the sight of blood.
>
> I can't stop, only the chocolate and cakes give me comfort, I hide my fat body from the world.
>
> Masturbation is agony, it leaves my body in pain for days.
>
> John hates me.
>
> Jane abused me.

AS PSYCHOTHERAPISTS WE LISTEN TO examples of suffering daily, attending to the nuances of past and present relationships. Are we listening for the clues to the repressed libido, the part-object relation of the paranoid schizoid position, or the repetition of the unconscious drives destabilizing the fiction of a unified ego?

Do these questions matter? In other words, how do our theory and training as psychotherapists influence our practices? Would you, on hearing someone in emotional pain, advise that person to go and see a post-modernist; or a modernist for that matter? Modernism and post-modernism are terms which express differing Western cultural ethoses. Each is characterized by its position on history, truth, power, morality, the human subject, masculinity, and femininity. It is not that there is just one exclusive theory of modernism or post-modernism—different writers construct specific conceptual frameworks which elaborate their understanding of the modern or the post-modern.

Modernism refers to a view of the subject as rational, having a stable identity which can be universally known. The subject is construed in terms of an essential representation. History is seen to be linear, teleological. Power is ascribed to the "one who knows" and who therefore has the right to legislate for the truth and value of others. Post-modernism, on the other hand, stresses the de-centering of rationality in subjectivity, the multiplicity of shifting identifications, the interweaving of language and subjectivity. In other words, emphasis is placed on psychic development as inextricably bound up with linguistic and social development. Consequently, post-modernists argue that subjectivity is not adequately theorized in terms of universal developmental mechanisms or stages occurring outside of a social/linguistic context. Emphasis on the linguistic/social character of subjectivity maintains shifting complexities and, through questioning fixed assumptions of the "human," allows for wider theoretical development. This is especially relevant for psychoanalytic analyses of subjectivity and to the question of whether or not psychoanalysis can move on from traditional oedipal interpretations of masculinity, femininity, and sexual desires in order to allow the theorizing required by new relational possibilities. History in a post-modern view is characterized by gaps, losses, repetitions, and changing perspectives.

Historically, modernity has been situated as emerging with the Enlightenment, exemplarily expressed in Kant's philosophy. Kant introduced a critique of traditionally held beliefs in favor of a notion of the human as characterized by the exercise of autonomous critical reason. The humanism of modernity conceives of the human as the subject who can know himself:

> The guarantee that everything that has eluded him may be restored to him; the certainty that time will dispense nothing without restoring it in a reconstituted unity; the promise that one day the subject . . . will once again be able to appropriate . . . all these things that are kept at a distance by difference.[1]

Michel Foucault, in his work on the history of sexuality, situates Freud as a modernist because of his positioning of the Oedipus myth as the cornerstone of psychoanalysis. Oedipus pursues the "truth" of his "identity" hidden from consciousness yet constituted by desire and sexuality. Identification is a crucial concept in psychoanalytic accounts of development and in the concomitant process of analysis. The assured polarities of mother-father, feminine-masculine are the dyad of identifications and repudiations attributed to the baby/child's gender and sexual identification. Moreover, it is this gender identification with its appropriate sexual alignment that psychoanalysis privileges. In our book *Wild Desires and Mistaken Identities, Lesbianism and Psychoanalysis*, Joanna Ryan and I have reviewed the major texts of the psychoanalytic tradition regarding their theories of lesbianism. Within these texts we identified recurring issues:

> The alignment of gender and sexuality in the notion of identification and desire; the reliance on concepts such as oral sadism and unconscious identification with the father as developmental explanations; the consignment of homosexuality to the pre oedipal and the narcissistic; the appeal to biological phenomena as constitutive of psychic reality; the *a priori* theorizing based on normative notions of innate heterosexuality; the obliviousness to countertransference problems stemming from the personal and theoretical position of the practitioner.[2]

The concept of identification is construed as representation. Knowing who or what you are is knowing that you are a man or a woman and knowing who or what you desire. Not knowing whether you are a man or a woman is designated as "hysterical."

Representation implies knowledge, a bringing-together, a representing of the past and diversity of knowledge by means of which the subject claims to know himself completely. Foucault and his successors offer critiques of the notion of personal identity as equated with sexual identity: "our sexuality reveals us to ourselves, and our desire to have this secret self-knowledge revealed drives us to engage in discourse on our sexuality."[3]

This is the celebrated critique of the "repressive hypothesis." Foucault argues that psychoanalysis analyzes sexuality in terms of repression and in doing so operates with a substantive notion of the "human"; with the notion of a "true" underlying sexual identity.

Judith Butler offers a fascinating critique of sexuality conceived in terms of identity politics. She argues that identity categories of, for example, lesbian, homosexual, heterosexual, etc. are inadequate because every "subject position" is a matrix of different power relationships which are not univocal. In other words, subjectivity is not a matter of a self-identical entity. Butler points out that installing alternative gender identities reproduces normative exclusionary practices which foreclose the questioning of gender and sexuality. Rather, she allows for differing subject positions while challenging the notion of universal foundational humans who know themselves in their "true" sexuality. According to Butler, "The subject is not a thing . . . but a process of signification within an open system of discursive possibilities."[4]

Post-modernists challenge humanistic modernism, with its ideal of the self who knows himself and is thereby free, by focusing on the contingency and specificity of our lives. The problem is not just that psychoanalysis has got it wrong in relation to homosexuality and got it right about heterosexuality, but rather that the psychoanalytic enterprise of equating human subjectivity with the truth of sexuality is a construal of human relationships in terms of a totalizing knowledge, the refusal of difference and otherness, and a neglect of relationships as ethically recalcitrant to full knowledge. This is why post-modernism is relevant to our psychotherapeutic practices; it keeps us alive to the dangers of imagining that we exhaustively know the psyche, and it keeps us alive to our responsibility to and the uniqueness of our relationships with each human being.

In psychoanalytic theory and practice homosexuality is considered to be non-pathological if it is surpassed, if it is seen as adolescent experimentation, as a preparation for "adult," genital sexuality. Developmental theory construed in terms of mechanistic, causal determinism, such as is the case for all the psychoanalytic writers who universalize homosexuality as pathological, precludes a questioning of its own methods and assumptions regarding truth, knowledge, and morality. Despite the rigor and sensitivity of some of their clinical material, their desire for a spurious universal metapsychology prevents them from hearing the specificity of the patient's speech. These psychoanalytic writers begin by *a priori* pathologizing homosexuality as a unitary phenomenon and then theorize the origins of the pathology they have assumed. This has a certain logical contradiction and merits psychoanalytic interest. Psychoanalysts such as Socarides who trace homosexuality back to pre-oedipal fixation resulting in disordered gender identity, primitive defense mechanisms, and fragile ego boundaries, consistently assert that all homosexuality is pathological and therefore consider the psychoanalytic task to be treating homosexual patients to change their sexual orientation. Here the complexities of love and hate are reduced to ascriptions of primitive eroticism involving the dyadic mother/baby.

We are indebted to post-modern analyses for pointing out that the body and its development is not a-cultural and a-historical. As I have argued earlier, sexual differences are bodily differences, and sexual identity

> permeates, mediates, and is mediated by all our social and cultural interactions. Sexual identity is not simply a question of isolated individuals repressing or discovering their "true" desires, or of a logical definition, but is variously inscribed in cultural, religious, legal and political systems and practices.[5]

Michael Foucault's work, as I have mentioned, on the history of sexuality indicates that sexual behavior is a matter of

> how the rendering of sexual behavior into discourses comes to be transformed, what types of jurisdiction and veridiction it is subject to and how constitutive elements of this domain come to be called "sexuality."[6]

Thus for Foucault the body does not give knowledge that is then merely transmitted by an essentially neutral language. What is categorized as normal/abnormal, natural/unnatural are social constructs arising out of power/knowledge relationships rather than factual distinctions given at the level of the body or of the individual psyche.[7] Elizabeth Grosz points to the traditional binary categories defining the body: "inside/outside, subject/object, active/passive, fantasy/reality, surface/depth."[8] Grosz challenges this dualistic opposition and points out that libidinal intensities are not confined to biologically determined zones but are interactions occurring on the surface of the skin and various organs. In her view, concepts of inside and outside need not be oppositional. Grosz argues that what she calls "surface effects" generate an underlying depth or consciousness just like the moebius strip, a continuous two-dimensional plane which when rotated in space creates an inside and an outside:

> Tracing the outside of the moebius strip leads one directly to its inside without at any point leaving the surface. This depth is one of the distinguishing features marking out the modern Western capitalist body from other kinds.[9]

In line with a post-modern perspective, I am strategically challenging a dualistic account of the body/psyche which is pervasive in psychoanalytic writing; that is, the claim that there is an inner world, an outer world, and that the developmental task is to link them by virtue of theories of phantasies and mechanisms of defenses and repressions. This is not to deny the importance of theories of development but it is to stress that arguments in terms of causal mechanisms are inadequate to the rich complexity of human bodily/linguistic development, to the development of the child in its relationship to others.[10] Neither am I discounting the crucial importance of the baby's early experiences prior to the acquisition of syntactical language.

From the beginning, the baby is in a relational, linguistic world, albeit pre-verbal, which influences the vicissitudes of adult relationships but not as causally mechanical. Psychoanalysts whose conception of the baby's earliest relationship as that to phantasied objects where the phantasies are postulated as being a-linguistic, not just pre-verbal, advocate baby-observation as crucial to learning about early developmental stages. Apart from the epistemological naieveté regarding "observation," such theorists could be accused of falling into the same mistake as did early social researchers like anthropologists, who mistakenly believe that they could "objectively" analyze cultures without attending to the significance of their own investigative presence for their results. It is important to emphasize that homosexuality and heterosexuality are not adequately theorized within a normative mechanical discourse—living lovers and haters are culturally specific in their self-understandings, their passions, and their mortalities.

In offering a critical appraisal of development construed in terms of causal mechanisms, I am not in any way discounting the pain, loss, terror, abandonment, abuse, and rejection that can plunge a young person into pathological, destructive relationships in the world. The question is whether psychoanalysts can acknowledge, theoretically and in practice, that a young person's homosexual orientation can lead progressively to mature adult relationships as a homosexual, or if it is necessarily regressive in adulthood.

The purpose of psychoanalytic case-studies is to illustrate common features and specific diversity and complexity. The "common features" within the clinical setting are traditionally rendered as indices of the pathological, which is open to "scientific" or at the least hermeneutical—that is, interpretive—regularization. Common features do arise in clinical work with people who are homosexual—often arising from the difficulties and strengths they struggle with in homophobic societies in which their choice of sexual partner is ridiculed, denied, or legally punishable. As Joanna Ryan and I emphasize in *Wild Desires and Mistaken Identities*, "if generalization is appropriate it is in the area of the structuring of lesbian oppression, rather than in anything supposedly inherent in lesbians."[11]

In the following case-material, adolescence is seen in light of the complexities of time and subjectivity elucidated by post-modern critiques rather than in terms of a monolithic teleological explanation of development.

Jenny distraughtly stated at her first session: "I don't know who I am, I'm two people and I feel I'm going mad," and proceeded to sob deeply. She was engaged to be married to a young man whom she said she loved very much but in planning her marriage had drawn closer and closer to a friend, a young married woman, who was to be her bridesmaid. The two women were affectionate with one another and Jenny found herself "daydreaming" about Claire and feeling a sexual longing to be with her. She was confused because she had a passionate sexual relationship with her fiance. Jenny was twenty-five, the eldest of three children—a brother and sister—and from a Northern working-class Catholic family. She had been successful and popular at school and in college and was looking forward to having her own home with John and setting up a family. Jenny quickly formed a positive transference to the therapist and said she felt "waves washing through her" of relief that she could even speak about her feelings for Claire. She had professed to having a wonderfully close family, a mother with whom she could discuss her boyfriends and a father with whom she discussed politics. She was brought up a Catholic and her criticisms of the Church were the only points of dissention with her parents. Gradually Jenny began to have erotic feelings for the therapist which she reluctantly spoke of; she thought that would mean the end of the therapy and that the therapist would find her so disgusting she would be instantly rejecting and angry. In holding this erotic transference, the therapist opened the space for Jenny to explore her earlier adolescent fantasies and a passionate sexual relationship with another girl at the age of fourteen.

Jenny and her friend, Rose, were part of a group of peers that "hung around together" at school and went to discos on Saturday nights. They dated boys and discussed relative merits of "dry kisses" and "wet kisses." Members of their clique often stayed in each other's houses, and Jenny and Rose frequently shared a bed in which they discussed their religious beliefs, the boys they fancied, school, and the freedom of the future until late at night. One night "for a laugh," Rose started kissing Jenny on the mouth.

Jenny experienced an overwhelmingly new bodily/sexual arousal. For the first time each of them declared passionate love for the other and swore that if the other were a boy they would get married and live together forever. The next morning Jenny found her pajamas "wet with white stuff" and was terror stricken, convinced she had turned into a boy—she had recently learned that boys had "wet dreams." She was too scared to mention it to anyone and felt it was a Divine retribution for being sexual with Rose.

Jenny's passionate lovemaking with Rose continued for two years during which time the girls continued to go out with boys. They worried about the sinful aspect of their relationship but concluded that it "couldn't be all that serious because it wasn't sex with boys." Jenny had heard about lesbians, women who dressed in suits like men, and she certainly did not want anything to do with them. She worried that Rose was getting more and more interested in boys and began to spend evenings of agony as Rose went out with Michael. Finally Rose told her that she was in love with him but that Jenny would always be her best friend. Jenny described agonies of loss, desolation, and deception as she tried to pretend to family, friends, and school that all was well with her. She began to furtively look up medical textbooks to see if they would tell her what was wrong with her; she hated herself and felt evil and dirty for desiring Rose. Jenny enjoyed her school life and began to go out with lots of boys in the hope of finding what Rose had found with Michael and of putting her secret behind her. She began to enjoy boys sexually and met John with whom she fell in love. She felt she had at last outgrown her desire for Rose. As this history unfolded, Jenny began having negative dreams about the therapist—who appeared as threatening, leading her to the edge of cliffs, and under the sea, and into houses with uncertain floors. The conflict between her love for John and her sense of herself and her future, and her longing for Claire, resulted in negative attacks on the therapist for not curing her of her lesbian feelings and for even allowing her to have explicit thoughts about an amorous future with Claire. Such a future seemed impossible; she would lose her family, her friends, her job (she was a teacher); she would be destitute and shunned; and John's life would be ruined.

Jenny's conflicting feelings in relation to sexual relations with men and women were a recurrent theme in her therapy for over two years. She married John but five months later had a brief affair with a lesbian colleague with whom she was able to share her growing confidence in her intellectual interests. This relationship, whilst terrifying in its intensity, seemed to open out for her the possibility of a mutually fulfilling adult lesbian relationship.

After eighteen months she decided to leave John and began a serious relationship with another woman.

This vignette illustrates how the therapist was able to hold open the possibility of Jenny's shifting desires without adhering to a notion of a fixed sexual identity as either "really heterosexual" (and therefore "normal"/ mature) or "really lesbian." Although it was difficult for her initially, the therapist also managed to be sufficiently open to the vicissitudes of Jenny's eroticized transference, an openness which, from our experience of supervising therapists (including feminist therapists), we have found to be rare. Rather than pathologize her lesbianism, the therapist enabled Jenny to explore her fear of sexual intensity with women. The psychoanalytic frame allowed for the working through of her merged intensity with her mother such that she could separate from her and, albeit painfully, forge a fresh relationship with her. This enabled Jenny to begin to discover an intimacy with another woman that allowed for difference and separateness. Jenny, like many psychoanalytic writers, had equated lesbianism with symbiosis and much of her analysis was concerned with her moving from such a "fixated" certainty.

For many psychoanalysts homosexuality is viewed primarily as a denial of difference, as narcissistic. Sameness of gender is assumed to be a barrier to "real" sexual desire. Such a position assumes that all features of a homosexual relationship pale into insignificance compared to the sameness of gender, including all other possibly important differences between the partners. In our experience it cannot be assumed that just because two people are of the same gender, they therefore experience gender in similar ways. In practice, many of the excitements, conflicts, and pleasures of homosexual relationships may well concern differences in the way gender is experienced and lived out, including how, as a woman, desire for and from another woman is felt and expressed. In this way gender can be an issue of difference between two people of the same gender, either constructively or destructively, consciously or unconsciously, depending on the relationship in question.

As Joanna Ryan and I stress in *Wild Desires and Mistaken Identities*:

> a consideration . . . of how psychoanalysis has thought about and dealt with homosexuality also offers many insights into perennial questions about psychoanalysis, such as the split-off nature of the social, the regressive use of the biological and the causal, the unreflective incorporation of social norms into notions of maturity, the difficulty of really letting the patient speak, and engaging with this, and finally, the complexities of rendering social forms of oppression psychoanalytically.[12]

Notes

1. Michel Foucault, *The Archeology of Knowledge*, translated by A. Sheridan (New York: Pantheon, 1972), 12.
2. Noreen O'Connor and Joanna Ryan, *Wild Desires and Mistaken Identities, Lesbianism and Psychoanalysis* (New York: Columbia University Press, 1994), 12–13.
3. James W. Bernauer and Michael Mahon, "The Ethics of Michel Foucault," in *The Cambridge Companion to Foucault*, ed. by Gary Gutting (Cambridge: Cambridge University Press, 1994), 129.
4. Jana Sawicki, "Foucault, Feminism, and the Question of Identity," in *The Cambridge Companion to Foucault*, 299.
5. O'Connor and Ryan, *Wild Desires and Mistaken Identities*, 22.
6. "Questions of Method: An Interview with Michel Foucault," in *After Philosophy End or Transformation?* ed. by Kenneth Baynes, James Bohman, and Thomas McCarthy (Cambridge: MIT Press, 1987), 116.
7. Michel Foucault, *The History of Sexuality, Vol. 1*, translated by Robert Hurley (Middlesex: Penguin, 1980), 5–11.
8. Elizabeth Grosz, "Bodies and Knowledges: Feminism and the Crisis of Reason," in *Feminist Epistemologies*, ed. by Linda Alcoff and Elizabeth Potter (New York: Routledge, 1995), 196.
9. Ibid., 198.
10. Maurice Merleau-Ponty, "The Child's Relations with Others," in *The Primacy of Perception*, ed. by James M. Edie (Chicago: Northwestern University Press, 1964), 96–155.
11. O'Connor and Ryan, *Wild Desires and Mistaken Identities*, 272.
12. Ibid., 13.

10

Psychoanalysis with Gay and Lesbian People

An Interpersonal Perspective

Richard Rutkin

MY FOCUS IN THIS ESSAY is not on the genesis of sexual preference nor on the psychodynamics of choice of love partner, nor is it on explications of variations of lifestyle. I intend to discuss an interpersonal psychoanalytic perspective on the psychoanalysis of the homosexual individual, and his or her issues and struggles in living and evolving a personally meaningful sensibility and way of life, including satisfying interpersonal relationships. My focus as an analyst is on the individual's feelings about her self within the context of her interpersonal relations, and not at all on her homosexuality, neither as a symptom nor as a character defect. I will first briefly comment on some historical psychoanalytic ideas about homosexuality, and then discuss my own interpersonal point of view on psychoanalytic treatment as it pertains to gay and lesbian individuals.

Freud, although seemingly compassionate and sensitive toward homosexuality in his personal life (Freud 1921, 1933, 1935), classified homosexuality as an inversion (carefully distinguishing it from a perversion [Freud 1919]), and an inhibition of normal development (Freud 1910, 1925) where pregenital libido instincts, bisexual in nature, are not sufficiently suppressed by successful resolution of the Oedipus complex (Freud 1905, 1915, 1916, 1922). He believed that the homosexual man, avoidant and anxious and fearful of castration, surrenders to a feminine identity, narcissistically choosing same-sex partners who, because of pregenital libido fixation, are loved as extensions of the self (Freud 1902, 1926). This position set the stage for subsequent psychoanalytic thinking on homosexuality, which, despite its extensive evolution, still principally revolved around the centrality of Oedipal issues and their lack of resolution (Fenichel 1930, 1945; Sachs 1923). Much of the later classical thinking, which focused on pre-Oedipal issues (Glover 1932; Klein 1932), spoke to stunted or pathological development of the ego and superego. More recent formulations are directed toward considering primitive defense mechanisms (Socarides 1978), fear of maternal separation (Bieber 1967), "pseudo-sexual" motives such as power and dependency needs (McDougall 1972), or pre-Oedipal developmental arrest and ego deformity (Bergler 1948). All of them place homosexuality on the pathology continuum.

It seems inevitable that psychoanalysis would pathologize homosexuality given the long-standing influence of Judeo-Christian tradition which holds homosexual behavior to be sinful because it contradicts the Biblical view that the purpose of sex is procreation rather than pleasure or relatedness (Bayer 1981). This historical view of homosexuality as sin readily led to modern psychology's only slightly less harsh perspective on homosexuality as pathology—a position just as insidiously negative, but seen by the mental health community as more humane. This pathological construction of homosexuality influenced psychoanalytic theorists to seek causes of its behavior, leading to the unfortunate and often destructive emphasis on "cure," that is, of course, the transformation from homosexuality into a heterosexual orientation. Even those psychoanalytic theorists who view homosexuality as a reparative attempt to achieve sexual pleasure when heterosexuality is undesirable, also see homosexuality as symptomatic of underlying pathology and needing to be cured through treatment (Bayer 1981; Kohut 1971, 1984).

Psychoanalysis's perspective on homosexuality as pathology dovetailed with society's views of homosexuality as wrong and deviant, serving to reinforce the anti-homosexual attitudes of many heterosexuals and homosexuals. The idea that a "mental science," medical in origins and mostly practiced by "doctors," would see homosexuality as "disturbed" and symptomatic gave credence and support to long-standing anti-homosexual bias. These attitudes may have been somewhat lessened by the 1973 American Psychiatric Association's decision to remove homosexuality from the

DSM II classification as a mental disorder, but nevertheless it continues to prevail, not only in society in general but in the mental health professions in particular. Whether the diagnosis of homosexuality, formally or informally, describes it as a pathology, or, most recently, as a condition or alternate lifestyle choice (DuBay 1987), mental health clinicians are often encouraged to urge corrective orientation treatment, reinforcing anti-homosexual feelings and beliefs in both the patient and the therapist.

Central to my conception of psychoanalytic treatment is a non-diagnostic perspective, focused away from biological and social factors emphasizing developmental pathology, and oriented toward bringing about changes in the patient's experience of self (Levenson 1972, 1983; Singer 1970; Wolstein 1960). Even the terms "gay" and "lesbian" can be seen as having diagnostic-like qualities, in that they connote stereotypes and sets of expectations about individuals. As such, they invite generalizations if one is not careful to avoid the pitfalls of applying labels to individuals. It is always dangerous, even if sometimes convenient, to use easily generalizable categories, lest they set a stage of "specialness" or "differentness," and orient or skew the perceptions of the analyst away from the uniqueness of the individual and toward the qualities of the generalization. The danger here lies in seeing not the woman but the "lesbian," not the man but the "black or African American," not the troubled twenty-seven-year-old person, but the "borderline." We in the mental health professions are all too familiar with the uses of derogatory stereotypes in classifying people. We have an unfortunate history of viewing people by their "diagnostic category," often in a dehumanizing and leveling manner, removing focus from the individual person and who she or he is to characteristics held in common with others who share certain of their circumstances. It then becomes tempting for the analyst to work toward getting the person to be a better "gay man" or a better "lesbian woman," rather than exploring and understanding the individual in his own right, with his own individual qualities, characteristics, and issues, including his or her homosexuality.

It is my working belief that people develop psychological difficulties not solely because of terrible things done to them in their childhood but because of their development of an elusive pattern of omissions, distortions, and misrepresentations of their early experience with others and consequently of themselves. This pattern endures and restricts their experience of themselves and others in the present. As I approach the psychotherapeutic work with a new patient, it is my preference to focus on and pay acute attention to my feelings, thoughts, and patterns of reaction—that is, to "experience" the "unique" individual who presents him or her self for treatment. Although I remain very aware of my patients' conflicts and distortions, I avoid attempts at diagnostic generalizations. Thus I am freer to "receive" the presenting patient in his or her own right and to gain understanding solely through interaction and relatedness as it develops during the interchanges that occur in the treatment itself. The goal of this process is to attempt to understand how the patient experiences his or her self in the world in terms of the unique patterns of feelings and beliefs she or he has regarding self and others, and to help to increase the patient's awareness and knowledge of these patterns.

My role as an interpersonal analyst is not to serve as an agent of change from one way of being to another, but rather to be a co-participant in the exploration into the patient's experience of the world. In the course of interacting with the patient in this manner, my own experiences and feelings about the patient and his or her issues become engaged and necessarily influence the nature and manner of our contact. It is thus inevitable that my feelings and experiences about homosexuality will strongly influence interactions with and feelings toward lesbian and gay patients and become one of the interactive factors that contributes to countertransference (Lewes 1988; McHenry and Johnson, 1993). Countertransference, of course, is not only determined by interactions between the patient and the analyst, but also has deep roots in the analyst's preconceived notions, feelings, attitudes, and prejudices that are brought to the work (Kwawer 1980). These underlying factors must be acknowledged and recognized by me as I clarify the motivations for my actions and words. Might my reactions have to do with my anxieties? With my attraction or arousal? With my less than aware fears or bigotry? If not acknowledged, these issues will inevitably distort the truth of what I say to and the manner in which I interact with the patient.

Although the unique and powerful effect of psychoanalysis as an instrument of emotional clarification and growth derives from elucidation of the patient's patterns (including limitations) of experience and action, leading to expanded awareness and the possibility of freer and less encumbered choice, the method also contains within it the danger of the patient being molded into the analyst's conception of idealized and preferred ways of living in the world. Put another way, the psychoanalytic interaction can persuade the patient to see and experience things as the analyst does

(Levenson 1983). If the analyst holds a preconceived notion about the direction of the analysis and what its outcome ought to be instead of being open to the unique individuality of the patient, activities in the direction of ideological conversion will follow, and improvement will be politicized or defined according to the analyst's own value system. Because of the patient's desire to cooperate with the analyst, this conversion can occur with the collusion of the patient (McHenry and Johnson 1993). A truthful (and therapeutic) examination of the patient's experience is then avoided, and the patient's growth and well-being are compromised.

It is thus vital for the analyst to realize the special circumstances that affect a homosexual individual whose ways of living in the world are seen as different and abhorrent, and even immoral, to many, and who is thus affected by prejudicial beliefs and attitudes from both without and within. Ignorance of a homosexual person's milieu would become a serious limitation to relating to his or her experience. This raises questions about the advantages and disadvantages about whether or not lesbian and gay patients should see heterosexual analysts (McHenry and Johnson 1993). Although I do not believe in the absolute preferability of such matching, time limitations account for this important topic not being more extensively addressed in this paper. Suffice it to say for now, it is the authentic engagement of two individuals, and not a contrived arrangement designed for easing the engagement, that contains the necessary therapeutic communication and encouragement to help the patient to engage his or her own authentic sense of self. Gender, sexuality, or other groupings of the analyst and the patient are less central then communicability, comfort, rapport, etc. Similarities such as gender or orientation in themselves do not assure engagement.

I believe that the patient's interactions with others, past and present, are the principle determinants of her experience and behavior and comprise the central focus of the analytic work. Therefore analysis proceeds as a detailed inquiry into all aspects of her interactions with others, with the major focus being on the relationship between the patient and analyst in the unique analytic dyad. In general, psychological difficulties arise when an individual limits awareness of self in the service of self-preservation and salvages aspects of individuality and a sense of dignity in the face of interpersonal demands, so that she renounces certain vital aspects of her self, resulting in a self-protective, albeit narrowed, world view. This narrowed and self-fulfilling view of the world and others represents how I see transference. From the intrapsychic point of view, during therapy sensibility, expectation, and perspective are transferred or projected from the patient's past and outside world to the person in the present circumstance, the analyst. In my interpersonal view, transference is the skewing of contemporary interactive reality, not by projection, but rather by the patient's particular manner of shaping and perpetuating her world view or reality in a way that transcends the actuality of the analyst. But it needn't be only the analyst who is distorted by the patient's transference. Transference, from my perspective, is an idiosyncratic and hence constricted and self-fulfilling way of viewing everything—a characterization and portrayal of the patient's reality and an invitation to the analyst and others to join in and maintain the status quo.

Homosexual people certainly share similar influences that can shape their personalities as well as their defensive/protective transferential patterns. Theses influences include their awareness of the enormous societal discrimination against homosexuality, the negative self-image that this discrimination often fuels, the frequent necessity of self-definition outside of the mainstream, and the need to cope with generalizations about oneself based on one's choice of a love partner. Yet, even within these patterns, I believe that individual differences still predominate and should be the fundamental focus of the analysis. To repeat, the focus of the analysis is the individual and her or his interpersonal issues and conflicts, and not a preconceived perspective nor set of symptom patterns or diagnoses.

To fail to realize and consider the complex common core of pathogenic societal influences on the development of the gay or lesbian individual is to ignore a central reality effecting growth and development and to naively miss the opportunity to gain real understanding of his or her circumstances. We are all continually exposed to and embedded in societal discriminatory perspectives, and it is thus inevitable that all of us hold anti-homosexual views within and outside of our immediate awareness. In fact, the gay or lesbian individual is most often infused with anti-homosexual feelings and attitudes in the form of self-denigration derived from societal identification, internalized as self-contempt. This is usually communicated through the transference (McHenry and Johnson 1993). A major aspect of analytic clarification of these patients' deepest feelings and beliefs about themselves and others occurs through a collaborative exploration of these influences in the transference.

Just as the concept of transference has evolved from being seen as strictly a projection of the patient's past onto the present circumstances to being understood as a personal skewing of the patient's current interpersonal reality in an idiosyncratic manner, countertransference has similarly evolved within the interpersonal perspective from being seen as the analyst's irrational response to the patient and her transference to being seen as the totality of the analyst's reactions to the patient and the treatment (Levenson 1983). Whereas in the past the analytic therapist viewed countertransference as undesirable encroachments or even unconscious childish reactions to be understood privately, it is now seen as the analyst's inevitable human response to the patient and as a source of vital information about the other person, sometimes even shared with the patient and explored together.

I believe that the major generalized countertransference issue for the heterosexual or homosexual analyst working with gay and lesbian patients concerns the analyst's own internalized prejudice against homosexuality. Whereas negative attitudes and beliefs about homosexuality appear fairly clearly in many theoretical constructions, negative reactions to homosexuality, except for blatant homophobia, are often far more subtle in analysts and become most clearly discernible in their countertransferential analytic reactions.These negative reactions might be psychodynamically rooted in the analyst's concerns about her or his own sexuality or in prejudices derived from prevailing cultural devaluations of homosexuality or ignorance and misconceptions about the functioning of homosexuals. Thus the analyst with unexplored negative feelings and reactions might choose to avoid exploration of or unconsciously collude with the patient in not identifying issues that might arouse anxiety, pain, guilt, or self-hatred in either of the participants. A common collusion in this regard, for example, might entail the lack of acknowledgment of the patient's homosexuality itself, creating an analytic environment where the avoidance of fundamental issues of sexuality are rationalized by the distortion that "after all is said and done, we're all basically the same," or by failing to recognize that the patient's tendency toward secrecy developed as self-protection in an actually oppressive and unsafe world. It is essential for the analyst to recognize, acknowledge, and extend the understanding of these feelings within him or herself, clarifying any distortion of his or her own needs and motivations while engaging the patient. Whatever its psychogenesis, unexplored countertransferential avoidance or distortion can readily lead to perpetuation of the status quo and an analytic outcome of little difference or change, instead of leading to the desired and increased ability on the part of the patient to be loving and accepting of herself, to have loving and significant relationships, and to have active and productive involvement with the society in which she lives while creatively seeking enhancement of her own identity.

References Cited

Bayer, R.B. 1981. *Homosexuality and American Psychiatry: The Politics of Diagnosis*. New York: Basic Books.

Bergler, E. 1948. Preliminary Phases of the Masculine Beating Fantasy. *Psa Q* 7: 514.

Bieber, I. 1967. Sexual Deviations. In *Comprehensive Textbook of Psychiatry*, ed. by A. Freednab and H. Kaplan. Baltimore: Williams and Wilkens.

DuBay, W.H. 1987. *Gay Identity: The Self Under Ban*. Jefferson, NC: McFarland.

Fenichel, O. 1930. Zur Psychologie der Transvestitismus. *Int. Z. Psa.* 16: 21.

———. 1945. *The Psychoanalytic Theory of Neuroses*. New York: Norton.

Freud, S. 1902. Analysis of a Phobia in a Five Year Old Boy. *Standard Edition* 10: 1. London: Hogarth, 1955.

———. 1905. Three Essays on the Theory of Sexuality. *SE* 7: 123.

———. 1910. Leonardo Da Vinci and a Memory of His Childhood. *SE* 11: 59.

———. 1915. Instincts and Their Vicissitudes. *SE* 14: 109.

———. 1916. The Libido Theory and Narcissism. *SE* 14: 237.

———. 1919. A Child is Being Beaten: A Contribution to the Origin of Sexual Perversion. *SE* 17: 175.

———. 1921. Letter to Jones. In *Body Politic*. Toronto: May Press, 1977

———. 1922. Certain Neurotic Mechanisms in Jealousy, Paranoia and Homosexuality. *SE* 18: 221.

———. 1925. Some Psychological Consequences of the Anatomic Distinction Between the Sexes. *SE* 20: 75.

———. 1926. Inhibitions, Symptoms and Anxiety. *SE* 20: 75.

———. 1933. Femininity. *SE* 22: 112.

———. 1935. Letter published in *Am J of Psychiat.* 107, 1951: 786.

Glover, E. 1932. The Principles of Psychiatric Classification. *J of Mental Science*.

Klein, M. 1932. *The Psychoanalysis of Children*. New York: Delacorte.

Kohut, H. 1971. *The Analysis of the Self*. New York: Intl. Univ. Press.

———. 1984. *How Does Analysis Cure*. Chicago: University of Chicago Press.

Kwawer, J. 1980. Transference and Countertransference in Homosexuality: Changing Psychoanalytic Views. *Am J of Psychother* 34: 72.

Levenson, E. 1972. *The Fallacy of Understanding*. New York: Basic Books.

———. 1983. *The Ambiguity of Change*. New York: Basic Books.

Lewes, K. 1988. *The Psychoanalytic Theory of Male Homosexuality*. New York: New Amer. Library.

McDougall, J. 1972. Primal Scene and Sexual Perversion. *Int J Psa* 53: 371.

McHenry, S.S. and Johnson, J.W. 1993. Homophobia in the Therapist and Gay or Lesbian Client: Conscious and Unconscious Collusions in Self-Hate. *Psychotherapy* 30: 141.

Sachs, H. 1923. Zur Genese der Perversionen. *Int Z Psa* 9: 172.

Singer, E. 1970. *Key Concepts in Psychotherapy*. New York: Basic Books.

Socarides, C. 1978. *Homosexuality*. New York: Aronson.

Wolstein, B. 1960. Transference: Historical Roots and Current Concepts in Psychoanalytic Theory and Practice. *Psychiatry* 23: 159.

11

The Evolution of My Views on Nonnormative Sexual Practices

Roy Schafer

I

IT IS PARTICULARLY IN CONNECTION WITH the psychology of women that the problems in Freud's theory of psychosexual development have been identified, articulated, and explained in detail and with much sophistication. A large part of this development may be attributed directly and indirectly to the efforts of feminist thinkers. Starting from this advance, it requires no great leap in reasoning to conclude that if the psychoanalytic psychology of women is problematic, then that of men, from which it purports to be derived, must be equally problematic. Expectedly, therefore, strong arguments have been advanced to show that this is so and on this expanded critical basis one readily sees that there is much to question about Freud's views on gay and lesbian sexuality, for these views have been derived from his phallocentric approach to the psychosexual development of both sexes.

There is no uniformity to be found in these many critiques. Inevitably, they have varied with the particular critic's school of psychoanalytic thought, personal predilections, and continuing access to new ideas and information from other fields of humanistic study. Also, they have built on one another and become ever more compelling. Beyond that, many feminist critiques have themselves been criticized as being too narrowly focused on gender relations and thus neglectful of large issues in the theories of sexuality in general (Rubin 1984).

To a modest extent I have participated in some aspects of these critical developments, drawing in part on the work of fine thinkers in many fields of study and in part on my own observations and reflections as an analyst (1974, 1978, 1992, 1994). While giving an account of the evolution of my views as promised in the title of this essay, I want also to explore some further aspects of the problems of nonnormative sexuality when looked at through the lens of Freudian psychoanalysis.

My account of my views will not abide by the conventions of chronological time. Although that kind of linear chronology might seem to be the basis for the clearest version, it is not that at all: insights and criticisms develop in bits and pieces that are packed with multiple implications, only some of which can be realized at the moment of conception. Like Heinz Hartmann's description of interpretations (1951), insights and criticisms have "multiple appeal," that is, all kinds of surprising consequences elsewhere in the mind than at the point of initial focus. This has characterized the evolution of my ideas and no doubt has been the case with many others who work in psychoanalysis. Additionally, if I give some idea of what I have evolved *to* before going too far back in my history, my retrospective account may be made more accessible. Consequently, much of what I shall say represents more of the present phase of my evolution: where I have arrived rather than where I started from.

I should also mention from the start that I am not going to refer to the vicissitudes of my personal development or the dynamic factors influencing me at present. These necessarily have contributed to the evolution of my views on psychosexuality, both normative and nonnormative. Yet in this respect, my silence expresses my agreement with Freud and many others: bringing intimate personal considerations to bear in expounding and assessing theoretical ideas is a two-edged sword; it settles nothing about lines of argument and the conclusions reached. We all have personal reasons for those aspects of reality that we see clearly and emphasize as well as for those we remain blind to or deplore out of bias. As many well know, Freud himself fell victim to this two-edged sword as have many analysts after him. For example, Freud tended to brush off feminist and other critiques of the psychoanalytic bias against nonnormative sexual orientations and practices as expressions of penis envy or other problems with sexuality. But raising the two-edged sword, one can respond to Freud's countercritical cries of "penis envy" with the cry of "castration anxiety" or of "repressed mother envy." And in the present context, one must finally say to all of this only, "So what?!"

The term phallocentric, however, is not party to these arguments, because when this term is properly used it refers to faulty and biased methodology and reasoning and not to personal intention. As a metaphor, however, "two-edged sword" itself conveys a phallocentric orientation in its symbolic linking of reasoned argument to the phallus.

II

I want next to take up directly the different sexual practices—both the normative or publicly conformist and the nonnormative or publicly individualized. It seems to me worthwhile to structure my thinking about sexual practices around the antithesis of curiosity vs. rushing to moral judgment, both positive and negative. Presumably, analysts are thoroughly committed to curiosity, including curiosity about the evolution of moral judgments and the way these are made and conveyed implicitly as well as explicitly. And yet if you read between the lines, you soon realize that in traditional Freudian psychoanalysis many moral judgments have been taken for granted as factual statements, while many other moral judgments have been presented as reasoned conclusions based on careful exercises of curiosity in the form of purportedly scientific investigation or, even more simply, uncontroversial reality testing.

Heinz Hartmann emphasized this point among others in his 1959 Freud Lecture, *Psychoanalysis and Moral Values* (1960), at the New York Psychoanalytic Society and Institute. There, he pointed out how, in child-rearing, parents and educators use words like "good" and "bad" among many ordinarily descriptive words as though they convey facts about things and practices, when in effect, if not in intention, they express moral preferences or imperatives. This is true in the case of gender development; specifically, when a boy is told, "Boys and men do this, not that; they are this way, not that way; they aspire to this, not that; they look good this way, not that way," and so on, he is being indoctrinated with moral prescriptions masquerading as factual descriptions. The indoctrination proceeds similarly in the case of girls.

What Hartmann did not go into, however, are the observations that show that children are pretty smart about these so-called realistic lessons. Children are not just great fabricators in fantasy; often, they do correctly take communication of facts as more than mere information. Consequently, they realize that what is being conveyed along with these "facts" is the warning that in the future they will be judged—loved and admired or scorned, punished, and emotionally abandoned—if they either do or do not conform to the norm without question or protest. Additionally, children go further in fantasy to envision extreme rewards and dire consequences if they get the so-called facts right or wrong. The rationalist parents who say later on, "But we never threatened; we only informed and explained," are naive about their own inner lives and the inner lives of their children.

I am emphasizing that we must remain aware how readily so-called normative facts are already infused with musts or ought tos and how they thereby serve to perpetuate the moral import and impact of the norms they embody. Emphasis on normative facts amounts to a two-sided attack: it both encourages identification with unconsciously held parental superego pressures, and at the same time it encourages projection of one's repressed nonconformist tendencies. Both of these developments then lead to persecutory attitudes toward that which is not normative in others. As I understand it, that's how it has played itself out with regard to gay and lesbian sexual orientations and practices, those much persecuted manifestations of the forbidden, the condemned, the unnameable, and therefore the unthinkable. And that is also how it has also played itself out between men and women, organizing intergender relations around sadism and masochism.

It was Freud who prepared us to understand these developments: how, through superego identification and projection, we persecute in others what we come to condemn and repress in ourselves. We persecute by abuse, derogation, ostracism, neglect, discrimination, and so on, sometimes grossly and sometimes subtly. Freud showed that what we do condemn is heavily conditioned by overt and implicit pressures; that it is not natural, not an inbuilt part of human nature to show sexual bias; in other words, that kind of discrimination thrives through nurture, not nature; history, not biology.

More is involved, however, than direct or disguised moral pressure. We have to take into account the coercive force of language. I touch here on a very large area of study and will single out for mention only one aspect of it that has already received much attention, fruitfully so. I refer to the organization of language and therefore of thinking in binary terms. Binary terms pervade identity formation and human relations. It is not just a matter of good and bad but also, and with special relevance to our topic today, masculine and feminine, heterosexual and homosexual, oedipal and preoedipal, genital and pregenital, paternal and maternal, active and passive, and so on and so forth. Contemporary critical theory has brought out how these binary arrangements set up implicit hierarchies of value in favor of the first term of the two. They also dichotomize much too much, and they introduce arbitrary assumptions about symmetry.

Much of Freud's formal theorizing was cast in binary and symmetrical terms, even though, clinically, his basic interpretations often did not observe the constraints imposed by his formal conceptualizations. In most of his clinical works he gave us mixed and asymmetrical cases, often called overdetermined, and that is just what we all usually encounter in clinical work: mixed cases and asymmetrics. These cases replace the balanced black and white contrasts, but there is still the assumption that what is mixed are hierarchically valorized and symmetrical opposites. And here we see how basic constituents of language control our thinking, just as they controlled much of Freud's thinking. We learn from the first to think of paternal-maternal or masculine-feminine as hierarchically valorized and symmetrical opposites. Even male and female bodies or genitals are divided up that way as in the case of the erect penis and the vagina as a hole to receive it, as though a "hole" is all there is to it and as though the vagina is the only "hole" and that that's all it's good for. Before modern anatomy took over, anatomists considered this vaginal "hole" the penis turned inside out; in effect, it was another form of setting up ranked opposites even while seeming to deny a fundamental difference between the sexes (Laqueur, 1989). The idea of "the opposite sex" epitomizes this way of constructing nature.

Much of my evolution as clinician and theorist has consisted in divesting myself more and more of the idea of opposites, seeing how much mischief has been sponsored by that way of thinking. And I have paid more and more attention to the binding and disruptive power of so-called symmetrical opposites in the thinking of my patients. So often it turns out that, for patients, what seems a simple linguistic convention represents, unconsciously, a powerful and simplistic moral bias, an overwhelming idealization, as well as persecutory or guilty orientations.

Psychoanalytically, the word "opposite" is usually inappropriate and misleading. The better word for it is "difference." The analyst's curiosity should be dedicated to defining and understanding differences. That kind of curiosity is individualizing; it downplays classifying and diagnosing. Thinking along these lines, the noted methodologist of anthropology,

Clifford Geertz, recommended "thick description" of the single scene or event or person (1973).

What has evolved in my thinking along with this divestiture of binaries is a tentative, if not suspicious, attitude toward all universalizing propositions about men, women, fathers, mothers, children, child-rearing practices, psychosexual development, and so on. To my mind, all the key issues of psychoanalysis are too saddled with these overambitious generalizations that push us toward classification and diagnosis, and that too often are based on questionable dichotomizations. They get in the way of empathic listening, curiosity, or graphic description. Reductionism replaces good phenomenology.

Given more time, I could take up at length how the shifts I have made enter into appraisals of need for treatment, therapeutic change, and termination. But all of that would take us too far afield for today's purposes.

To return now to the different sexual practices: It is these sorts of nonconformist practices that threaten particularly those who are polarized by binary thinking who have, on this basis, become fiercely normative. Polarized men need to buttress their own identities by surrounding themselves in fact or fiction with "dumb cunts" and deriding, ignoring, or defeating other sorts of women, if they can even get past using "dumb cunt" to cover all women. In an equivalent way, many polarized women hope, in *their* binary terms, to develop a solid feminine identity by making sure to marry a man and have children at no matter what psychic cost to them and to scorn those women who don't share these goals; at the same time, they may reduce all men to "brutes." For both types of threatened people, to be normative or conformist is to be worth something, to be justified, to be safe from persecution in the inner world and the outer world.

We are dealing here with what has been called the process of naturalizing, that is, making it seem simply natural as well as factual that people follow the norms and defend them vigorously, if not brutally, even murderously. It was one of Freud's great contributions to denaturalize prevailing convictions about the sexual innocence of children and related convictions about the effects of disgust, shame, guilt, and fear. At the same time, however, and going in the opposite direction in his mode of theorizing and generalizing, he appears now to have been further naturalizing the idea of a heterosexual, genital, reproductive culmination of development. Thus, he could not go all the way with the curiosity that led to his being able to denaturalize as much as he did. When it came to gay and lesbian sexuality, he stopped short. He viewed these sexualities as manifestations of arrested development. For him they were, by implication, forms of pathological development. Ostensibly a nonjudgmental conclusion, implicitly it did reaffirm in a pseudoscientific way the normative morality of his time. For there is no impermeable line between the ideas that there is something different about someone and something wrong with that someone, and as a next step, between the ideas that something is wrong psychologically and something is wrong morally. That's why, for instance, children and grown-ups feel humiliated and vulnerable by admitting publicly that they need psychological treatment—and, of course, far more vulnerable in the case of acknowledging gay and lesbian proclivities.

What Freud did in the realm of sexual orientation and practices was to mistake a norm as a fact of nature. How he came to do so and what that acceptance entailed I took up in my first large contribution to this topic in the early 1970s, just about twenty years ago. Thus, having for the most part given an idea of what I have evolved to as well as developed a broad intellectual context for my ideas about sexual differences, I shall review a few of the main theses in that article, "Problems in Freud's Psychology of Women" (1974). Not only do I still stand by these theses, I now believe that already then I was involved in an historical trend that, in one form or another, has been achieving ever-wider acceptance among analysts and at least some segments of the general population. Or, if not acceptance, then at least recognition as a point to be debated, as it is being debated still today. In recounting these earlier theses, however, I won't avoid filling them in further with considerations that date from later years, including the present time. As I stated earlier, I do not see a linear rendition as necessarily the most valid or informative telling of history.

III

A central part of my argument then (and now) is that Freud's Darwinism led him to adopt what I called an evolutionary ethic. Specifically, he viewed the individual as the carrier of the reproductive organs and substances designed to guarantee the survival of the species. Above all, there was to be the successful transmission of the germ plasm from generation to generation. From this point of view, it seemed to him to follow that psychosexual development should culminate in genital, heterosexual, reproductive orientations. Anything else would go against the plan of nature. Whatever its vicissitudes on the way to that endpoint—and, as he showed, there are various phases, modes, zones, pleasures, and pains to encounter along the way—only the one endpoint is to be considered natural.

It was in this way that Freud naturalized and moralized normative sexual practices. He did not see that he was making an unwarranted leap from biological theory to moral judgment when he assumed that development *ought to* culminate in reproductivity. Also, he did not see that he was making a moral judgment when he reasoned that, because development *can* proceed to reproductivity, it is *only* the reproductive heterosexual who is the mature, normal, healthy, fully developed person, the better off person, and so, by implication (which he would have consciously repudiated), the person who is a better sort of person than others who have developed differently. Once Freud idealized this form of development, other forms had to be seen as immature, unfortunately arrested, perhaps irremediably so, although under ideal circumstances they might be amenable to the growth-enhancing method of psychoanalysis. Just as in his phallocentric way he regarded the clitoris as a stunted organ, he regarded those who diverged from the norm as stunted people. In his personal stance, he was tolerant; in his analytic formulations, he was not.

Freud was not lacking in what he took to be sound empirical evidence to support his position. He did always aim to be dispassionately objective, and, to be accurate about it, he did a lot better in this emotionally highly charged realm than the bulk of his contemporaries. What I believe happened is that when he looked in depth at his sample of homosexually inclined patients, he saw much unconscious sexual conflict involving fear, envy, rivalry, resentment over feelings of damagedness, narcissistic excesses, and so on and so forth. This seemed to be the evidence that clinched his point—as though it was not already in his mind as a preconception and a value judgment (see, e.g., Freud, 1954). In fact, however, nothing conclusive follows from Freud's observations of homosexually inclined patients, for every heterosexual patient in analysis shows the same or similar conflicts, and it was Freud himself who introduced us to this perception.

There is more behind Freud's conclusions. There is the further observation that for many heterosexually active patients, curative effects seemed to derive from the analysis of these unconscious complications of gender identity and predilection. Again, however, nothing conclusive follows from this observation either. Of the various reasons why this is so, I want to emphasize one in particular: Freud's Darwinian ideology committed him to bringing his "immature" patients to heterosexual reproductive positions, and for their part almost all of his patients, too, were committed to this goal. Insofar as they were motivated in their analytic work, they wanted to get rid of their unconscious "perverse" and "inverse" tendencies, for that's what their pathogenic repressions seemed now to be about. Freed from these repressions, and helped toward a mixture of renunciation, sublimation, and continued repression, they could hope to succeed in achieving genital heterosexual love, reproductivity, and pleasure instead of suffering. They and Freud were together in this.

I believe that, by and large, it is still that way in the analytic treatment of the great majority of patients. Heterosexual tendencies are taken for granted; it is conflict over them that is to be examined, understood, and reduced. In contrast, homosexual tendencies are considered central to psychological problems, and it is the temptation to act on them in fact or fantasy that is to be examined, understood, and reduced. Strong cross-gender identifications must be modified, pregenital fixations loosened so far as possible, and the troublesome homosexual tendencies finally subordinated to heterosexual genital primacy. Ideally, the patient will accept a degree of latent homosexual leaning as natural but idealize its expression through aim-inhibited friendships, empathy, creativity, and so on. Renunciation is the goal. Nowhere in Freud is evidence of his recognition of the line of argument developed, for example, by Judith Butler (1990): using Freud's own explanation of the passing of the Oedipus complex in his monograph "The Ego and the Id" (1923), she draws other conclusions. Specifically, she read Freud to be showing that identification with the lost oedipal object—the parent of the opposite sex—should favor homosexual resolutions of that complex. Freud mentioned this problem but did not deal with it effectively.

With these points, we have entered the thickets of Freud's idealizing of compulsory heterosexuality and his characterization of the young child as polymorphously perverse. Polymorphous, yes, but why perverse? "Perverse" was meant to include the homoerotic, too. Here, we must confront the general idea of perversion. The *Shorter O.E.D.* says on Perversion, "turning aside from truth or right; perversion to an improper use; corruption, distortion" (1973). We should not overlook the fact that the history of the word perversion includes major legal and religious ideas of impropriety. On that account, "perversion" and "perverse" can be seen to be all the more loaded with moral connotations. Significantly, the illustrative quotation given in the *O.E.D.*, from Bacon, is "Women to govern men . . . slaves (to govern) freemen . . . (are) total violations and perversions of the laws of nature and nations." The *O.E.D.*'s choice of example naturalizes moral condemnation of feminists as well as nonnormative psychosexuality. Remaining for a moment in this etymological context, we can recognize the same bias in the use of the word *straight* for normative sexuality: straight as opposed to what?—crooked, twisted, off the mark?

What, then, might we assume was between the lines of Freud's use of the word "perverse" when he spoke of pregenital sexuality as being polymorphously perverse? I would say that in his theorizing Freud was looking backward from the teleologically prescribed endpoint of Darwinian sexual development. We can anticipate this conclusion from the word pregenital, for that word implies that one is speaking of matters that the individual ought to get beyond. It is implied that it is not enough to stay with the words oral, anal, or phallic-exhibitionistic; it is required to abide by the prescriptive use of the prefix "pre."

In addition to moralizing genitality as the allegedly natural endpoint, I think an aesthetic value judgment is also implied in the idea of genital primacy. Freud argued that oral, anal, and phallic are all well and good as subordinate features of adult sexual life, but that it would go against the ideas of integration and maturity if, instead of sublimating them, one were to linger too long over, or be altogether gratified by, their sensuous potential. Here, the specific forms of integration and maturity that Freud was idealizing derived from his teleology of reproductive sexuality. His idealization includes implications of being decorously pleasing as well as being stable and efficient, or perhaps more exactly being decorously pleasing just because one is stable and efficient. In addition to its being the era of Darwin in metaphors of reality, it was also the era of the idealized powerful machine. Many concepts of beauty and art smack of that unexamined aesthetic value judgment; that is, the judgment that normative moral correctness is essential to beauty. Aesthetics serves as a vehicle for moral prescription—among many other uses, of course.

It seems to me, therefore, that in this respect Freud was working in conformity with the moral and aesthetic dictates of his culture, and so he was effectively using the language of that culture in a way that further fenced us all in. Today we realize more than ever that language is not just a tool of thought or a vehicle. Words teach us what to think as well as how to think and how not to think. The power is in the word, and parents and educators may themselves be regarded as the vehicles for the words of history, culture, material necessity, and distributions of power. Thus, for example, in the case of the United States military, the effort to combine the words gay and hero or gay and fighter fails; it falls on deaf ears in the chambers of Congress, too, as well as amongst the largely unthinking public that elects this Congress. The combinations are unthinkable. Heroes have to be heterosexual men—by definition—and women, whether lesbian or not, couldn't possibly, really, reliably fight well; at least natural women couldn't. Ask Sam Nunn. This is not a digression. We are not that far from the thinking of the average traditional analyst or at least from what is prescribed for his or her thinking by the analytic literature and the teaching in training institutes. We tend to be indoctrinated by the extreme naturalization not only of normative sexual practices but of prevailing gender differences—the oppositeness of the sexes, so-called.

To begin with, I mentioned curiosity as being the antithesis of rushing to moral judgment. Assuming that psychoanalysis is defined by its particular form of curiosity about the human mind in human relationships, let me now frame this question: "How would the consistently curious analyst think and speak about these matters?" I've been trying to illustrate some aspects of this way of thinking in what I have presented in my critique thus far. I will be doing more of the same in the remainder of this essay. Obviously, there can be no one way: we are dealing with individual differences in both parties to an analysis.

To continue the argument, I want to return to the prefix "pre." The word pregenital, on which I have already commented, is closely allied to the word preoedipal, even though it does establish a somewhat different center of interest. I maintain that "preoedipal" is also a teleological, implicitly moralistic term. It naturalizes a normative development that has been, from Freud on, usually understood in the sense of the positive oedipal, the crystallization though not the culmination of heterosexual development. The negative oedipal Freud identified and emphasized especially in "The Ego and the Id" (1923). He regarded it as the seat of crystallized homosexual love as well as the capacity to identify with the opposite sex. Nevertheless, the negative oedipal remains as neglected in most of his formal theoretical writings as does the mother in his case histories. Further, in his theories this neglected woman generally remains the unarticulated sex object of the oedipal boy and rival of the oedipal girl. Therefore, preoedipal refers to what is pre*heterosexual* as well as pre*genital*.

In my 1974 article, I argued—and I am not claiming priority here for every detail of this argument—the arbitrariness of Freud's attributing to penis envy so dominant a role in the lives of all women. He attributed this envy directly to the shock of discovering, at the phase-appropriate moment, the anatomical difference between the sexes (1925). He asserted that the shock is instantly mortifying to the girl, so much so that then and later there remains imprinted on her mind a lasting sense of inferiority that serves as the basis for penis envy. Back then, I argued that Freud had stopped short of asking what he might have been expected to ask if he had continued to exercise his enormous curiosity; specifically, he didn't ask, "What would there have to be about the girl's development prior to this moment that would make her that vulnerable and would lead her to that position?" But to ask this question is to acknowledge the central role of the child-mother relationship in all psychic development of both sexes. Freud did acknowledge that role somewhat a little later on, but it is apparent that he did so with some uncertainty or ambivalence, for in his concluding "Outline" (1939) he backtracked from this acknowledgment.

Looked at in this light, the prefix "pre" seems to me out of place when discussing the gratifications, frustrations, attachments, and fears during the very first years of development. All of these have to be taken up first on their own terms; their subsequent transformations, if any, should not intrude at the very beginning. At each point, they should be approached with unhampered curiosity. There should be no implication that they are not yet the real thing. Certainly, they usually undergo important transformations during the remainder of development, and Freud did pay much fruitful attention to these developments in the case of both boys and girls. Nevertheless, my entire argument suggests to me that, if anything, the most fitting alternative term for the oedipal is post-dyadic.

"Post-dyadic" preserves the sense of continuity and transformation in development that is so essential in psychoanalytic thinking. "Post-dyadic" has greater heuristic potential. The oedipal triangle is, then, "post-dyadic"; the dyadic is not "preoedipal." Today, many analysts are working on this assumption even though they may not always realize it or say so publicly. To put the matter most conservatively, however, I would assert that, in psychoanalysis, the words pregenital, preoedipal, perverse, and inverse are disorienting as well as judgmental, and so they tend to limit further and further extensions of curiosity about the individual case.

IV

When I began to read psychoanalysis as a sophomore in college, at which time I began my passionate and faithful adherence to it, I had already been thoroughly indoctrinated with all the conventional sexual biases in and by the world in which I grew up. This indoctrination had the forceful assistance of my unconscious infantile fantasy life, itself a variable that was not by any means independent of my upbringing and general cultural-linguistic conditioning. Consequently, Freud's point of view seemed to me inexorably logical, realistic, and scientifically secure. When, some fifteen years later, I began my psychoanalytic training in seminars at the Western New England Psychoanalytic Institute, it all still seemed that way to me. Everything I read and everything I was taught reinforced this point of view. Certainly, tolerance and curiosity were strongly supported, but unconsciously one was discouraged from questioning the established psychosexual order, the presumably natural order of things in the psychosexual realm. Compliance was richly rewarded. Mine was. And, to be sure, the tolerance and curiosity were those of the superior other.

Once I began to teach Freud in my institute, however, some five years after that, I began to formulate, fleetingly, inadmissible questions about Freud's point of view. Briefly, I became aware that Freud's position did not hang together and that it included bias. Nevertheless, it took some more years before I paid much attention to these questions. It became harder and harder to teach Freud's psychosexual theory with conviction. Partly, this was because candidates, too, had begun to raise hard questions.

By then, we were all in the protest period of the late 1960s and early 1970s when almost anything previously taken for granted as natural or right or as part of nature was being thrown into question. At that time, saying "the Establishment" was also a way of saying (to paraphrase the Clinton campaign), "It's history, stupid, not biology." Intellectually at least, sexual mores were being challenged, reexamined, and revised. At that time I was working therapeutically with undergraduate students at Yale University. Expectably, they were into all kinds of sexual experimentation and question-raising, too. Further, it was the time of the drop-out, the pill, the mind-altering substance, and co-education, each of which raised further difficult questions. It was a time when therapy itself came to be widely regarded as part of the problem rather than part of the answer. All this questioning went to the point where many clinical students regarded it as a matter of principle never to come to class. In retrospect, I would say that as a result of all these social changes and pedagogical experiences I was prodded to pay more and more attention to my half-repressed questions.

During this time I was studying closely ego psychology and its psychosocial ramifications. Outside of psychoanalysis, I was reading about interpretation in many fields: the humanities and social sciences, especially in literary criticism, cultural and intellectual history, the philosophy of history, other branches of philosophy, anthropology, and feminist papers of that period and earlier. I was becoming more and more sensitized to how culture-bound, time-bound, and gender-bound perspectives establish what we're supposed to take for granted about gender roles, sexual orientations, and distributions of power in general, and equally sensitized to the rhetoric of dominant perspectives. I began to see more clearly that we are limited in what we look for, in what we can see when we do look, in the vocabulary available to us to conceive it and tell it, and in the criteria of solid evidence we use; also that there are many presuppositions we must remain blind to, and so on and so forth. If I had read only psychoanalysis, I would never have gotten as far as I did in being alert to how far ideology extends into what is circulated in psychoanalysis as established fact.

In psychoanalysis, for example, it seems like a straightforward technical principle that in doing character analysis one must render what is ego-syntonic ego-alien, thereby making it possible to analyze pathological character traits. That's the way one develops in the patient motivation for therapeutic change. Taking a second look, however, one realizes how much space this technical principle leaves for the analyst's personal values to be imposed on the patient. Here we need think only of the ego-syntonic homosexual orientation in whatever way that is structured in character, and of how so many analysts tried to make these orientations ego-alien or else resignedly thought it was hopeless even to try. It was much the same with those women who had developed in an assertive, competitive way and were not committed to, or even oriented toward, settling down at home as a wife and mother.

Another example of much broader scope was the valorization of universalized theory, the kind of theory that Freud was overeager to develop. This valorization continues to burden us in today's plethora of all-encompassing theories of personality development, gender definition, and much more. This theorizing tries to explain too much too fast. Freud's (1954) letters show that he couldn't wait to universalize his formulation of his own Oedipus complex or his interpretation of castration anxiety and penis envy. Today we realize that with all the gains that accrue to understanding and therapeutic efficacy from his rapid generalizations, there also accrued built-in negative valuations of women, femininity, and all unconventional sexual orientations and practices. Today, there are more analytic child development theories than one can count, and none of them is based on absolute, incontrovertible value-free factual findings. They can't be. I believe that this valorization has not yet been sufficiently studied.

In any case, as, back then, I read more, thought more, and brought my wider reading and critical theory to bear, I began to teach more effectively and challengingly, and from that change came my 1974 essay on the questions I have been discussing today. I have been at it ever since and not only in the area of sexuality. I have been trying to show in all my writings that all aspects of psychoanalytic theory need to be constantly reexamined with sustained curiosity and with references to newer developments in critical thinking. I keep on finding more and more to challenge, more and more that doesn't hang together, and more and more stimulation of curiosity. Being curious is what goes best with being consistently analytic, especially when it is curiosity about the structure of thought and the entailments of presuppositions and, of course, about moral judgments hidden in the language we use when speaking of individual differences, sexual and otherwise.

References

Butler, J. 1990. *Gender Trouble: Feminism and the Subversion of Identity*. New York and London: Routledge.

Freud, S. 1923. The ego and the id. *The Collected Papers of Sigmund Freud* 19: 3–66. London: Hogarth Press, 1961.

———. 1925. Some psychological consequences of the anatomical distinction between the sexes. *The Collected Papers of Sigmund Freud* 19: 243–258. London: Hogarth Press, 1961.

———. 1939. An outline of psychoanalysis. *The Collected Papers of Sigmund Freud* 23: 139–207. London: Hogarth Press, 1964.

———. 1954. *The Origins of Psychoanalysis: Letters to Wilhelm Fliess*. Trans. E. Mosbacher and J. Strachey. New York: Basic Books.

Geertz, C. 1973. *The Interpretation of Cultures: Selected Essays*. New York: Basic Books.

Hartmann, H. 1951. Technical implications of ego psychology. *Psychoanal. Quart* 20: 31–43.

———. 1960. *Psychoanalysis and Moral Values*. New York: International Universities Press.

Laqueur, T. 1989. *Making Sex: Body and Gender from the Greeks to Freud*. Cambridge, MA: Harvard University Press.

Rubin, G. 1984. Thinking sex: Notes for a radical theory of politics. In *The Lesbian and Gay Studies Reader*. Ed. by H. Abelove, et al. New York and London: Routledge, 1992, 3–44.

Schafer, R. 1974. Problems in Freud's psychology of women. *J. Amer. Psychoanal. Assn.* 22: 459–485.

———. 1978. *Language and Insight: The Sigmund Freud Memorial Lectures, 1975–1976, University College, London*. New Haven: Yale University Press.

———. 1992. *Retelling a Life: Narration and Dialogue in Psychoanalysis*. New York: Basic Books.

———. 1994. Gendered discourse and discourse on gender. In *Psychoanalysis, Feminism, and the Future of Gender*. Ed. by J. H. Smith and A. M. Mahfooz. *Psychiatry and the Humanities* 11: 1–21. Baltimore and London: Johns Hopkins University Press.

The Shorter Oxford English Dictionary on Historical Principles. 2 volumes. Revised edition by C. T. Onions (1973). Oxford: The Clarendon Press.

12

Psychoanalytic Theories of Lesbian Desire

A Social Constructionist Critique

Erica Schoenberg

> The essence of man is no abstraction inherent in each single individual. In its reality it is the ensemble of the social relations.
>
> —Marx, 1976, *Six Treatises on Feurbach*

> Folks are dumb where I come from, they don't have any learnin'. Still they get from A to Z, doin' what comes naturally.
>
> —Irving Berlin, *Annie Get Your Gun*

"THIS HAS BEEN A WEEK FROM HELL," a patient of mine is fond of stating to begin her sessions. And so it has been for me, I think now, having immersed myself for the past week in the psychoanalytic literature about female homosexuality. Although I am vacationing on a beautiful lake in New Hampshire, I have spent much of the time frenzied, the hairs on the back of my neck standing up, rage boiling within me and feelings of impotence making me alternately want to scream or sleep. For in its consideration of lesbians, the psychoanalytic discourse resembles, and is as abhorrent as, its pre-feminist stance towards "that other group of people who would forever remain incomplete—women" (Lewes 1988, 236). Characterized by inferiority, "narcissistic mortification" (Chodorow 1994), and loss of their psychic core, psychoanalytic accounts condemn both groups to a life of endlessly awaiting restitution of the lost penis which will finally make them whole. Which is to say that psychoanalytic theories of lesbians are no more than a recycled, but more vitriolic, version of the socially conformist, reactionary, phallocentric propaganda that characterized theories of women. Oppressive prejudice masquerading as fact; ideology in the guise of science.

Although Harris (1991) tried to take heart in the belief that in the work of the last two decades, "the organizing fantasy of women as castrated has been definitively undermined [and that now w]omen have their own desires and processes of identification and object choice" (245), her claim is belied by even the most casual perusal of the literature on lesbians. Khan (1979, cited in O'Connor and Ryan 1993, 86), for example, states that the female homosexual has "exaggerated penis-envy," and that her masculinity complex defends against a "deeper sense of genital inadequacy." Kernberg (1976, cited in Chodorow 1994) takes as given the "dominance" of the paternal penis" (55) and makes the oedipal girl's "achievement" of heterosexuality contingent on both her and her mother's recognition of the inferiority of their own genitals. Interestingly, Kernberg is totally out front in acknowledging the socially conformist nature of his "scientific" tying of gender identity to heterosexuality, noting that "stable sexual identity and a realistic awareness of the love object . . . *includes social and cultural* in addition to personal and sexual ideals" (52, emphasis added).

How can it be that the psychoanalytic discourse about lesbians is so appallingly insular, untouched by feminist critique? For at least two reasons, I think, both of which merit consideration. The first is the total absence of participation, until recently, of gay and lesbian analysts in the discourse. The reason for this invisibility is, obviously, the very problem under discussion—bias and discrimination in psychoanalysis, which have made our numbers negligible in institutes and in the field at all. The hatred and stigmatization of gay men and lesbians has also made it very risky until recently for any analyst to present controversial ideas about lesbians, since this could subject the author's own sexuality to suspicion, with possibly dire professional consequences. One's ideas implicate one's identity and one's identity discredits one's ideas. This vicious cycle forecloses dissent and innovation. The question is, then, why such closed-mindedness on the part of the psychoanalytic community, why such a panicked investment in maintaining the status quo? For it is surely panicked to conclude that lesbians are impaired in their capacities for empathy and whole-object love because they preferred gross motor activity, which is not "real" play, to doll play, the true creative expression of play in girls (Dorpat 1988).

This is not a description of reality; it is an attempt to create and prescribe reality—"normal" girls must play with dolls (and lesbians never do). Again, gender role prescription—girls will be moms—is interwoven with the sexual object-choice prescription—girls will be heterosexual (and, of course, monogamous) so that they can give birth to and take care of these babies. The assertion that the wish for a baby is an inborn gender characteristic and that, consequently, lesbians are not able to become their "biologically determined female selves" (Siegel 1988) is consistent with this line of thought.

It is in this incarnation, psychoanalysis as Big Brother (Foucault 1978), regulating and prescribing desire, that psychoanalysis itself created the second condition that insured its insularity. That is, by promoting homogeneity and the maintenance of social order, psychoanalysis constructed a discourse of normality that brainwashed most of its practitioners. The canons of psychoanalysis described libido as "naturally" generative and heterosexual. And since for many adherents psychoanalysis had replaced religion, its "Truth" was unquestioned. The psychoanalytic discourse so persuasively painted reality as straight that until the 1970s it did not occur to even many gay men and lesbians that homosexuality could be an acceptable and enhancing life choice (Duberman 1991).

Thus the power, tenacity, and credibility of psychoanalytic beliefs about sexuality have been enormous. Ostensibly descriptions of what is "natural," they have defined and structured the ways in which most of us conceive and live our sexualities. However, neither our ideas nor our sexual practices reflect nature.

> There is no essential, undifferentiated sexual "impulse," "sex drive," or "lust," which resides in the body due to psychological functioning and sensation. Sexual desire . . . is itself constructed by culture and history from the energies and capacities of the body. . . . [T]he body, its functions, and sensations [are] potentials [and limits] which are incorporated and mediated by culture. The physiology of orgasm and penile erection no more explains a culture's sexual schema than the auditory range of the human ear explains its music. (Vance 1991, 877–78)

This paper is grounded in a social constructionist view of sexuality as rooted in culture rather than biology. My project is to examine psychoanalytic assumptions about lesbians in order to unmask what appear to be "common-sense" verities about sexuality and expose them as narratives constructed in accordance with particular social and historical configurations. For example, the very idea that a person can be defined by her sexual behavior, i.e. that there is such a thing as "a lesbian," is a relatively recent one (McIntosh 1992; Weeks 1989). Homosexual behavior may be universal but homosexual identity is a cultural phenomenon of the last hundred years. It is only by placing psychoanalytic theory in a social and historical context that its assumptions and biases can be exposed and examined. I will therefore begin at the inception of psychoanalytic theorizing about sexuality and progress to contemporary views of lesbians. In this way I hope to clarify the way in which a specific set of ideas about lesbians came to feel given by nature rather than developed by individuals living and thinking in a particular time and place with their own relation to society and to power.

Psychoanalysis and Sexuality

The psychoanalytic discourse on sexuality emerged within the context of the secularization of European society. By the end of the nineteenth century, doctors and psychiatrists such as Freud, Krafft-Ebing, and Havelock Ellis were replacing priests as arbiters of morality and standard bearers of social norms. Their work constituted a revolution in the meaning of sexuality, which now assumed a significance in social and psychic life heretofore unknown. Although non-procreative sex had long been associated with sin in Christian tradition, sexuality had not previously been seen as reflecting any fixed, classifiable, or determinate aspect of the individual. Sexual preferences, such as for the gender of a partner, could be classified and evaluated, but were not considered any more personally revealing than was dietary preference (Halperin 1990). The ancient Greeks, for example, considered the gender of the object inconsequential; a passion for women implied one for men as well. Since in their eyes sex was an expression of social power relations, with the older, richer partner doing the penetrating and the younger, poorer partner being penetrated, partners in classical Athens "came in two kinds, not male and female, but active and passive, dominant and submissive" (Halperin 1990, 50). Even dreams, the key to hidden sexual desire for later psychoanalytic theory, were not thought to have underlying sexual significance for the ancient Greeks. Rather, since they saw sex as derived from the social rather than the social as derived from the sexual, Artimedorus, a master dream analyst of the second century A.D. assumed that all dreams, even sexual ones, were really about something other than sex (Halperin 1990).

For the new turn of the century medical priesthood, however, sex represented the critical organizing principle of an individual's psychic life, the basis of personal satisfaction; in short, the "truth of our being" (Foucault 1978). And as sex became foundational, sexual deviance replaced sin as the locus of social regulation (Weeks 1989). And, quite significantly, it was deviance in general and sexual deviance in particular that made psychiatry a growth industry. That is, just as Joseph McCarthy's existence and power required an endless supply of Communists to sustain it, the medical establishment's prominence and authority were sustained by a supply of deviants to ferret out, expose, and preferably cure. This need for deviance resulted in the rise to significance and reification of behaviors that had not in the past been considered meaningful in any way.

> The machinery of power that focused on [sexuality] did not aim to suppress it, but rather to give it an analytical, visible and permanent reality: it was implanted in bodies, slipped in beneath modes of conduct, made into a principle of classification and intelligibility, established as a raison d'etre and a natural order of disorder. Not the exclusion of these thousand aberrant sexualities, but the regional solidification of each one of them. The strategy behind this dissemination was to strew reality with them and incorporate them into the individual. (Foucault 1992, 18)

For the new heresies in this contemporary morality play, nineteenth-century sexology gave "strange baptismal names" (Foucault 1992, 18) such as Krafft-Ebing's zoophiles and zooerasts. And so, in 1892, this group that depended on deviance for its survival gave birth to homosexuality; heterosexuality, which of course could not exist within the deviant counterpart which would establish its "normality," arrived in 1900 (Halperin 1990). The creation of homosexuality as a clinical entity transposed "the practice of sodomy into a kind of interior androgyny, a hermaphrodite of the soul. The sodomite had been a temporary aberration: the homosexual was now a species" (Foucault 1992, 17–18).

During the past century this linkage of psyche with sexuality came to pervade our cultural consciousness, giving shape to many of our most fundamental beliefs about ourselves. The foundational ideas of this discourse were that sex is biologically given, an expression of one's essence prior to domestication by society. Thus, sex was the expression of one's primordial self, "the property of individuals . . . [which] may reside in their hormones or their psyches" (Rubin 1984, 276). This property was not distributed equally, however; men and women were "naturally" opposite and complementary in their sexual characters. For men, sex represented "an overpowering natural force, a 'biological imperative' located in the genitals, [especially the wayward male organs] that sweeps all before it . . . like hamlets before an avalanche" (Weeks 1989, 13). For women, on the other hand, sexual desire was thought by late nineteenth-century sexologists to be totally lacking, even in their romantic lives.

This narrative of men and women as incommensurable entities with stable, inherent, dichotomized essences was, however, a relatively new one, specific to its time and place. The pre-Enlightenment story, for example, was dramatically different, conceiving of us all as one sex on a continuum; women were essentially men lacking in vital heat or metaphysical perfection (Laqueur 1990). Since vital heat was related to reason, friendship was equated with males, and women, whose reason was inadequate to restrain their passion, were equated with fleshiness. With the dichotomization of sex, these ideas, which dated back to antiquity, were replaced with their opposites. Now it was men who were seen to have an insatiable desire for sex, while women were seen to seek relationship and to be in the majority "not much troubled with sexual feelings" (Laqueur 1990, 3). Furthermore, during the Renaissance the vagina was viewed as an internal penis, suggesting that complementarity lies in the eyes of the beholder, a function not of any objective condition, but rather of our underlying theories about difference or about what does and does not count as evidence.

> In terms of the millennial traditions of Western medicine, genitals came to matter as the mark of sexual opposition only last week. Indeed, much of the evidence suggests that the relation between an organ as sign and the body that supposedly gives it currency is arbitrary, as indeed is the relationship between signs. The male body may always be the standard in the game of significance, but it is one whose status is undermined by its unrepentant historical inconsistency. (Laqueur 1990, 22)

However, despite the recognition by nineteenth-century science of the morphologically androgynous embryo, psychoanalysis reified biology, asserting the "natural" complementarity of the sexes. When theorized with the foundational conviction that the "true" purpose of sex was reproduction (rather than, for example, pleasure), heterosexual genital relations were inevitably valorized while all other sex was framed as an inherently unnatural, defective, and abnormal arrest of the "natural" order of things (Schafer 1974). Adrienne Rich (1983) calls this "compulsory heterosexuality," by which she means belief in a "mystical/ biological heterosexual inclination, a 'preference' or 'choice' which draws women to men" (637). Her thesis is that there is nothing mystical or biologically determined about female heterosexual object choice. Rather, there are compelling social forces, both overt and covert, which channel women into heterosexual romance and marriage. Rich and others (e.g., Rubin 1975; Weeks 1989) cite many such forces which permeate and structure all aspects of society.

First there are the violent and obvious means of enforcing heterosexuality, such as rape, clitoridectomy, pimping, selling of daughters and brides; then there are the more mundanely institutional ways, such as prescriptions for full-time mothering, which keep women out of the job market entirely, and the segregation of women in lower paying jobs, which keeps women dependent on men's incomes even when they do work; then there are the more informal or subliminal forms of control, such as language, e.g., the word "slut" which keeps girls in line and inhibits sexual experimentation; and finally there is the inundation of literature and the visual media with heterosexual images, the food for heterosexual fantasies (Chodorow 1990), while images of lesbians, celibates, or other "deviants" are virtually nonexistent and typically pejorative when they do appear.

Additional pressure for sexual conformity emerges from the profound social consequences attached to one's rank in the hierarchy of sexual acceptability. Those high up in the hierarchy, e.g., legally partnered heterosexuals, reap the advantages of the privileged—certified mental health, respectability, legal rights, institutional support, and material benefits. The price paid by those whose sexual behaviors cause them to fall lower on the totem pole is enormous—they are presumed to be mentally ill and often dangerous, they are stared at, beaten up and ostracized, their jobs and homes are jeopardized, they cannot take advantage of the financial benefits of partnership, such as sharing health insurance. The list could go on and on. These are not insignificant consequences and they provide intense pressure toward shaping sex (Rubin 1984).

Thus, rather than constituting a spontaneous and natural "dance of the chromosomes"—the irresistible and barely repressible force of nature held in tenuous check by "the thin crust of civilization" (Weeks 1989, 25)—the sexual pairing of men and women is a rigorously and relentlessly enforced social product which exists in order to promote specific social goals. One of these goals, the subordination of women to patriarchy, is justified by the concepts of sexual difference and heterosexual complementarity (Wittig 1993).

> The division of labor by sex can therefore be seen as a "taboo": a taboo against the sameness of women and men, a taboo dividing the sexes into two mutually exclusive categories, a taboo which exacerbates the biological differences between the sexes and thereby *creates* gender. The division of labor can also be seen as a taboo against sexual arrangements other than those containing at least one man and one woman, thereby enjoining heterosexual marriage. (Rubin 1975, 178)

Psychoanalysis has been instrumental in creating and enforcing the doctrines which maintain existing power relations. The doctrines of the natural complementarity of the sexes, of the naturalness and superiority of heterosexuality, and of the bifurcation of the psychological and the social all legitimize the status quo. For by locating the individual in the sexual, personal, interior world, politics, economics, and other social phenomena came to constitute the public, the exterior "realm of culture, society and history" (Padgug 1992, 48). Thus, as individuals came to conceive of their true personal essence as their sexuality, they increasingly detached themselves from realities of work and class, which were then experienced as external. However,

> far from being a necessary or intrinsic constituent of the eternal grammar of human subjectivity, "sexuality" seems to be a uniquely modern, Western, even bourgeois product—one of the cultural fictions that in every society gives human beings access to themselves as meaningful actors in their world. (Halperin 1990, 42)

Psychoanalysis, which has been extraordinarily influential in writing the story of sexuality that imbues our lives with meaning, is a powerfully coercive aspect of ideology. By installing a belief in the individual unconscious, the psychoanalytic narrative locates sexual meaning and motivation in the deepest part of the self. As sex is understood to embody cultural meaning rather than biology, however, it becomes clear that far from reflecting our most inward, authentic, and private experience, sexuality is "shared, unnecessary/ and political" (Rich 1983). And with this relocation the locus of desire also moves from the genitals to "the most important [sexual] organ in humans, [the one that] is located between the ears" (Vance, cited in Weeks 1989). It is our cultural narratives, embodied in psychoanalytic theory, that determine who and what we desire. As long as our thinking is hobbled by the idea that "a narrative of the female Oedipus complex must account for the little girl's turning from the mother to the father in the course of this phase of development" (Ogden 1987, 485), or that we are "innately heterosexual" (Chasseguet-Smirgel 1964), there can be no vision of femaleness apart from the "*idea* of nature that has been established for us" (Wittig 1993, 103).

All women are implicated in theorizing lesbian desire, the realm of women as subjects and objects of desire distinct from men. It is in this space, a "space hard-won and daily threatened by social disapprobation, censure, and denial, a space of contradiction requiring constant reaffirmation and painful renegotiation" (De Lauretis 1993, 142) that the very notion of female desire can be interrogated. Theorizing lesbians is the site of freeing all women from a discourse that cannot conceive female desire without the ubiquitous phallus. However, there can be no such free space until the demonizing ideas which currently occupy it are deconstructed. Psychoanalytic theorizing of lesbians embodies and perpetuates this demonization. Viewed through the lens of the social constructionist critique developed above, Big Brother peers out from behind our most basic psychoanalytic convictions.

The Psychoanalytic Story of the Lesbian

Lesbians presented a problem for psychoanalysis. For if women were "naturally" passive and passionless, even in their "normal" relations with men, how to explain their passion and motivation with one another? The only possible answer given the narrative of naturally bifurcated and complimentary sexes was a complete inversion of a woman's sexual nature. She had, as Freud (1955) said of his female homosexual, to have "changed into a man." Thus, a gendered split is created between "desire and identity, between having and being" (O'Connor and Ryan 1993, 54). If being one gender prescribes love of the other, then same-sex desire is anomalous and unnatural and must "mean" pathological cross-identification. "A woman who loves a woman must be a man or be like a man or wish to be a man" (Magee and Miller 1992, 72). There is no theoretical space for "feminine," i.e., not pathologically cross-identified, women to love women. In fact, in psychoanalytic theory there really is no homosexuality since, due to the gendered split, all desire is theorized heterosexually. Thus, women who love women do not actually exist in this story at all.

> The feminine occurs only within models and laws devised by male subjects. Which implies that there are not really two sexes, but only one. A single practice and representation of the sexual. . . . That a woman might desire a woman 'like' herself, someone of the 'same' sex, that she might also have auto- and homosexual appetites, is simply incomprehensible. (Irigaray, cited in De Lauretis 1993, 142)

However, in spite of the fact that turn-of-the-century sexology invented the idea of "the lesbian," and regardless of the fact that there is no theoretical space for a woman who desires another woman, psychoanalysis has proceeded as though "the lesbian" is a real, unitary, and diagnostic entity and is replete with accounts explaining her dynamics (e.g., Chasseguet-Smirgel 1964; Eisenbud 1982; Khan 1993; McDougall 1970, 1980, 1985). There are several common themes in these narratives which can be summarized as follows:
(1) There are only two sexual stories—one normal and the other deviant or perverse. The former posits heterosexuality as the "achievement" marking successful traversal of the oedipal conflict. The latter posits lesbian sexuality (and all alternative forms) as developmental failure.
(2) Sexual object choice reflects essential truths about the psyche. Heterosexuality signals health, mature love, and true object choice. Homosexuality signals narcissism, regression, and gender disturbance.
(3) According to the laws of nature, female desire exists only in relation to male desire. Penises of all sorts—be they envied, feared, or castrated, play a starring role; in fact, there is no story without them. A woman's love of another woman is equated with or reduced to male identifications and desire.

All psychoanalytic narratives of a woman's desire for another woman base this desire in normal development gone awry. In even the most sympathetic renditions, the young lesbian develops because she cannot "succeed" in traversing the "normal" path. So, for example, while Eisenbud (1982) insists that the lesbian's solution to her problems is "progressive, not regressive" (86), and that "lesbian orientation . . . at its origin . . . [is] a forward step instated by the ego in an effort to attain effective mystery" (99), this origin is still depicted as an unfortunate, abnormal deviation from normal development, i.e., "the child has been excluded from 'good enough' or 'long enough' primary bliss [and therefore] seeks inclusion by a sexual bond and sexual wooing" (86). The implication is that the heterosexual girl's developmental path is not littered with pathology-inducing obstacles in this way. In other narratives the young lesbian is too competitive with or hateful of an autocratic, absent, or neglectful father (Deutsch 1944); or identified with rather than desirous of the father (Horney 1924). All roads originate in her being "too" something, in excess or deficit, and lead to an immature, aberrant solution. In most accounts her problems with her father and masculinity are considered primary.

In order to more fully examine psychoanalytic theorizing of lesbians, I now turn to the work of Joyce McDougall, a well-respected analyst who has written extensively in this area. Her work, while representative of the main themes in the literature, is usually considered at the progressive end of the spectrum (compared to hard-liners such as Socarides, e.g., 1979) in that it is seen as sympathetic to lesbians. However, as this discussion, which is based on "Homosexuality in Women" (1970), *Plea for a Measure of Abnormality* (1980), and *Theaters of the Mind* (1985), will make clear, McDougall's work is a pathologizing diatribe against lesbian desire. Although she has recently attempted to appear more tolerant and contemporary (e.g., her assertion [1985] that there are "homosexualities," some of which are healthy, rather than one single, inevitably pathological homosexual condition), her basic thesis remains unchanged. Nor has McDougall's belief in her own privileged knowledge of "Truth" been disturbed by the self-reflexivity which troubles many theorists in our postmodern times.

In McDougall's view, lesbians are "perverts," people "who do not make love like everyone else" (1985, 245). (Did you know that all people make love the same way?) Describing the term perversion as too pejorative, she coins her own term for such unfortunate aberrant practices—"neosexualities." This term warrants unpacking, since its putatively neutral prefix, neo, promises greater tolerance than its predecessor did. McDougall defines "neosexualities" as "delusional" creations (273), such as the use of "mirrors, whips, fecal matter, or partners of the same sex" (246) which are designed to ward off psychosis by denying the basic realities of castration (252) and of the difference between the sexes (249). Thus her term masks, but leaves unaltered, the same pathologizing message about lesbian desire. Furthermore, by suggesting that homosexual practices are new, McDougall manages to covertly undermine lesbian desire by denying its historical existence and thus raising further suspicions about its status.

McDougall makes use of this rhetorical strategy, which pretends to convey one message while in fact conveying a quite different one, in other ways as well. For example, she advises analysts against "label[ing] the sexual deviant according to [the latter's] sexual practice alone [since this] is an artificial approach that ignores the rest of the personality . . . and [gives] partial and indeed biased information regarding another human being" (246). However, she goes on to say that "perverse sexuality is but one manifestation of a complex psychic state in which anxiety, depression, inhibitions and narcissistic perturbation all play a role" (247). Thus, while cautioning on the one hand against psychological evaluation based on sexual practice, she concludes on the other hand that this very practice is the red flag signaling character pathology.

With these disingenuous devices in mind, I turn now to a more careful look at McDougall's theory. Here again we find that beneath a pretense to sympathy and tolerance lies a marginalizing and pathologizing message. The basic story line is as follows: The little girl idealizes the mother, who is described as "beautiful, gifted, charming. She is endowed with all the qualities the daughter lacks" (1980, 107). At the same time, mother is felt to be rigid and controlling and to demand the girl's total and exclusive commitment. It would be disloyal and dangerous to be independent of her or to be interested in a relationship with father, whom mother openly devalues. Thus, while mother is "usually represented . . . as the essence of femininity and in no way a masculine *phallic* personality, [she] is nevertheless felt to have secretly destroyed the father's value as an authority figure, and to have aided the child in denying this phallic-genital qualities" (1980, 102, emphasis added).

Father, for his part, is "neither idealized nor desired. If not totally absent from the analytic discourse, he is despised, detested, or denigrated in other ways. . . . [H]e is often presented as ineffectual and impotent; there is no feeling of a strong, loving father nor of a man whose character might be considered as essentially virile" (1980, 95). Sometimes father is described as terrifyingly dangerous and physically threatening. "One has the impression of a little girl in terror of being attacked or 'penetrated' by her father" (1970, 184).

Due to this family configuration, the little girl, who is consumed with envy and rage, lacks help in separating from mother. "Behind the 'castrated' image . . . lies the image of the father who has *failed in his specific parental role*, leaving his small daughter prey to a devouring or controlling and omnipotent maternal image" (1980, 101–102). Father is then, in this scenario, "lost as a love object" (105) and is instead identified with a "mutilated image" for which "the ego runs the risk of suffering merciless attacks from the superego" (106). Rather than want him or love him, the little girl "becomes" him. Accompanying this identification is the "wishful fantasy . . . [of] total elimination of the father and creation of an exclusive and enduring mother-daughter relationship" (108). Attachment to mother as "mother's phallus" (115) allows the fantasy of continued union while simultaneously protecting the daughter from "enthrallment and submission to these omnipotent aspects of the mother imago" (121). The "penis wish" plays a prominent role in the story since for "homosexual women [it] not only exist[s] to repair a fantasied castration but it is also intended to keep dormant any *feminine* sexual desires" (123, emphasis added). She concludes that, in homosexual women, the "fantasy of being castrated is more profound, more globally disturbing, than in the case of women who have developed neurotic symptoms or neurotic character traits to cope with castration anxiety at its different levels" (126).

Thus, the "homosexual way of life," which requires "two problem parents" (91) for its production, is a denial of castration, a denial of the difference between the sexes, and thus a denial of sexual reality and gender reality (1980). Therefore, while McDougall describes herself as emphasizing "the positive aspects of the homosexual relationship," i.e., "the fact that the girl, in making a homosexual attachment, is making a bid for freedom from the real mother as an external obstacle" (1970, 206), she has no doubt that "this venture is doomed to fail in its aim" (1970, 206) since "few of the basic conflicts are resolved and . . . the new relationship contains the seeds of its own destruction" (1980, 132). The homosexual "pays dearly for a fragile identity which is not truly her own. Yet she is compelled to play this role, for the alternative is the death of the ego" (1970, 210).

To be a woman who desires other women is, then, to be on the edge of psychotic states of depression, dissociation, and psychic death (along with kleptomaniacs and alcoholics, whose psychic structure is "almost identical" [1970, 175] to that of lesbians). In fact, it is an amazing accomplishment that lesbians manage to walk around at all, given the extent to which our personalities are constructed of pathological introjection, fragile ego identity in general, disturbance of body-ego perception, symptoms of depersonalization, splitting, denial, hatred, envy, and fear.

It should be noted, however, that McDougall's entire discussion is based on the treatment of a mere handful of women, all of whom are extremely disturbed. Some carry large knives with them in their pocketbooks to protect them from dangerous men such as taxicab drivers (1980). Another boasts that she hasn't bathed for weeks, knows that she stinks and loves it (1970). One of her patients banged her head against the wall "until I came to my senses" (1980, 93) upon finding out that her lover would unexpectedly be away for a few days. Another, when faced with the same situation, was "overwhelmed by feelings of depersonalization of psychotic dimensions [and] could control her anxiety only by stubbing out burning cigarettes on her hands" (1970, 204). And another wanted to have her breasts removed and hallucinated having a penis (1980, 123). Yet despite the prominence of serious characterological problems of all sorts, McDougall apparently believes that lesbians constitute a unitary group of which these women are representative. Sexual orientation is viewed as the encompassing dimension which defines them and overrides all other categories.

McDougall's approach is grossly problematic for other reasons as well. For one, she confuses a narrative account of her patients' lives with a causal account (Schafer 1992). That is, McDougall's theory does not "explain" why these women desire other women. I have no doubt that some lesbians resonate with some aspects of the story she constructs, e.g., a mother with whom the girl is overinvolved and from whom she has difficulty separating, in part due to an absent or emotionally remote father. However, other lesbians did not come from a family like this—and many heterosexual women did. Adult desire cannot be reduced to any causative set of family relations. Some lesbians were closer to their mothers than to their fathers, while for others the reverse holds true. Similarly, the fact that a woman has sex with a man says nothing about the extent or type of involvement she had with either of her parents. Nor does it "mean" that she likes or can be intimate with men or with anyone else in her world.

Despite this, the implication in McDougall's work—and in virtually all psychoanalytical accounts of lesbian development—is that there is a particular family configuration that "causes" heterosexuality and that, furthermore, this family configuration is the "normal" one, which is presumably free of pathology, or at least which involves minimal pathology. It is "deviation" from this constellation and "failure" to traverse the "natural" developmental path to adulthood that is then thought to "account" for lesbian desire.

However, the whole idea of a "normal" family is an anachronism, a remnant of the Western-European fantasy of homogeneous, patriarchal life, held dear and reified by a group succinctly described by a patient of mine as "white men in suits" and their "wannabees." The concept of a normal developmental story denies the diversity and complexity of contemporary life in which children grow up in all possible family constellations, including single-parent homes, homes with two moms or two dads, homes headed by grandmothers or aunts—or grandfathers or uncles, for that matter—homes with neighbors, foster families, or institutional groups, orphanages, or in some places gangs of kids who try to take care of each other. In addition, environments vary according to the customs and values of each religious or racial group or class, the psychological make-up of the members, and the goodness-of-fit between the individual child and the surroundings. All children deal as best they can with the conditions they encounter (Horney-Eckardt 1988), but there is no "normal" condition; stories are as diverse as the number of children there are, since each child's experience in any situation is unique. It is patently absurd to contend that heterosexuals as a group have a more pathology-free upbringing or fewer "problem parents" than homosexuals. If heterosexuality equaled mental health, we psychoanalysts would never treat straight patients. Such simple-minded fictions are not depictions of "reality." They are ideological tools to justify and promote the status quo. And they have caused great pain to lesbians as well as to their families.

However, McDougall's entire vision is based on such rigid, unquestioned prescriptions for normality. This is unequivocally (and presumably unintentionally) revealed in the title of her book, *Plea for a Measure of Abnormality* (1980). While ostensibly "pleading" for the right of lesbian desire to exist, McDougall has no doubt that it is abnormal, as if normality were objectively defined and written in stone—and as if she were privy to its laws. Two positivist and essentialist assumptions about normality, related to the biases discussed above, constitute the foundation of her argument. The first is that gender and sexuality are inseparable, i.e., that femaleness "means" loving men. The second, a direct consequence of the first, is that there is, therefore, a "correct" way to experience feminine desire. Needless to say, lesbians do it wrong.

Let's take a careful look at each of these and at how they play out in McDougall's theory. As discussed above, the idea of a gendered split means that femaleness is synonymous with the desire for men, i.e., with heterosexuality. Thus, McDougall (1970) attributes a woman's desire for another woman to "*a desire to be the father*, and therefore masculine" (172). Here again we see that it is impossible for lesbian desire to exist in this theory. Love between two women must involve a man. But why need it be "masculine" to love a woman? Without an essentialist confounding of sex and gender, there is no reason why it can't be feminine for a woman to love a woman. Furthermore, what does masculine mean if all of us identify to some degree with the important people of both genders in our world? Although McDougall acknowledges that cross-sex identifications contribute to the richness of personality even in "normal" cases, she seems to believe that she should determine the ratio and kind of same-sex vs. cross-sex identifications which will insure health.

McDougall is also convinced that a woman's love for another woman reveals a repudiation of and "disparaging attitude to men" (1970, 176). But why should this be so? As O'Connor and Ryan (1993) put it:

> If I am offered tea or coffee . . . and I choose tea, does this mean I have repudiated coffee or my desire for it? The answer may depend on all the surrounding considerations, events and feelings contributing to my choice. If I were to say, "I'd love some tea, the sort you have smells delicious," it is hardly appropriate to describe me as having repudiated coffee. I haven't accepted coffee, but neither have I repudiated or rejected it. Nor have I given any indication of not liking coffee, or having any feeling about it that would lead me to reject it for itself. (42)

McDougall's biases just keep on coming. Most astonishingly, she maintains that lesbians "maintain the *illusion* of being the true sexual partner to another woman" (1980, 88, emphasis added). The arrogance of this statement truly takes my breath away. I assume that McDougall has never made love to another woman, yet she nevertheless knows that the experience is deficient and unsatisfying. In addition to being arrogant, however, the statement is ludicrous in a psychoanalytic sense. The psychoanalytic project is the elaboration of personal meaning, which is a matter of psychology, not of biology. "True" sexual partnership emerges from one's inner world and from a sense of psychological fit with another person—not from the presence or absence of a penis.

In truth, the absence of penises in lesbian love strikes me as far less remarkable than McDougall's (and psychoanalysis's) obsession with them. Is it "normal" (as McDougall's colleague's teen-aged daughter wonders) "to talk so often about penises" (1980)? How did penises get to be so important, anyway? After all, as Schwartz (1992) has noted, they just hang there most of the time. McDougall allies herself with the French psychoanalytic tradition in this debate, installing the physical (penis) as the symbolic (phallus) and asserting its centrality in both psyche and culture. But what purpose other than the shoring up of patriarchy can it serve to insist that "if adults are to enjoy their sex lives without excessive guilt or anxiety, the phallus, symbol of power, fertility, and life, must also come to represent, for both sexes, the image of narcissistic completion and sexual desire" (1985, 267)?

Perhaps McDougall "doth protest too much" in contending that "true" feminine pleasure depends on the genital "complementarity" between the sexes, since as Shere Hite (1994) has documented, sex for many heterosexuals leaves a lot to be desired. Hite found that because coitus is often insufficiently stimulating (and because many men think that the insertion of their penises in a woman's vagina *should* be sufficient), "many women never or often irregularly orgasm during sex with men" (170). This, she feels, may account for many women's lack of interest in and passivity during sex. Certainly heterosexual women's complaints about their husbands, both as emotional partners and as lovers, are legion. Yet McDougall promotes the superiority of heterosexuality as self-evident, while trashing lesbian love as a manifestation of "underlying hatred and general ambivalence" (1980, 101).

That the theoretical system is intractably pathologizing is revealed in McDougall's comment that "the overt homosexual . . . has met with severe impediments to the harmonious integration of her homosexual drives" (1970, 173). An open-minded observer might think that a woman who loves other women has, in fact, achieved an eminently successful integration of these drives. However, no evidence can disrupt McDougall's prejudice; all data is assimilated to it. Because she is convinced of her own privileged view of human functioning and consequently of her right to define normality, she does not hesitate to impose a set of prejudices on a population of patients and call it theory. Thus, while putatively impartial, her account calls my way of loving hate and condemns many women's deepest feelings of passion, connection, and love to the garbage. Only women like McDougall can be "real" women in her story.

Finally, McDougall is convinced that for a woman to desire another woman is to seek sameness in a panicked denial of difference. Obviously this view reduces all interpersonal difference to genital difference. What about differences in temperament or cognitive style or professions or body type that might enhance one woman's attraction for another? And could not greater sameness potentiate heightened intimacy? In addition to being remarkably limited and stereotyped, McDougall's view is decidedly nonpsychoanalytic in its conviction that the physical gender of the sex object determines the psychological meanings and layerings of fantasy that the lover experiences. This has been taken up by Butler (1991) in her discussion of how gendered fantasies of the beloved may have no correspondence to physical gender, nor need fantasies of oneself during sex (or at other times) be restricted to one's own physical gender. Thus, to designate a sexual encounter as homosexual or heterosexual requires negotiation of a labyrinth of meanings and fantasies which are fluid and changing.

> If a sexuality is to be disclosed, what will be taken as the determinant of its meaning: the phantasy structure, the act, the orifice, the gender, the anatomy? And if the practice engages a complex interplay of all of those, which one of these erotic dimensions will come to stand for the sexuality that requires them all? (Butler 1991, 17)

If a woman makes love with a woman while fantasizing herself a man with a woman, does that confer heterosexuality on the encounter? And is it then more mature? If a woman enjoys being finger-fucked or using dildos or other sex toys, does that mean she "really" wants a man?

To my mind considering the issue in 1994, there is no meaningful use for the construct of sexual identity. Sexuality is not an idealized, coherent, fixed entity which expresses an underlying sexual essence. Rather, I believe that sexuality is a fluid, dynamic process which assumes different forms at different times. For example, the anecdotal evidence I gather from my practice suggests that choice of same-sex partners is greatly on the rise on college campuses. Is this because a certain percentage of coeds were "really" homosexual all along but just conformed to heterosexual norms in the past? Or because all of a sudden the percentage of overinvolved mothers and absent fathers (or whatever family configuration is considered etiological) has greatly increased? I doubt it. A more persuasive answer is, I think, that at this point in history homosexual object choice is becoming more of an option. And, since it's on the menu, people are going to try it. As with other aspects of identity (Mitchell 1991), sexuality forms and reforms, is shaped and reshaped depending on the circumstances in which it appears. "There is no 'natural' condition for the human; there is only one or the other social construction that is in the state of building, repair or collapse" (Gagnon 1991, 274).

Recognizing our biases about "natural" sex will promote a more neutral, evenhanded examination of patients' sexualities. By freeing our inquiry from its normative theoretical straightjacket, we allow true analyses of the rich variety of personal meanings that sexual behavior will have for different individuals. For example, women I treat who love other women often feel that they must renounce any attraction for men that they feel in order to truly come to terms with being lesbians. But where is it written that we should not be attracted to different people, both men and women, at different times? Why should sexual desire be permanent, unitary, and restrictive?

The charge that "their work is one of the significant, even culpable, forces in contemporary life" (Cushman 1994, 803) is inconceivable for most analysts. We hope that we are freeing our patients, not acting as their prison guards. However, until we realize how saturated our theories are with ideology, how infused our psychology is with politics, we will continue to function as Big Brother, despite our best intentions. Not until we recognize that heterosexuality as we know it is an artifact of our culture and that sexual object choice "means" nothing inherent about who we are, will psychoanalysis have the opportunity to extricate itself from its current role of enforcing conformity and return to its original, radical, analytic mission.

Note

1. Many people contributed to the preparation of this manuscript. Thanks to my study group on sexuality, in the early days composed at different times of Diane Burhenne, Ann D'Ercole, Tom Domenici, Stephen Frommer, Debra Gold, Ronnie Lesser, Melanie Suchet, and Carole Vance, for the stimulating discussions that helped me to develop and clarify these ideas. Thanks to Adrienne Harris for her generosity in guiding me through earlier drafts; to Rita Frankiel for helping me to find my own voice; and to Michelle Price for their helpful comments. And especially thanks to Ronnie Lesser for her input on this paper and for her intelligence, boundless curiosity, and vision.

References Cited

Berlin, I. *Annie Get Your Gun*. Decca Records.

Butler, J. 1991. Imitation and Gender Insubordination. In *Inside/Outside: Lesbian Theories, Gay Theories*. Ed. by D. Fuss. New York: Routledge.

Chasseguet-Smirgel, J. 1964. *Female Sexuality: New Psychoanalytic Views*. Ann Arbor: University of Michigan Press.

Chodorow, N. 1994. Heterosexuality as a Compromise Formation. In *Femininities, Masculinities, Sexualities: Freud and Beyond*. Lexington: University Press of Kentucky.

Cushman, P. 1994. Confronting Sullivan's Spider: Hermeneutics and the Politics of Therapy. *Contemporary Psychoanalysis* 30 (4): 800–844.

De Lauretis, T. 1993. *Sexual Indifference and Lesbian Representation*. New York: Routledge.

Deutsch, H. 1944. *The Psychology of Women*. New York: Grune and Stratton.

Dorpat, T. 1988. Forward. In E. Siegel, *Female Homosexuality: Choice Without Volition*. Hillsdale, NJ: Analytic Press.

Duberman, M. 1991. *Cures: A Gay Man's Odyssey*. New York: Dutton.

Eisenbud, R.J. 1982. Early and Later Determinants of Lesbian Choice. *Psychoanalytic Review* 69: 85–109.

Foucault, M. 1978. *The History of Sexuality, Volume I*. New York: Pantheon.

———. 1992. The Perverse Implantation. In *Forms of Desire: Sexual Orientation and the Social Constructionist Controversy*. Ed. by E. Stein. New York: Routledge.

Freud, S. 1920. Psychogenesis of a case of homosexuality in a woman. *Standard Edition* 18: 145–74. London: Hogarth Press, 1955.

Gagnon, J. 1991. Commentary on "Toward a Critical Relational Theory of Gender." *Psychoanalytic Dialogues* 1 (3): 73–76.

Halperin, D. 1990. Sex Before Sexuality: Pederasty, Politics and Power in Classical Athens. In *Hidden From History: Reclaiming the Gay and Lesbian Past*. Ed. by M. Duberman, M. Vicinus and G. Chauncey. New York: Meridian.

Harris, A. 1991. Introduction, Symposium on Gender. *Psychoanalytic Dialogues* 1 (3): 243–46.

Hite, S. 1994. *Women as Revolutionary Agents of Change: The Hite Reports and Beyond*. Madison: University of Wisconsin Press.

Horney, K. 1924. On the Genesis of the Castration Complex in Women. *International Journal of Psychoanalysis* 5: 50–65.

Horney-Eckardt, M. 1988. Psychoanalysis Is Alive and Well: Meeting the Challenges of Diversity. *Journal of the American Academy of Psychoanalysis* 16 (4): 417–30.

Irigaray, L. 1993. *Speculum of the Other Woman*. Cited in T. De Lauretis. Sexual Indifference/Lesbian Representation. In *The Lesbian and Gay Studies Reader*. Ed. by H. Abelove, M. Barales, and D. Halperin. New York: Routledge.

Khan, M. 1993. Cited in N. O'Connor and J. Ryan. *Wild Desires & Mistaken Identities*. New York: Columbia University Press.

Laqueur, T. 1990. *Making Sex: Body and Gender from the Greeks to Freud*. Cambridge: Harvard University Press.

Lewes, K. 1988. *The Psychoanalytic Theory of Male Homosexuality*. New York: Simon & Schuster.

Marx, K. 1976. Sixth Thesis on Feuerbach. In K. Marx and F. Engels. *Collected Works*. Volume 5. New York: International Publishers.

Magee, M. and Miller, D. 1992. "She Foreswore Her Womanhood": Psychoanalytic Views of Female Homosexuality. *Clinical Social Work Journal* 20 (1): 67–87.

McDougall, J. 1970. Homosexuality in Women. In J. Chasseguet-Smirgel, *Female Sexuality: New Psychoanalytic Views*. Ann Arbor: University of Michigan Press.

———. 1980. *Plea for a Measure of Abnormality*. New York: International Universities Press.

———. 1985. *Theaters of the Mind: Illusion and Truth on the Psychoanalytic Stage*. New York: Basic Books.

McIntosh, M. 1992. The Homosexual Role. In *Forms of Desire: Sexual Orientation and the Social Constructionist Controversy*. Ed. by E. Stein. New York: Routledge.

Mitchell, S. 1991. Contemporary Perspectives on the Self. *Psychoanalytic Dialogues* 1 (2): 121–147.

O'Connor N. and Ryan, J. 1993. *Wild Desires & Mistaken Identities*. New York: Columbia University Press.

Ogden, T. 1987. The Transitional Oedipal Relationship in Female Development. *International Journal of Psychoanalysis* 68: 485–98.

Padgug, R. 1992. Sexual Matters: On Conceptualizing Sexuality in History. In *Forms of Desire: Sexual Orientation and the Social Constructionist Controversy*. Ed. by E. Stein. New York: Routledge.

Rich, A. 1983. Compulsory Heterosexuality and Lesbian Existence. In *Powers of Desire*. Ed. by A. Snitow, C. Stansell & S. Thompson. New York: Monthly Review Press.

Rubin, G. 1975. The Traffic in Women: Notes on the "Political Economy" of Sex. In *Toward an Anthropology of Women*. Ed. by R. Reiter. New York: Monthly Review Press.

———. 1984. Thinking Sex. In *Pleasure and Danger: Exploring Female Sexuality*. Ed. by C. Vance. New York: Routledge and Kegan Paul.

Schafer, R. 1974. Problems in Freud's Psychology of Women. *Journal of the American Psychoanalytic Association* 22: 455–59.

———. 1992. *Retelling a Life*. New York: Basic Books.

Schwartz, D. 1992. Commentary on Jessica Benjamin's "Father and Daughter: Identification with Difference—A Contribution to Gender Heterodoxy." *Psychoanalytic Dialogues* 2 (3): 411–16.

Siegel, E. 1988. *Female Homosexuality: Choice Without Volition*. Hillsdale, NJ: Analytic Press.

Socarides, C.W. 1979. A Unitary Theory of Sexual Perversions. In *On Sexuality*. Ed. by B.T. Karasu and C.W. Socarides. New York: International Universities Press.

Vance, C. 1989. Cited in J. Weeks. *Sexuality*. New York: Routledge.

———. 1991. Anthropology Rediscovers Sexuality: A Theoretical Comment. *Social Science Medicine* 8: 875–84.

Weeks, J. 1989. *Sexuality*. New York: Routledge.

Wittig, M. 1993. One is Not Born a Woman. In *The Lesbian and Gay Studies Reader*. Ed. by H. Abelove, M. Barale and D. Halperin. New York: Routledge.

Part 3

Lesbian and Gay Psychoanalysts

Their Encounters with Anti-Homosexuality

13

Anti-Homosexual Bias in Training

Jack Drescher

Introduction

WHEN I WAS A PSYCHIATRIC RESIDENT in the early 1980s, I attended a Manhattan dinner party where I sat with a heterosexual psychiatrist with whom I was casually acquainted. A cultured and successful woman, although not a psychoanalyst herself, she had undergone several personal analyses and was highly regarded by her psychoanalytic colleagues, some of whom were my supervisors. We had friends in common, including the gay man who introduced us to each other and whose visit to New York had prompted our gathering. We spoke about my interest in psychoanalytic training and I voiced my pessimism about obtaining it because of discriminatory policies of analytic institutes toward gay people. She suggested, in her sincere and charming way, and much to my astonishment, "Why do you have to tell them?"

Because I am the Co-Chair of the Committee on Gay and Lesbian Issues of the New York County District Branch of the American Psychiatric Association, many lesbian and gay colleagues have shared with me their professional experiences of discrimination. My personal experiences of anti-homosexual bias are the result of my willingness to adopt an openly gay voice in a professional community that has been either unwilling or reluctant to hear them. The different perspectives on talking about homosexuality in the above example represent a cultural gap between heterosexuals and gays. To a heterosexual psychiatrist, avoiding an open discussion of one's homosexuality makes perfect sense: "Get the training and don't make an issue of it." To gay psychoanalysts struggling to integrate their personal and professional identities, it is a complex issue intimately related to one's character and integrity.

A scholarly man recently reminded me that "suffering in itself does not confer dignity upon the sufferer." I found his heterosexual perspective useful in writing about the history of bias against lesbians and gay men in the mental health professions. I wish to avoid the unfortunate tendency within conservative organizations to label any historical discussion of injustice as "political correctness." Some analysts have used this label to dismiss points of view that they either disagree with or do not want to hear (Trop and Stolorow 1993). This is not an uncommon phenomenon within psychoanalytic organizations, where clinical theory is frequently used to rationalize an institutional unwillingness to change and where dissent from orthodoxy is frequently ascribed to character pathology.

It should be emphasized that psychoanalytically oriented institutions are not alone in practicing anti-homosexual bias. I am, however, more familiar with the nature of discriminatory psychoanalytic practices based on my experience as a psychiatrist and as a psychoanalyst and my work with both the Committee on Gay and Lesbian Issues and the Gay and Lesbian Psychiatrists of New York. Even as I write these words, I am haunted by the derisive psychoanalytic characterization of homosexuals as "injustice collectors" (Bergler 1956; Nicolosi 1991, 428). It is an attitude that assumes the grievances of gay people are either unjustified or exaggerated, or that gay people are too touchy and unforgiving. It is an attitude reinforced by a psychoanalytic belief that lesbians and gay men have only themselves to blame for the ongoing experiences of hatred and prejudice with which they must contend on a regular basis.

Historical Contributions to Bias

In its early years, it did not appear that the psychoanalytic movement would discriminate against lesbians and gay men. Freud's public positions on homosexuality were quite tolerant for his time. He believed homosexuals should not be excluded from analytic training and signed a public appeal to decriminalize homosexuality in Austria and Germany (Lewes 1988). One of Freud's closest associates, Sandor Ferenczi, persuaded the police of Budapest to stop arresting a female transvestite on grounds that she suffered from a mental disorder (Stanton 1991). In contrast to the nineteenth century's religious view of moral degeneration and its scientific theory of nervous degeneration concerning homosexuality, Freud made a magnanimous gesture in which he embraced not only homosexuals but the homosexual within everyone: "Psychoanalytic research is most decidedly opposed to any attempt at separating off homosexuals from the rest of mankind as a group of special character . . . it has found that all human beings are capable of making a homosexual object-choice and have in fact made one in their unconscious" (Freud 1905, 145).

Freud, of course, was a human being with many contradictions. Despite his social tolerance for homosexual rights, he had deeply held beliefs about the expected normal outcome of psychosexual development:

> The final outcome of the sexual development lies in what is known as the *normal* sexual life of the adult, in which the pursuit of pleasure comes under the sway of the reproductive function and in which the component instincts, under the primacy of a single erotogenic zone, form a firm organization directed towards a sexual aim attached to some extraneous sexual object. (Freud 1905, 197, emphasis added)

He strongly believed in the hierarchical primacy of genital heterosexual intercourse and later wrote:

> Since normal intercourse has been so relentlessly persecuted by morality—and also, on account of the possibilities of infection, by hygiene—what are known as the perverse forms of intercourse between the two sexes, in which other parts of the body take over the role of the genitals, have undoubtedly increased in social importance. These activities cannot, however, be regarded as being as harmless as analogous extensions [of the sexual aim] in love relationships. They are ethically objectionable, for they degrade the relationships of love between two human beings from a serious matter to a convenient game, attended by no risk and no spiritual participation. (Freud 1908, 200)

Obviously, the sexual activity of homosexual lovers precludes the insertion of a penis into a vagina. Because his theory, grounded in nineteenth-century Darwinism, elevated that form of sexual activity above all the others, Freud planted the seeds for the subsequent "scientific" rationalization of anti-homosexual bias in psychoanalytic training. How could an analyst be certified as psychologically mature enough to do analytic work when he or she persisted in behaving in a sexually immature way? By extension, analytically oriented programs that were not even training psychoanalysts used similar criteria when training psychiatrists, psychologists, and social workers.

The other important historical figure who laid the groundwork for continued discrimination against lesbians and gay men in the United States was Rado (1969). Although his theories did not limit themselves to the issue of homosexuality alone, they had an enormous impact on the psychoanalytic writers who would later specialize in "cures" for homosexuality (Bieber, et al. 1962; Socarides 1968). Rado rejected Freud's psychological embrace of homosexuality, refuted bisexuality, and offered his own "adaptational" explanation for homosexuality. He was the prototype of the *Nuclear Family Analyst* (Drescher forthcoming): This is the analyst who dresses up his personal beliefs and prejudices about sexuality and relationships as a scientific theory. The science of the theory draws upon Darwinian evolution. Simply put, each man and woman is an individual bound by the evolutionary need to survive and procreate. The nuclear family is seen as a biological achievement, rather than a social one. To fulfill the evolutionary mandates of survival and procreation, couples must be monogamous and have stable, long-term relationships so children can be reared until they reach adulthood. Homosexuality, heterosexual promiscuity, and short-term relationships are pathologized because they threaten the family unit's survival and reproduction. The nuclear family analyst believes evolution is something akin to an anthropomorphic force that expects us to behave in ways for which we have been evolutionarily designed. The fact that penises fit into vaginas is scientific proof of the heterosexual destiny of human beings. According to Rado:

> The male-female sexual pattern is dictated by anatomy. Almost as fundamental is the fact that by means of the institution of marriage, the male-female sexual pattern is culturally ingrained and perpetuated in every individual from earliest childhood. Homogeneous [that is, homosexual] pairs satisfy their repudiated yet irresistible male-female desire by means of shared illusions and actual approximations; such is the hold on the individual of a cultural institution based on biological foundations. This mechanism is often deeply buried in the individual's mind under a welter of rationalizations calculated to justify his actual avoidance of the opposite sex.... Why is the so-called homosexual forced to escape from the male-female pair into a homogeneous pair? This brings us back to the familiar campaign of deterrence that parents wage to prohibit the sexual activity of the child. The campaign causes the female to view the male organ as a destructive weapon. Therefore the female partners are reassured by the absence in both of them

> of the male organ. The campaign causes the male to see in the mutilated female organ a reminder of inescapable punishment. When the never-recognized fear and resentment of the opposite organ becomes insurmountable, the individual may escape into homosexuality. The male patterns are reassured by the presence in both of them of the male organ. Homosexuality is a deficient adaptation evolved by the organism in response to its own emergency overreaction and dyscontrol. (212–13)

Demonization of Homosexuality

Discrimination and bias within psychoanalytically oriented mental health fields resembles forms of prejudice against both racial and religious minorities. Historically, psychoanalytic attitudes of anti-homosexual bias resembled anti-semitism in many ways. The hated and feared homosexual interloper had to be kept out of psychoanalysis as forcefully as possible. Lewes (1988) noted a post-war phenomenon in psychoanalytic literature's "repeated use during this period of the chilling phrase *a solution to the problem of homosexuality*" (232). Nazi anti-semitism, however, was a form of racism. Jews were considered to be members of an inferior racial group, and membership in that group was bound up in a person's essence. Like the color of one's skin, one could not deny its constitutional presence within an individual and there were severe penalties for Jews who tried to pass as Christians.

Psychoanalytic prejudices against lesbians and gay men more closely resembled traditional European anti-semitism where two options were available to Jews. One was to continue practicing the Jewish faith and remain a despised or tolerated second-class citizen. The other was to convert to Christianity and receive more of the rights of citizenship. Conversion, from either Judaism to Christianity or from homosexuality to heterosexuality, offered an alternative to membership in the hated minority group. Isaac Bashevis Singer (1969) wrote of Polish Jews who converted to Roman Catholicism in order to gain entrance into Polish society. While always regarded as converts, they were allowed some access to social networks and institutions that excluded Jews.

The Marranos were Jews who converted to Christianity during the Spanish Inquisitions but secretly practiced Judaism, sometimes hiding their beliefs from their own children, who were raised as Christians.

> Thanks to such disguise, they could attend universities, pursue the liberal professions, serve in the army, and remain in touch with the aristocracy and the court. This schizophrenic existence was not without its difficulties.

> Because of the instability it created, such dual identity led to bitterness and disillusionment, frustration and cynicism. In danger of being discovered, as was frequently the case, the Marranos were subject to attack and ridicule. Living in or between two worlds, they sharpened their sensitivity and found literary expression in humor and satire. (Lazar 1972, 18)

It is not surprising that many lesbian and gay people underwent a psychoanalytic conversion process but kept their homosexual activities secret in order to protect their public identities. In the era of reporting analyses, it was not unusual for gay people to hide their sexual orientations from their own analysts: for example, gay men in training analyses would have to remember to say "she" when they meant "he."

European Christians could not understand why Jews would not accept Christianity, a religion they believed superseded Judaism. One explanation was to seek biblical evidence of the willful stubbornness of the Jews. A church in Rome stands before what used to be the entrance to the Jewish ghetto. An inscription in Latin and Hebrew says, "You Jews are a stiff-necked people." A similar view emerged within the psychoanalytic community of the stubborn lesbian or gay male patient who refused to accept a psychoanalytic conversion to heterosexuality. "Thus, through a complicated system of negation, disavowal, and displacement, he [the sexual deviant] will often claim that he is not perverse, that he was born homosexual, transvestite, etc., that is to say, his sexual pattern is a necessary part of his identity. . . . The pervert frequently believes too that he holds a special secret concerning sexual desire and may even claim that he has discovered the true secret" (McDougall 1980, 61–62).

A psychoanalytic "clinical picture" emerged of the lesbian or gay man trying to get into training programs. This view grew out of a combination of Freudian theory, later psychoanalytic theory, and heterosexual cultural prejudices. Like other demonizing myths, such as the Christian notion of the avaricious Jew or the white man's anxieties about the sexually prolific black man, these stereotypes served to rationalize discrimination against a minority group. The story was repeated, in part or in whole, in the psychoanalytic literature, at conferences, at institute training meetings, in individual supervision, and in analysis. It goes something like this: "Homosexuals are sexually immature; they are either developmentally arrested or regressed and are subsequently restricted to immature sexual practices and relationships. They are sexually impulsive and a presumed danger to patients they might treat." It was the common wisdom of psychoanalysis that homosexuals are incapable of forming meaningful, long-term relationships. Lesbians and gay men were treated as sociopaths if they tried to hide their homosexuality during interviews for training. In fact, the psychoanalytically influenced DSM-I listed homosexuality among the sociopathic disorders until 1968 (Bayer 1981). Because "motivated" homosexuals had the opportunity to undergo psychoanalytic conversion to heterosexuality (just as every Jew has the opportunity to accept Christ), refusal to accept these terms of admission was seen as evidence of either impudence or moral turpitude.

Don't Ask, Don't Tell

The recent controversy over permitting lesbians and gay men into the U.S. armed forces illustrates parallels in the social dynamics of military and psychoanalytically oriented institutions. Both cultures excluded "overt" homosexuals from entrance into the system. If a lesbian or gay man managed to bypass the initial screening procedure and managed to enter the system, they lived in constant fear of discovery and expulsion. In addition, both groups reviled homosexuality as a danger to values they were trying to perpetuate. Although closeted gay members served admirably in the military and in psychoanalysis, once discovered they had to be extruded in order to reinforce shared heterosexual values and to perpetuate heterosexual stereotypes about homosexuality. The stereotypical belief that lesbians and gay men do not make good soldiers and prey upon vulnerable heterosexual colleagues parallels psychoanalytic beliefs about lesbian and gay therapists. Two psychoanalytic biographies illustrate this point.

The biography of Anna Freud (Young-Bruehl 1988) takes great pains to reassure us that she was *not* a lesbian. She never married but the close, live-in relationship she had with Dorothy Burlingham is described in platonic terms. The biographer refers to the rumors of Anna Freud's homosexuality as unsubstantiated and spread by her enemies, presumably among the Kleinian school. To her defenders, an asexual analyst is preferable to a homosexual one. This is also true in the interpersonal psychoanalytic community. Harry Stack Sullivan never married; he "adopted" and lived with Jimmy Sullivan, a younger man from another social class (Perry 1982). Though his biographer alludes to their sexual relationship, she never defines it. To further cloud the issue, she goes so far as to say that Jimmy was a young catatonic delivered into Sullivan's care by a friend who found him on the street. In that sense, she mirrors the attitudes within Sullivan's institute where discussing his homosexuality is more discomforting than talking about his early psychosis. A gay colleague at the White Institute told his analyst that he had heard Sullivan was gay. The analyst responded, both defensively and somewhat coyly, "How do you know? Do you know anyone who slept with him?" I have no claim of special knowledge about the sexual lives of these two important analysts. I merely wish to draw attention to the attitudes within psychoanalytic culture that the contributions of Anna Freud and Sullivan are somehow diminished if it is true that they were homosexuals. Conversely, their psychoanalytic legacies are defended if those who suggest that they were gay are discredited. The underlying, unconscious belief is that gay people have nothing meaningful to offer the field of psychoanalysis except as paying patients seeking treatment.

In the military debate, the heterosexual majority was unwilling to accept the evidence that lesbians and gay men can perform their duties admirably. There are psychoanalysts who maintain similar prejudices. Some are public about their beliefs (Socarides 1994), while others express them privately. Until very recently, the absence of "out" lesbian and gay psychoanalysts made it impossible to disprove their claims. "Don't ask, don't tell" emerged as a political compromise in the debate on lesbians and gay men in the military. After the American Psychiatric Association deleted homosexuality from its Diagnostic and Statistical Manual in 1973 (Bayer, 1981), a "don't ask, don't tell" approach toward lesbians and gay men spontaneously evolved in segments of the psychoanalytically oriented mental health fields. This approach was certainly preferable to the exclusionary attitudes it replaced but certainly did not go far enough in respecting the rights of lesbian and gay mental health professionals. In fact, more than twenty years after the deletion of homosexuality from the diagnostic manual, where are the openly lesbian and gay training and supervising analysts?

John* was a psychiatrist accepted for psychoanalytic training at a classical institute in the early 1960s. On the first day of his training analysis, he told his analyst that he was a homosexual. The analyst told him to sit up. The analyst demanded to know how he had gotten through the screening process. John told his analyst that none of his interviewers asked any questions about his sexual orientation. The analyst told John that "the matter" would have to be reported to the training committee and he terminated the session. Within a week, John officially withdrew from that institute. This occurred at a time when psychoanalytic training was a major step toward advancement in academic psychiatry and psychology.

Mark*, a fellow resident during my psychiatric training, was interviewed at another residency program in the late 1970s. After what seemed to be a reasonable, professional interview, his interviewer said, "I'm going to ask you three questions that I ask everybody. First, are you psychotic?" Mark said no. "Are you a substance abuser?" No, again. "Are you a homosexual?" Mark said he was. The interviewer said "I'm sorry, but I don't think homosexuals should be allowed to become psychiatrists." Mark burst into tears, presumably providing his interviewer with further proof of his unsuitability for psychiatric training.

In the late 1980s, Richard* was a psychologist in psychotherapy supervision. Richard was openly gay with this supervisor who held an important position at an institute he was considering for training. She liked him and his work very much. She explained she could arrange his admission interviews with three analysts who would not bring up his sexual orientation as long as Richard did not to bring it up either. If he was accepted for admission, he was not to speak openly about his homosexuality during the entire course of training, either in classes or supervision. He was, however, free to discuss it in his training analysis which was not a reporting analysis. Those were the conditions for her assistance. Richard declined and got his training elsewhere as an openly gay man.

"Psychoanalytic Coyness" (Drescher, forthcoming) is an attitude of insincerity seen in some analysts when they discuss their feelings about homosexuality. It results from the conflict between the unconscious hatred or anxiety these heterosexual analysts feel towards gay people and the analysts' self-representations as caring and tolerant individuals. Overt expressions of psychoanalytic coyness are usually provoked by drawing attention to the analysts' prejudices. Coyness emerges as a very clever intellectualization or rationalization intended to cover up the analysts' true feelings or intentions.

When I applied for psychoanalytic training in 1988, a friend at an American-affiliated institute asked if I was applying there. I told her that her institute did not accept gay people. She was surprised and did not believe me and asked her training analyst about my statement. He confirmed that it was true. In a *classic* case of psychoanalytic coyness, hiding his contempt behind his false compassion, he told her, "Blind people should be entitled to all the rights and privileges of sighted people but you don't want them to fly a plane." One of my interviewers at an institute where I did apply was clearly uncomfortable with my being openly gay and questioned me extensively about an early heterosexual experience including questions about my orgasms and those of the woman. He did not seem curious about my long-term relationship with a man; the only question he asked about my partner of many years is what he did for a living and then he changed the subject. At the end of the interview, sensing his discomfort, I asked how my being gay would affect my application. He told me I had asked "a false question." I said I did not know what a false question was. He said if I were a heterosexual applicant, I would not automatically be accepted to the institute. I said that it was not a false question because I'm sure he knew there were other institutes that did not accept gay people. He responded "It will neither help you nor hurt you." Apparently this was the case, since I was admitted to this institute.

I applied for residency training in 1979. At one program, my interviewer, whom I shall call Dr. X, said "Tell me about your intimate life." I paused and told him I was gay. Dr. X seemed taken aback by my admission. After he paused for a moment he said, "Well, how long has your longest relationship lasted?" He might have responded by asking "Are you currently in a relationship?" I immediately understood that he was referring to a psychoanalytic stereotype about homosexual pathology, in this case that homosexuals are unable to maintain long-term relationships. This made me feel very defensive in the interview and I decided I did not want to go to that program and did not include it in the internship match. Coincidentally, my impression of Dr. X was later validated by two episodes. My fellow resident Mark* began analysis with Dr. X upon the recommendation of an analytic supervisor. Mark was interested in psychoanalytic approaches but Dr. X told him that Mark would not be accepted as a candidate in the psychoanalytic institute where Dr. X taught. It was the policy of that institute to exclude "overt homosexuals." Although Dr. X said he disagreed with the policy, there was nothing he could do about it. I have heard of similar experiences from several gay psychiatrist colleagues interested in analytic training who went into analysis with training analysts from the 1950s through the '80s. One gay psychiatrist was in treatment with the director of training at an institute. After telling her prospective patient that he would not be accepted by the admissions committee, she added that he was fortunate. This meant he could have a "real," non-reporting analysis, safe from the prying eyes of others. My colleague tells this story as an illustration of his analyst's kindness, as do all the others who have told me similar stories. All of my colleagues feel that their analysts helped them. I have no reason to doubt the kindness of these analysts but I always wonder what ethical principles underlie their affiliation with institutions that practice discriminatory policies with which they disagree.

The second follow-up account of Dr. X occurred recently in my private practice. A patient was referred for medication treatment by his analyst who is a psychologist. The patient had been in treatment with Dr. X for over twenty years, many of them devoted to "curing" the patient of his homosexuality. The patient had been married, was now divorced, and is currently self-identified as gay. He told how he left Dr. X. While talking about his growing belief that homosexuality might be genetic, he remembers the analyst called him stupid. The patient left the session in an agitated state. Dr. X called the patient at home, something the patient commented on as remarkable because the analyst had never done that before. The analyst expressed his concern for the patient who replied, "You called me stupid." Dr. X clarified his position and said, "I didn't say you were stupid, I said the idea was stupid." The patient answered, "Well, it's the same thing, isn't it?"

The supervision of trainees provides a unique opportunity for the transmission of anti-homosexual prejudices within the mental health fields. The supervisor in the teaching relationship has the power to influence the career of his or her student. This provides unique opportunities to inculcate trainees into heterosexual orthodoxy as well as to punish them if they do not conform. During my residency training, my psychotherapy class was taught by a psychiatrist with an interest in psychoanalysis, though he was not a psychoanalyst himself. In class, he repeatedly disagreed with residents who cited the DSM-III assertion that homosexuality per se was not a mental disorder. He also did it in a way that indicated that he had nothing but contempt for those who disagreed with his position: "I don't give a damn what the DSM-III says" was a milder version of a repeated oath in class.

I also had this psychiatrist for individual psychotherapy supervision and we met repeatedly to discuss referrals for a potential psychotherapy case. One day we reviewed the chart of a seventeen-year-old girl referred for treatment after her family found out she was having a relationship with an older woman. The supervisor said to me, "How do you think your being a homosexual will affect the treatment of this patient?" I had never had a conversation with this supervisor about myself and was completely taken by surprise. I replied, "Who said I was a homosexual?" He said, "Someone told me you were." I asked who had told him. "I don't remember," was his reply. I told him I had no interest in continuing the discussion. He became defensive and sputtered, "I thought you were open about it." Apparently he saw no relationship between his stated public opinions about homosexuality in class and my defensive reaction to his question. I wrote a letter to the residency training director describing the incident. This infuriated the supervisor who resented my making his behavior public. What I learned from that painful experience, which ended in our mutual agreement to terminate supervision, was how exposing unacceptable behavior by supervisors through appropriate channels could sometimes end that behavior in my presence.

At a workshop designed for lesbian and gay residents to share coping strategies in their psychiatric residencies (Drescher 1992), thirty trainees attended. They were from large cities and small university towns. In a spontaneous discussion of their residency programs, all of them talked about stressful learning situations with analytic supervisors and teachers. In didactic courses, senior analysts discussed homosexuality as psychopathology and challenged residents to defend the position that it was normal. When supervisors made judgmental remarks about gay patients, residents either missed supervision or changed supervisors without giving the real reason for doing so. Anxious about the critical opinions of analytic supervisors, residents would not talk freely about their personal responses to patients. Lesbian and gay residents discussed the difficulty of finding a therapist in a community where pathological viewpoints about homosexuality were the public expressions of psychoanalytic thinking. Some delayed their own treatment until they could move to a different academic environment.

Because of legitimate concerns about advancement and promotion, lesbian and gay residents are rarely willing to argue with supervisors who espouse anti-homosexual views. They are somewhat prepared for anti-homosexual bias in residency because of the cultural biases they experienced prior to training. When supervisors talk disparagingly about gay people, it is not uncommon for lesbian and gay trainees to protectively hide further in the closet.

Between heterosexual supervisors and trainees, the intimacy of the supervisory relationship offers an opportunity for the transmission of bias to the next generation. Sometimes the results of these encounters can be surprising. A psychiatric resident starting psychotherapy supervision with a senior analyst was presenting her new patient. The patient was a gay man in the first year of medical school. The supervisor questioned why this man had even been accepted into medical school because, as she told the resident, homosexuals had enormous difficulties controlling their impulses.

She explained that when homosexuals got to the third year of medical school and had to do physical examinations, they were not able to control those impulses toward patients. The resident, who was heterosexual, told the supervisor that she had worked with gay attending physicians, residents, and medical students throughout her albeit brief career and considered them fine physicians. The resident refused to continue in supervision with the analyst and requested a change of supervisors.

A heterosexual colleague told of a supervisory experience from his residency. He was presenting the case of a gay man to a psychoanalyst for psychotherapy supervision. The supervisor remarked that homosexuality was not a human way of relating. By this he meant that homosexuals did not look each other in the face when they made love because they practiced orogenital and anogenital sex. My colleague thought for a moment and then told his supervisor the following story. Several years earlier, he had a girlfriend who suffered from recurrent vaginal infections. During those times, they were unable to have sexual intercourse in their usual way so they practiced anal intercourse. He assured the supervisor that it was in fact quite possible to have anal intercourse face-to-face. The supervisor had nothing further to say about the inhumanity of homosexuality.

Conclusions

At the conference in "Perspectives on Homosexuality" that prompted this book, a heterosexual analyst made the point that there was discrimination in psychoanalysis *in the past*, that it was isolated to some "neurotic individuals" and that it was more likely to be found in medical psychoanalytic institutes rather than psychology institutes. I commented that his discussion reminded me of the post-war German phenomenon of sorting out the good Germans from the bad ones. This led him to declare that my characterization was unacceptable to him because he did not believe the analogy was applicable. He tangentially added that he did not believe Attica was equivalent to the Holocaust and therefore refused to even consider what I had said. Another heterosexual analyst declared that comparisons with Nazi Germany were "invalid" because no atrocities had been committed within psychoanalysis. As a child of Holocaust survivors, it was not my intention to trivialize the Holocaust but to draw attention to the way in which groups deal with the issue of "assigning blame" after a terrible event has happened. I prefer to leave it to the reader to determine where one draws the line between atrocity and abuse.

The relationships between an analyst and analysand or a supervisor and supervisee can be used for many purposes. Both relationships thrive in an atmosphere of safety whose intimacy can foster growth in patients and apprentice therapists. This is the ideal goal of any analyst or supervisor. When analysts try to promote their own belief system to protect their own interests or those of their institutes, they may find themselves experiencing a conflict of interest. When an analyst has such a conflict, it is possible that patients and supervisees may be harmed, particularly when noncompliance with the analyst's or his institution's goals for training or therapeutic outcome lead to humiliation, bad evaluations, demotion, or expulsion.

Several points need to be emphasized in an examination of the history of anti-homosexual bias within the psychoanalytically-oriented mental health professions. First, it is important to acknowledge that times and attitudes have begun to change and now we can talk about incidents of discrimination that used to happen frequently and also how that discrimination occurs today. Second, it is useful to show how institutional bias was rationalized by clinical theory. Third, the history of anti-homosexual bias illustrates the point that it is extremely difficult to separate a scientific theory from the cultural matrix in which theories are formulated. Fourth, we are reminded how vulnerable patients and trainees are to the human frailties and prejudices of their analysts and teachers. Finally, we see how discrimination works: usually behind closed doors, often insidiously, and ultimately corrupting the ideals of the institutions in which it flourishes.

Note

*The names of various people discussed in this essay have been changed.

References Cited

Bayer, R. 1981. *Homosexuality and American Psychiatry: The Politics of Diagnosis*. New York: Basic Books.

Bergler, E. 1956. *Homosexuality: Disease or Way of Life*. New York: Hill and Wang.

Bieber, I.; Dain, H.J.; Dince, P.R.; Drellich, M.G.; Grand, H.G.; Gundlach, R.H.; Kremer, M.W.; Rifkin, A.H.; Wilbur, C.B.; Bieber, T.B. 1962. *Homosexuality: A Psychoanalytic Study*. New York: Basic Books.

Drescher, J. 1992. *Lesbian and Gay Residents: Survival Strategies for the Nineties*. Component Workshop Presentation, American Psychiatric Association, May 1992, Washington, DC.

———. *Psychoanalytic Attitudes Toward Homosexuality*. (In Press).

Freud, S. 1905. "Three Essays on Sexuality." In *The Standard Edition of the Complete Psychological Works of Sigmund Freud* 7: 123–246. Translated and edited by J. Strachey. London: Hogarth Press, 1962.

———. 1908. *"Civilized" Sexual Morality and Modern Mental Illness. SE* 9, 177–204.

Isay, R. 1989. *Being Homosexual: Gay Men and Their Development*. New York: Farrar Straus and Giroux.

Lazar, M. 1972. *The Sephardic Tradition: Latino and Spanish-Jewish Literature*. New York: W.W. Norton.

Lewes, K. 1988. *The Psychoanalytic Theory of Male Homosexuality*. New York: Simon and Schuster.

McDougall, J. 1980. *Plea for a Measure of Abnormality*. New York: International Universities Press.

Nicolosi, J. 1991. *Reparative Theraphy of Male Homosexuality: A New Clinical Approach*. Northvale: Aronson.

Perry, H.S. 1982. *Psychiatrist of America: The Life of Harry Stack Sullivan*. Cambridge: Harvard University Press.

Rado, S. 1969. *Adaptational Psychodynamics: Motivation and Control*. New York: Science House.

Singer, I.B. 1969. *The Manor*. New York: Farrar, Straus and Giroux.

Socarides, C. 1968. *The Overt Homosexual*. New York: Grune and Stratton.

———. 1994. Response [to Judd Marmor], Letter to the Editor. *Psychiatric News* (May 20).

Stanton, M. 1991. *Sandor Ferenczi: Reconsidering Active Intervention*. London: Jason Aronson.

Trop J., and Stolorow, R. 1993. Reply to Blechner, Lesser, and Schwartz. *Psychoanalytic Dialogues* 3 (4): 653–656.

Young-Bruehl, E. 1988. *Anna Freud: A Biography*. New York: Summit Books.

14

The Difficulty of Being a Gay Psychoanalyst During the Last Fifty Years

An Interview with Dr. Bertram Schaffner

Stephen B. Goldman

Introduction

DR. BERTRAM SCHAFFNER IS AN important figure in the professional fields of psychiatry and psychoanalysis. He is a gay man who has consistently been committed to improving the self-esteem of both gay patients and therapists. In addition to his numerous and significant contributions to psychiatry and psychoanalysis during a long and prominent career, he is the author of numerous papers and one widely admired book, *Father Land* (1984), which examines authoritarianism within the German family. In collaboration with Margaret Mead and Ruth Benedict, he conducted cross-cultural research in the Caribbean Islands, and in 1958 he founded the Caribbean Federation for Mental Health, focusing on matters of public mental health and mental hospital policies in the Caribbean Islands.

Dr. Schaffner has written extensively on working with persons with HIV/AIDS, has taught classes on the subject, and has led numerous groups for patients and physicians affected by this disease. As President of the Gay and Lesbian Psychiatrists of New York and as Chairman of the Committee on Human Sexuality of the Group for the Advancement of Psychotherapy,

Dr. Schaffner has been in the forefront of those psychiatrists dealing openly and tolerantly with gay and lesbian issues.

In short, Dr. Schaffner's compassion, eloquence, and commitment have inspired several generations of psychoanalysts. It is with this in mind that Dr. Goldman interviewed him.

Dr. Goldman has actively promoted fair treatment for gay and lesbian people within psychology since the early 1970s. As a member of the Gay Academic Union, he successfully lobbied to delete "homosexuality" as a mental illness from the Diagnostic and Statistical Manual of Mental Disorders. He was a member of the Lesbian and Gay Caucus of the American Psychology Association, which developed into Division 44: The Society for the Psychological Study of Lesbian and Gay Issues. In his private practice, Dr. Goldman sees many gay clients and has worked extensively with people with HIV/AIDS and their partners and families.

Goldman: Bert, I'd like to hear whatever you have to say about your life as a gay man and a gay psychiatrist; and especially about the evolution you have observed in this world over your eighty-one and a half years, in the professional world as a physician, in the psychoanalytic world, and, finally, in the evolving world of gay people in this country.

Schaffner: This is a very timely moment for our discussion because of the historic conference which resulted in this book. This conference was the first one organized by gay and lesbian psychologists to discuss homosexual issues on an equal professional footing with their straight peers. It is also timely because this year is the twenty-fifth anniversary of the famous Stonewall riots which have come to symbolize the beginning of the gay rights movement as we know it today.

I grew up in a small town in western Pennsylvania, suffering acutely over being a "sissy"; rebuffed by my adolescent schoolmates because I had studied dancing and appeared with a girl partner in a recital of classic dance, for which I don't think I was ever forgiven. I was written up in the high school yearbook as "Most Likely To Succeed," but also as "leaving my girlish grace to Ann Pennington" in the Class Will. This may have left me with the naive feeling that I would have few intellectual or professional roadblocks in life, but only problems over sexual appearances. How much I had to learn!

Goldman: And you understood from an early age that you were, as they say, "different"?

Schaffner: Right, but I was also specifically aware of my sexual interest in men from about the age of three.

Goldman: You were not repressed?

Schaffner: No, I felt my impulses were natural, and I was very comfortable with them until my parents learned of my activities with other children in the neighborhood. I was made to feel wicked, and I grew up feeling that I was someone to be avoided. My isolation was compounded by the fact that I was promoted three years ahead of my age group and sat in classes with children of twelve who would have nothing to do with a boy of only nine. My fears of being exposed as gay led to some difficult experiences. In summer camp, at age 16, I was asked whether I had had sexual contact with a man who had identified me as having been his sexual partner. Although I was told that I should be examined because he had syphilis, I totally denied having had sexual relations with him out of my paralyzing fear of anyone in my family and social circle finding out about my "disgraceful" life. Naturally, I secretly consulted a physician as soon as I could leave the camp, and fortunately had not contracted the disease.

Needless to say, I could hardly wait to move out of my hometown for Harvard, 500 miles away, where I arrived at the tender age of 15, again over two years younger than my classmates. My dormitory mates refused to have me along on their trips to football games and visits to New York with their dates. I found a small circle of gay friends in Cambridge, but once this was discovered by my classmates, they ostracized me; I felt as though I were wearing a "Scarlet Letter." To make matters worse, my father opened a letter addressed to me by a gay friend and then forbade me to return to college. I was only able to persuade him to change his mind by threatening suicide. As a result of these many troubles, I convinced myself that I should "cure" my homosexuality by transferring to a coeducational college. With my academic record of straight As, I was readily accepted by the Dean of Swarthmore College, although he expressed puzzlement as to why I was transferring. Naturally I could not tell him the truth.

I continued to do well academically, but I certainly made no progress in changing my sexual orientation. In fact, my primary conscious confusion was about the selection of a vocation. Fortunately, at a tea honoring Rhodes Scholars hosted by the President of Swarthmore during my junior year, I met a doctor from a nearby pharmaceutical corporation with whom I fell in love. It was his strong feeling that I would make an excellent doctor, and I am still grateful for his helpful advice. Thus, much to everyone's surprise, I decided to major in premedical studies, requiring an extra year in undergraduate school; I graduated as an M.D. from Johns Hopkins Medical School in 1937 at the age of 25.

Goldman: I believe you served in the Army, too. Were you a doctor then, and did your homosexuality influence you in any way?

Schaffner: In October 1940, I received my draft notice. Although some men used their homosexuality as a means of evading military service, I did not, partially because I felt that as a Jew I had a duty to fight against the Nazis, and probably also because I felt that I could somehow survive as a gay man in the military. Luckily the Army allowed me to complete my psychiatric residency at Bellevue Hospital, thus enabling me to enter service as a doctor and an officer. As for any influence my homosexuality may have had in this capacity, during the first four years of my service I screened draftees to determine their psychiatric fitness to be in the Army. Officially, my job was to detect and weed out homosexuals. Since men rejected for homosexuality suffered prejudice, public disgrace, and even loss of livelihood, I felt it important to prevent such consequences by finding other legitimate reasons for their rejection. However, when I discovered gay draftees who strongly desired to serve in the Army, I did my best to determine whether they were strong enough to survive. If I believed they could succeed, I approved their papers.

Goldman: So both groups were fortunate to have you be their interviewer: the ones who wanted to serve and the ones who would probably not have functioned well. I presume you were in the minority among the interviewers, because you were sensitive to the gay issue and would do your best both for the candidate and for the military service.

Schaffner: Thank you, Steve, for understanding what I did at the time. It was not easy because it contravened current military regulations and policy. And, unfortunately, that military policy has not yet changed; in fact, today it is even somewhat worse.

Goldman: How did you get along in the Army?

Schaffner: Although I survived five and a half years in the service, it was not entirely without difficulty. My first four years were spent in cities within the United States which allowed me a comfortable social life with gay friends. In August 1944 when I was transferred to a remote military camp prior to going overseas, life changed completely. Suddenly I was once again isolated from friends who knew and accepted my sexual orientation. This isolation threw me into a panic which I did not know how to resolve within the military setting. Fortunately, my Commanding Officer granted me leave to consult a New York City psychoanalyst recommended by civilian friends. This was my first contact with psychoanalysis, and a fortunate one. The visit did help to relieve my panic; in a way, it also influenced my eventual decision to study psychoanalysis.

Goldman: During this first session, were you open with the analyst about being gay, and if so, what was his response? Did he accept your being gay?

Schaffner: He didn't condemn me, but he certainly regarded my homosexuality as an illness and urged me to seek treatment at the the end of my military duty. Of course, this was the accepted viewpoint in 1944, almost thirty years before the American Psychiatric Association removed homosexuality from the DSM list of mental illnesses.

Goldman: In terms of your own professional development at that point, were you interested in becoming a psychoanalyst?

Schaffner: Yes, I was already a psychiatrist and quite aware of psychoanalysis. Yet I was ambivalent about it since I had graduated from Johns Hopkins where Dr. Adolph Meyer had a well-known bias against psychoanalysis.

Goldman: Did you train with him?

Schaffner: Yes, while I was a medical student, he had been my professor of psychiatry.

Goldman: Did he have great influence on you?

Schaffner: No, because somehow I already surmised that psychiatry alone could not help me understand gayness or how to live with it. I yearned to be at peace with my own gay life and to help others do the same.

Goldman: But you already had a sense that psychoanalysis could be a way to live with yourself as a gay person? What drew you to psychoanalysis?

Schaffner: You must remember that in those years, the 1930s through the 1960s, psychoanalysis was in its heyday, revered as the true answer for life's questions and the cure for all sexual problems. In today's terminology, I really wanted to be able to "come out," to be unashamed of being gay, to accept myself, and to be free from my own internalized homophobia. I wanted to be able to live with it and not be constantly anxious and uneasy. And, of course, I wanted to have a happy love relationship.

Goldman: What were your experiences with coming out to your family?

Schaffner: Unlike today's young people, for whom it can often be easy to come out to parents (the world has changed a great deal since my childhood 70 years ago), I did not have a good experience when I told my mother at age 13 that I was gay. She was morally shocked; she also felt personally hurt because she interpreted it to mean that I did not like her. She never accepted my homosexuality and continued throughout her life to imply that it was really due to an unwillingness to accept the responsibilities of marriage. In 1938, when I was 26, my mother met my lover and subsequently dreamt that *I* had died and that *she* married him!

Goldman: What about your father?

Schaffner: After my mother's bad reaction and my father almost succeeding in ending my college education because of it, I never made any further attempts to discuss my sexual orientation with him. However, in the latter part of his life I felt that he knew and had arrived at peace of mind about me. We grew rather close to one another before his death.

Goldman: Was psychoanalysis helpful to you as a gay man?

Schaffner: Yes and no. I had to change analysts twice before I found one who truly helped. When I returned to New York City in 1946 I began psychoanalysis with the analyst whom I had consulted in 1944 before going overseas. At this time, I told him I was now planning to apply for training at the New York Psychoanalytic Institute and requested a letter of recommendation from him. He informed me that admission would be out of the question because of my homosexuality. This was a shock to me on many levels. I had never been refused admission to any academic institution. I also could not conceive of a satisfying professional life without psychoanalytic training. For the first time in my life, I experienced my homosexuality as a major, catastrophic liability for which I could not see any solution. I was refused admission to both the New York Psychoanalytic Institute and the Columbia University Psychoanalytic Institute. That same first Freudian analyst, of course, had one strike against him in terms of our analytic relationship for being the bearer of the bad news about the New York Psychoanalytic Institute. But besides that, he did not interact with me in terms of my real needs to understand and accept my homosexuality. Instead, he spoke in Freudian jargon which I did not find helpful, e.g., "You are afraid of the teeth in your mother's vagina." He also insisted upon my lying on his couch. One day I turned around and found him asleep. That was the last straw! I remained in a state of shock for nearly a year until I learned of the new, unorthodox William Alanson White Institute of Psychoanalysis, and applied there. I was interviewed by three analysts, among them Dr. Janet Rioch and Dr. Erich Fromm, both of whom were cordial and accepting of my homosexuality, about which I was very frank. I was admitted and began psychoanalytic training in 1949. The White Institute's founder was Dr. Clara Thompson, whose guiding spirit was Dr. Harry Stack Sullivan, a courageous, innovative, gay psychiatrist. It seems ironic that the Institute, whose entire curriculum is based on Sullivan's theory of interpersonal relations, remained reluctant to publicly acknowledge his homosexuality until only two years ago.

My next analyst, Dr. Clara Thompson, was genuinely willing to work with me as a homosexual. However, she must have harbored the feeling, then prevalent, that homosexuality was subject to modification or even reversal as a result of good psychoanalysis. Unfortunately, this may have led her into being overly trusting of me when I suggested becoming engaged to a remarkable woman I had met while working with Military Government in Germany. Apparently, Dr. Thompson failed to grasp my transference to her, i.e., my need to please her (as I would have wanted to please my mother) by getting married and being, in my mother's words, "able to take responsibility toward a woman." Clara reacted as if the expressed wish to marry were true instead of a neurotic transference. When she believed me and mistakenly went along with my plan, I had a dream that I was flying to Europe to meet my fiancee, in a plane that had no roof and which was flying upside down! The next morning I realized that a marriage, if allowed to take place, would so completely violate my psychological self, that it could affect my sanity. I had to save myself from such a tragic travesty. I decided not to marry. In addition, since I also shared in the lack of understanding that this had been a transference phenomenon, I decided not to continue working with Dr. Thompson.

I stayed with my third analyst, Dr. Grace Baker, for thirty years. She was a graduate of the Baltimore Psychoanalytic Institute and had been herself trained by Dr. Harry Stack Sullivan and Dr. Frieda Fromm-Reichman. She was excellent in helping me deal with my feelings of prudishness, inadequacy, inferiority, and intrinsic evil and guilt. She also helped me to accept differences in people.

Goldman: Was she a straight or gay and did it make a difference?

Schaffner: No one I knew, knew for sure. There were rumors that she was lesbian; her closest male friend was a gay psychiatrist. Looking back, it is clear now that this did make a difference. I also see that I often really wanted to ask her about her sexual orientation, but did not dare. Remember, it was 1955! She had made numerous references to the importance of professional discretion and protecting one's private life. After her death I realized that although she had liberated me in many respects she had really not freed me from the sense of guilt and shame over my homosexuality. She had indeed helped me tremendously to understand my relationship to women but had neglected the crucial, essential work on my relationship to men.

Goldman: Was she still your therapist at the time of her death?

Schaffner: Yes, and, interestingly enough, for ten years I did not seek another therapist. Did I somehow feel I had had enough therapy? I prefer now to believe that I truly did not know what I needed. Then a severe crisis in my relationship with a lover forced me to examine my life once more, and for the first time, I deliberately chose a gay male therapist. Probably I had unconsciously come to terms with the fact that I must deal with my remaining homophobia.

Goldman: And how was that experience?

Schaffner: Well, Dr. Goldman, I hope you don't mind my talking about you, because you were the therapist I chose. I am happy to express my gratitude to you. Our work was very helpful. For the first time, I was able to recall and relive the pain and grief of my early relationships with my father, brother, and other males. For the first time, I became aware of how much I had actually wanted my father's love and interest. Previously I had not remembered that I wanted him to help me to learn how to associate with other people and to defend me from my mother. It astonished me to become aware of how much I had respected him and that his behavior toward me had left such a powerful impression. I came to know a side of myself that I had not recognized while working with women therapists. You helped me rediscover my fundamentally positive feelings toward men and myself, both as a man and a homosexual. For the first time, I felt united and whole. Then at last, I was able to extricate myself from the destructive relationship in which I had remained too long. My self esteem and my sense of well-being improved.

Goldman: Well, it's clear you have a lot of strengths and adaptive capacities; despite the travails of growing up as a gay person, your intellectual abilities—and your certainty that you could rely on them—and a self-acceptance even during unhappy or depressed periods allowed you to come through some rough times. You are unusually honest with yourself.

Schaffner: Thank you!

Goldman: Tell us about working as a psychoanalyst who happened to be gay during the '50s and '60s. How did it feel practicing before people felt free to speak about these things?

Schaffner: Well, I felt at the time that I was one of very few gay analysts and that I had a kind of obligation: I particularly wanted to deal with gay patients so as to help them feel acceptable and hopeful of leading a fulfilled life. I think I saw myself as useful and beneficial. But at the same time, I was going through much self doubt of my own, wondering if I could really be helpful. I hoped I could assist by being a role model with whom they might identify.

Goldman: Did you see many gay patients at this time? Did your practice move in that direction?

Schaffner: Yes, especially after 1980, when I became president of the Gay and Lesbian Psychiatrists of New York and began to "come out" in my private life and to other professionals.

Goldman: Did you develop a reputation, and did people like the idea that they could come to you when looking for a gay psychiatrist?

Schaffner: Well, I had many patients from the theater in the early days, from the theater and the arts. I did try, unsuccessfully, to control who knew and who did not. I thought I was being very careful whom I told. But I had a big shock when Jim Cattell, the editor of the *Psychiatric News* at Columbia, called up one day to say, "I have a patient here who isn't sure if he's homosexual or not, but he wants to see a gay psychiatrist, so that's why I'm calling you." I shall never forget that moment, the first time a straight man had said that to me, bluntly and directly, matter-of-factly, without acrimony or disapproval. In a certain way, I felt relieved. I thought, "OK, the jig is up," but then I had to reformulate my life. Until then I had been persuading myself to believe that there was still some degree of secrecy and privacy. At that moment, I realized that there was not.

Goldman: But don't you think that was true of most gay people, that nearly everyone had the notion that they could live double lives?

Schaffner: Yes, and it created a great deal of tension. In those days, I was really afraid to to let other gay psychiatrists know that I was gay, for fear that they might tell someone else.

I also tried an experiment to see how straight analysts would react to finding out. The first straight psychoanalyst and his wife whom I told continued being personally very friendly to me. However, my own psychoanalytic institute stopped referring patients to me almost completely.

Goldman: Really?

Schaffner: Yes. It caused me to start withdrawing from the White Institute. I stopped taking part in their activities because I wasn't sure I was still welcome.

Goldman: What was it like to be in training there as a gay candidate?

Schaffner: Not altogether comfortable. First of all, I assumed that I was the only gay candidate. Later I learned differently. I never referred to my own sexual orientation in classes, only in the privacy or "safety" of supervision, and I was afraid of my fellow candidates' reactions. Although I was elected President of the Psychoanalytic Society and even received an award from the Institute, I still held myself aloof socially until about 1990, when the combination of my therapy with you and the courage of some of the younger candidates who formed what we now call "The Gay White Way" enabled me to reenter the Institute's social and professional life as a comfortable, self-respecting, and "non-slinking" human being.

Goldman: And this was only in the mid-1980s?

Schaffner: Yes. Also, and probably due to the fact that I withdrew from active participation in the Institute's social and academic life, I did not seek or receive promotion to the positions of supervising or training analyst. However, during the last four years, there has been a marked change. The Institute has become aware of its own share in causing me to feel isolated and unwelcome and, since 1993, has gone out of its way to give me recognition. I have just been appointed Supervising Analyst. I probably should have been a Training Analyst by now, but in view of a newly-instituted ruling, one has to serve five years as Supervising Analyst before becoming a Training Analyst.

Goldman: Do you think your appointment as Training Analyst was prevented because you asserted your gayness?

Schaffner: Yes, and please don't forget that I withdrew from the Institute as well. It was reciprocal: they rejected, and I withdrew.

Goldman: Were you involved in any of the American Psychiatric Association's activities declaring homosexuality not to be a mental illness?

Schaffner: No, that took place when I was not participating in psychiatric organizational activities or even attending APA conferences. In those years, 1968 to 1980, I led a rather withdrawn, private life.

Goldman: And what about now? Bring us up to date with what it's like at this point in your life. You've been associated with the Gay and Lesbian Psychiatrists of New York for a long time. How did that come about?

Schaffner: In 1981 or '82 I learned of the formation of the Gay Caucus of the American Psychiatric Association and experimented for the first time in a gay consciousness-raising group. Afterward I felt the need to become more openly involved and accepted an invitation to join the recently formed Gay and Lesbian Psychiatrists of New York. It seemed a really daring step to take, saying in effect, "I don't care anymore who knows I'm gay." Six years later, I began to fight for a Committee on Human Sexuality at the Group for the Advancement of Psychiatry. With the generous help of Professor John Spiegel, the Committee was established in 1989 with myself as Chairman. The Committee is now writing a report on Antihomosexual Bias in Psychiatry.

Goldman: Wonderful. What else can you tell me about your work with AIDS and with HIV+ patients?

Schaffner: Six years ago, Dr. Stuart Nichols and I started a support group for HIV+ physicians, who were then the target of enormous public hysteria. They had a need for totally reliable, absolute confidentiality, and at that time felt they could not trust their secrets to most other physicians. This support group, conducted without fees, still continues. For three years now, Dr. Mark Blechner and I have been teaching a course in psychotherapy with HIV+ patients. I am now Medical Director at the William Alanson White Institute's HIV Clinic, of which he is the founder and Director.

Goldman: Do you believe that AIDS has accelerated the process of psychiatry coming to terms with homosexuality and viewing it in a different light?

Schaffner: Very much so. In the last two years, over 50% of the papers at the APA Conferences deal with HIV-related issues and homosexuality. Originally psychiatrists went along with the perception that AIDS was a gay disease, but time has shown us otherwise. Today's therapists are not surprised whenever AIDS pops up in their practice. They are now becoming able to deal with aspects of this disease. Yet I strongly believe that they need to develop much more understanding of the unique problems when treating homosexual patients in their practice.

Goldman: Your life and career have certainly helped to make the psychiatric and psychoanalytic professions aware that gay people *are* human beings. I want to thank you for taking the time to discuss with me your experiences as a gay man and as a gay professional during the enormous and encouraging historic developments for gay people of the last half century, an evolution that is still in progress and to which you have contributed in a very major way.

15

A View from Both Sides

Coming Out as a Lesbian Psychoanalyst

April Martin

IT WAS 1978 AND I WAS twenty-nine. I'd had my doctorate in clinical psychology for three years, had a private practice, and was in psychoanalytic training. Happily heterosexual, I thought of myself as tolerant of homosexuality—not one of those analysts who wanted to change a committed lesbian or gay male identity. Naively, I also thought that tolerance was all I needed and that analytic technique would handle the rest. I was unaware of my own homonegative feelings, heterosexist biases, and just plain ignorance.

I also had no idea that my life was to change irrevocably—that I was soon to find myself deeply and passionately in love with a woman. When the dam finally burst it was as astonishing to me as to those who knew me. An allergy to conscious deception rendered me unable to spend any time at all in the closet, and I immediately told everyone my good fortune. Mercifully, being in love is a state of derangement which softens the blows of the world, making it easier to throw caution to the wind.

For many months my feelings had been gathering momentum but could not break through the shock and disbelief of my consciousness. I can recall the degree of excitement I felt at seeing her, but I skillfully ignored the implications of it. In her presence I merely thought I had the flu.

On one eventful evening, I closed up my office and with no particular thought to where I was going, found myself drifting toward what I'd heard was a women's bar—a place in the Village called the Duchess. "What are you doing?" flashed through my mind, but too faintly to alter my course. About to walk in, I panicked as I noticed one of my patients across the street. I returned her greeting in my best professional manner, walked nonchalantly past the Duchess, then circled the area in a five block radius for the next hour. Finally, compelled by something on which I could not afford to reflect, I returned to the scene of the crime and slipped through the door.

With no idea what to expect I ordered a glass of wine. Someone sat down next to me, asking when I'd realized I was a lesbian. Flustered, I replied that I wasn't a lesbian and didn't know why I was there. Though I rarely drink, within a couple of hours I'd had four glasses of wine—a quantity sufficient for me to lose all inhibition. In a dizzying blur I danced, I flirted, I gave out my phone number, I even kissed a woman quickly on the lips. I walked home grinning, let myself into my apartment, and proceeded to have the most violent anxiety attack I have ever known.

The worst part of it was not, "What would my mother think?" or "Does this mean I'll never have a normal life?" No, the most terrifying aspect of it was, "Have I just thrown away the professional life I have worked so hard to attain?" Somehow I knew I was strong enough to withstand whatever rejection might come from family or from society at large. But the field of psychoanalytic psychotherapy was the source of all of my livelihood, most of my community, and much of my intellectual stimulation. Throughout years of training the masters of my field had described homosexuals as narcissistic, perverted, arrested in their development, unreconciled to their genders, harboring fear and hostility toward the opposite sex, incapable of mature love, and doomed to unhealthy relationships. I had assumed they must be correct. In misery and fear, I realized that I had just cast myself out of the garden.

Within days I fully acknowledged to myself that I was irredeemably in love with a woman and there was nothing to do but tough it out. The world is not interested in the complexities of one's romantic or sexual inclinations, so there was no use trying to split bisexual hairs about the fact that all of my prior relationships were with men. My life would be with a woman and that made us lesbians. But I had never met, read about, or even heard of a lesbian psychoanalyst, much less a respected one. The American Psychological Association and The American Psychiatric Association had by that time already recognized homosexuality as a normal variant of adult sexuality, but psychoanalysis has historically seen itself as more sophisticated than the rest of the mental health profession. The thought of self-important purveyors of neo-Freudian dogma reducing my life, love, home, and dreams to a sexual perversion or an infantile state of development was both infuriating and unbearable.

It was awfully hard deciding what to wear. When you are subjected to societal oppression, you are forced to construct an identity around it in order to survive. My first few forays into lesbian feminist circles of that era had introduced me to the tyranny of political correctness, complete with dress code. Eschewing the bondage of patriarchy meant no heels, no makeup, no skirts, no frills, and no style. I wore this uniform to my psychoanalytic seminars as a show of solidarity with sisters to whom I'd barely introduced myself. It didn't help that I simultaneously stopped smoking and gained twenty pounds, making me feel like comedian Robin Williams's quip that a lesbian is "just a large woman in comfortable shoes." At the same time, weary of feeling defiantly unattractive, I found myself purchasing some of the most beautiful and expensive clothes I had ever owned—soft draping silks in stunning prints with flowing skirts. In sartorial schizophrenia, I'd break stride with lesbian feminism and appear in splendor, eliciting "oohs" of approval from classmates that only deepened my discomfort. No matter what I wore I felt I was in drag.

As a heterosexual, I had basked in the liberal, self-congratulatory benevolence which comes easily to those in dominant power groups. Now, the heterosexual planet appeared very different, viewed from my freefall in the outerspace of a marginal subculture. Being a lesbian lent a different cast to the smallest acts of life. Suddenly categorized by my sexuality, I squirmed to think that even while I spoke about politics or the weather, people were trying to envision my sex practices. (Some later admitted they *were*.) The same things I'd done or talked about when I'd been involved with a man—going away for the weekend, shopping for a bedroom set, going out dancing—now seemed disturbing to people when I indicated that I did them with a woman. Simply signing a greeting card from both of us was tantamount to a brazen declaration—"flaunting," some called it. Many times a day I had to search for the courage to be honest, wrestling with fear and enervation.

As much as the world overemphasized the sexual content of my new life, it also ignored the seriousness of my relationship. Relatives and friends would "forget" to invite my spouse to an event, and had to be repeatedly, politely reminded that we were fully tenured partners in life. Paperwork forms asked me to identify myself as "Married," "Single," "Widowed," or

"Divorced." There was no category "Deeply committed to soulmate, legally prohibited from marrying."

Little offhand things I'd said in all good will to gay and lesbian patients over the previous years now revealed their subtle heterosexist underpinnings—the "compassionate" and subtly demeaning view I'd had of a gay man's sexual practices, the pursuit of dynamics that could have "caused" a lesbian's sexual orientation. How casually I'd assumed that heterosexual life was more natural, healthy, easy, mature, without ever thinking I was prejudiced. How arrogant I'd been to assume that I was equipped to help people whose experience, until now, had no parallel in my own. How many important questions I'd failed to ask, issues I'd failed to raise, options I'd failed to offer, because I had no frame of reference in which to formulate them.

These were errors that reflected not just our society's pervasive homonegativity, but also the hubris of psychoanalysis itself. One of my teachers stated emphatically that any well-trained analyst should be able to effectively treat any patient, regardless of gender, personality, style, or any other factor. The assumption that psychoanalytic inquiry was "pure," unaffected by the belief system of the analyst, was pervasive at the time (and still holds sway in many quarters). It was paralleled by the belief that our conceptualization of the self and its development rested on something "scientific," and was therefore immune to the political and social tides of the era. As is the nature of orthodoxies of all persuasions, those who questioned whether the Emperor wore clothes were considered beings whose sight had not fully evolved.

I was not the only lesbian in my training program, but it would be another decade before I knew that. (I have since met others, some of whom are still afraid to have their orientations known by colleagues who could demean them or hurt their careers.) As the lone visible representative of homosexualities, I found myself a reluctant but obvious spokesperson. Gay issues came up in class, and I tried to convey what I was learning through my leap of circumstance. Intellectual debates about theories of homosexuality ensued, for which I often felt ill-equipped. A colleague pressed, "Don't be offended, but . . . how do you know you *don't* have a disorder?" It was clear to me that I did not have the high ground in discussions of whether people like me were fully human.

One colleague boasted grandly that due to his sterling efforts his lesbian patient had decided to embrace heterosexuality. Today, I would challenge him immediately, armed as I now am with the research and writings of scholars of the last decade, and having treated many refugees from analyses which had persuaded them that renouncing their homoerotic desires would gain them both mental health and their analysts's respect. At the time, though, I just sat speechless and impotent. None of the other analysts in the room took issue with him.

A few years later, I approached the head of my training program about the possibility of offering a course on gay and lesbian issues in treatment. He was one of my most loving supporters and thought the course a good idea, but told me frankly, "They won't sign up for it. They don't feel they need it. We know that already from their response to ethnic minority issues."

Gradually I came to understand that my experience as a lesbian, far from endowing me with some authority, was a fact that served to discredit any opinions I had on the subject of homosexuality. "Well, of course you would say that," someone retorted, as if my personal investment in supporting gays and lesbians completely obliterated the knowledge on which my views were based. Heterosexuals, however, can apparently uphold the supremacy of heterosexuality without self-interest clouding their vision.

On a social level, there was the embarrassed and awkward silence when I inserted mention of my life partner into conversations about my colleagues' husbands and wives. It was as if I'd just brought up my family shame in polite company. Not long ago a lesbian student approached me at a meeting. She was, at that time, a candidate at a psychoanalytic institute where, several years prior, I had taught and supervised. She said, "They used you in one of my classes as an example of the most inappropriate case of self-disclosure they had ever encountered." The incident reported was that when I was pregnant with my first child, I revealed to the group of analysts I was supervising that I was actually expecting two children because my lover was pregnant as well. This student's class unanimously agreed that it was obscenely improper of me to have revealed my situation. The saddest part of this story, besides having the joyful creation of my family reduced to an unmentionable, is that the (closeted) lesbian therapist felt she had to concur for her own professional safety.

As open as I was, when our first two children were born I felt too vulnerable to put a notice in my institute's newsletter. Neither did I turn to this community for solace when our son died some months later. Those few who reached out to me despite my withdrawal have my undying gratitude. By our third child's birth I summoned my courage and it appeared in print with the other birth announcements of that issue.

Thankfully, the isolation of those years has largely ended—at least for me. Lesbian, gay, and bisexual analysts and therapists have created a significant network of support and intellectual stimulation. Heterosexual analysts, who for years were absent when my gay or lesbian colleagues and I gave talks and workshops, are now filling out the audience. People no longer blink as we trade stories about our children's adolescent trials and where they go to school. My wardrobe probably still betrays a lack of cohesiveness, but consistency may not be as important as I once thought it was. I can't say I feel safe in psychoanalytic circles in general because veiled—and even overt—prejudice is still rampant. But I no longer feel totally alone, and I can manage with that.

Unfortunately not everyone is so lucky, and fear is still a realistic and palpable presence for many in my profession. I know closeted gay and lesbian analysts who expect to be ruined if someone finds out. Some of them hate themselves. Some lie to their analysts. Many do nothing to contradict supervisors who presume their heterosexuality, and join in affirming its superiority. They may avoid presenting gay patients in conferences or supervision for fear of revealing the things that their knowledge and compassion leads them to say in sessions. Or they may work clinically in ways that are emotionally distant—in the guise of analytic neutrality—so that even their gay and lesbian patients will not discover their secret. The climate of the field continues to discourage psychoanalysts from coming out, perpetuating invisibility and isolation.

Paradoxically, one of the most maddening criticisms I hear as an activist for lesbian and gay issues is that there is no prejudice in this field. Those of us who attempt to express the frustrations of heterosexism, a need for support, or the desire to change homonegative language and precepts in teachings are often portrayed as mad soldiers hurling grenades at phantom enemies. "It was only ever a tiny minority," we're told, "none of the rest of us has ever felt there's anything wrong with someone being homosexual." At one time, my voice might even have been among theirs. Now I know better.

Meanwhile, my respect for the metaphors of psychoanalysis has deepened over the years, even as my dismay at its limitations and rigidities has increased. Psychoanalytic models come closer than anything else in the mental health field to addressing the poetry of the soul. They provide imagery and language that seeks access to the most private realms of human pain and joy. Without such imagery, we might be limited to recitations of behavioral symptoms and improvement, and miss opportunities for healing on a deeper level.

This is a time in world history when movements toward orthodoxy are gaining ground. The existential sufferings of uncertain life and certain death have created a hunger for easy truths. I am hopeful, however, that psychoanalysis may be outgrowing its defensive reliance on dogmatic assertions. We know more than we ever did about cultural diversity in general, and the roles that power, prejudice, and politics play in the psyche. I look forward to the creative ways in which psychoanalysis will embrace this knowledge as it moves forward into the next century.

Part 4

Conclusion

16

The Shaping of Psychoanalytic Theory and Practice by Cultural and Personal Biases About Sexuality

Mark J. Blechner

THIS BOOK IS THE RESULT OF an extraordinary conference—"Perspectives on Homosexuality: An Open Dialogue"—which took place at New York University on December 4, 1993. The conference was a special event for many reasons. It brought together heterosexual and homosexual psychoanalysts to discuss sexuality with each other. It included both gay and lesbian analysts, which went against the previous tendency of psychoanalysis giving disproportionate attention to homosexuality in men. It included psychoanalysts of many different schools. Finally, it culminated in a sense that the meeting had been illuminating and educational, and that there was hope that psychoanalysis could escape from the tradition of anti-homosexual prejudice that has marred much of its history. The organizers of the conference, Drs. Lesser and Domenici, accomplished a major feat in bringing together such a disparate group and having it work out so productively.

All of the speakers at "the Conference" (as I will refer to it) are included in the present collection, with the exception of Richard Lasky, who declined to have his paper published. There are also several additional papers which were written after the Conference. The task of discussing such a wealth of material is not an easy one. It would be impossible in the space available to respond in detail to so many varied viewpoints on so many topics. Rather than try to achieve the impossible, I am going to focus on several significant issues raised by the papers. These include: 1) the special issues of development of the gay and lesbian in a homophobic and heterosexist society; 2) the misunderstanding and misinterpretation of this experience by many psychoanalysts, and some possible correctives; 3) the relation of sexual orientation and gender identity; 4) the role of language, culture, empirical data, and biology in these issues; 5) how psychoanalytic theory and practice are related to the mores and taboos of the culture, with special attention to the related histories of psychoanalytic attitudes towards women and towards homosexuality; 6) the different forms of hatred, bias, and ignorance in the psychoanalytic treatment of homosexuals; and 7) some alternative directions that psychoanalytic theory and practice might take in the future.

We all know the French saying: "Plus ça change, plus c'est la même chose. (The more things change, the more they stay the same.)" I think that the inverse of this saying is also true and important for a consideration of psychoanalysis and homosexuality: "The more things *don't* change, the more they *don't* stay the same." This adage applies to many areas of life, certainly, for example, to love relationships, where stasis and rigidity do not usually lead to stability. It also applies to psychoanalysis. In the brief hundred years that psychoanalysis has existed, we have seen how many previously held assumptions look questionable, misguided, or false in light of our retrospective awareness of the quirks in our culture. Freud's daring in his time to talk to the teenage Dora about sexuality today seems to miss the point; now many of us see his lack of inquiry into the corrupt dynamics of Dora's family and his collusion with the agenda of Dora's father as more problematic than her supposed internal struggles with sexuality. We may blanch today when we hear about the many hours and dollars spent on helping women graduate from clitoral to vaginal orgasms through psychoanalytic treatment in the years before Masters and Johnson. And many of us feel shame and embarrassment when we learn that in the nineteenth century there was an accepted psychiatric diagnosis of drapetomania (Cartwright 1851/1981; see also Wakefield 1992) which was the pathological wish of a slave to gain his freedom. No doubt in a hundred years our great-grandchildren will experience those same uneasy feelings when they analyze how we are trapped by the axioms of our culture and how we derive from them what we naively consider to be scientific principles of human psychic functioning.

In his views of sexuality, Freud was at the vanguard of radical thinking, breaking many of the prudish conventions of his time. Over the years, however, American psychoanalysis has become, more and more, the voice of conservatism. Psychoanalysis today tends to follow the culture rather than lead it progressively as it once did. One important exception to this conservatism are some of the very forward-looking papers assembled in this book; another exception has come from some feminist psychoanalysts, who have placed themselves on the cutting edge of psychoanalysis by radically criticizing, from within the field, the prevalent male, heterosexual assumptions. This ferment of ideas has already led to changes in our thinking, not only about sex, gender, sexuality, and sexual orientation but about our fundamental assumptions, including the role of mothering in development and the unfolding of object relations. At the forefront of this reconsideration are several colleagues at New York University, including Jessica Benjamin, Muriel Dimen, Virginia Goldner, Adrienne Harris, and Sue Shapiro. Their reformulation of psychoanalytic thinking brings with it not only the fresh vantage point of feminism, but also the insights of disciplines from outside parochial psychoanalysis, including anthropology, sociology, and philosophy.

The more psychoanalysis includes people from different viewpoints and different backgrounds, the more vital it will be, and the more it will safeguard itself from misguided conclusions. Adolf Grünbaum's (1993) recent book, *Validation in the Clinical Theory of Psychoanalysis*, rightly criticizes organized psychoanalysis for its lack of rigorous hypothesis-testing, and its mixing up of causation and correlation. We know how often in our field such possible misreadings of causality have long gone unquestioned. In the field of schizophrenia, for example, the concept of the schizophrenogenic mother held sway for a long time, with the idea that a mother's behavior caused her child's schizophrenia—a terrible burden of blame that should not be dispensed without the greatest certainty. It took a long time for the alternative hypothesis to be given equal consideration—namely, that having a schizophrenic child might shape a mother's behavior (Blechner 1995).

A similar, possible misreading of data may have taken place in the psychoanalytic understanding of parenting patterns and homosexuality. Goldsmith (1992; see also Isay 1989) has analyzed the long-held psychoanalytic notion that a parental pattern of a domineering mother and an absent or passive father lead to a son's becoming gay. Let's ignore for the moment the fact that this pattern was observed primarily in gay *patients*, who are not a representative sample of gay men in general. Goldsmith points out that with those gay patients where this pattern does exist, the child's homosexuality could be *causing* the pattern of relationships with the parents, rather than the parental pattern causing the homosexuality. He proposes that the father's distance may be caused by his discomfort with his son's sexuality that he senses, perhaps unconsciously. The mother, in her turn, may act in a way that takes for granted a certain eroticism between herself and her son, which a straight[12] son might experience as an enjoyable, reciprocal flirtation; a gay son, however, may experience the same behavior as intrusive and domineering because it is not reciprocated.

An empirical test of these very different hypotheses remains to be done. But it shows the significance of getting varied viewpoints into our psychoanalytic discourse. On the topic of homosexuality, the garnering of alternative, experience-near viewpoints has been hampered by the exclusion of lesbians and gays from the psychoanalytic establishment. It's not enough to say concerning prejudice in psychoanalytic institutes, as Richard Lasky did at the Conference, that "some do and some don't." This is an example of what Drescher (1992) calls psychoanalytic coyness on the subject of homosexuality. More truthful is that *most* psychoanalytic institutes do discriminate, and some, if any, don't. Or perhaps, all do, but some do it less than others, as Drescher illustrates. Even if they admit open gays and lesbians for training, most major institutes, Freudian or not, do not promote them very far after graduation. Bertram Schaffner's experiences (see Goldman, in this volume) as an openly gay analyst for the last half century are a moving account of courage, integrity, and the struggle against external and internalized homophobia. Schaffner was promoted to the position of Supervising Analyst at the William Alanson White Institute only in 1993, at the age of 81. To my knowledge, no openly gay analyst been made a training analyst at a major American psychoanalytic institute.

Dimen (in this volume) tells us of the gay man who, upon hearing Hamer's results about a possible genetic cause of homosexuality, tells an interviewer, "I'm not gay because my parents did anything wrong." Dimen writes, "There was no blame, no right, no wrong, just a natural fact. Just the facts, ma'am. No emotion." Of course, she is right that underneath the manifest wish for "just the facts," there probably was a great deal of emotion. There was the emotion of guilt, and a desperate search for relief from guilt. This man had probably endured the same self-hating questioning that most gay men and lesbians go through when they realize that their sexuality—which is something that can have as much of a feeling of "true-self" as one can imagine and can be one of the great pleasures in their lives—is labeled wrong, sick, bad, hateful, sinful, pathological, and dangerous. Gays and lesbians hear this from society, and, more often than not, their parents tell them the same story. Usually, the children of ethnic, racial, and religious minorities can counter the hateful image projected onto them by society with the loving "reflected appraisals" they receive from their parents and families. Most lesbians and gay men do not even have that parental support growing up. As Rutkin astutely points out, is it any surprise that many gays and lesbians learn to be secretive, and might harbor a wish to be straight?

This poses a very important clinical problem for analysts. We all know how risky and complicated it can be for an analyst to set a therapeutic goal that is different from the patient's. Yet at the same time, there are some therapeutic goals that at least deserve thorough scrutiny, and among those especially is the wish on the part of the analysand to change something essential about his or her nature that is the target of irrational hatred by significant others. For years psychoanalysts offered gay patients the prospect that they could change their sexual orientation if they wanted to. Many of those analysts cannot be faulted; they were taught that such change was possible and desirable. Many of them meant well, and, keeping in mind Hartmann's concept of adaptation, thought they were helping their patients to survive best in the world that existed. And sometimes they were able to get gay and lesbian patients to have heterosexual experiences, sometimes even to marry and have children. The patients terminated therapy, and the analysts thought that they had achieved their goals and went on trying to achieve them with other gay and lesbian patients.

The trouble with such treatments often did not appear fully until after termination, although there may have been signs before (Blechner 1993). For gay men and lesbians who have grown up with parents who are homophobic, the dangers are enormous of re-enacting in the analysis the relationship of trying to develop a false, straight self that will please the straight parent/analyst. And by the time the patient realizes that this has happened, the analysis may be terminated, and a spouse and children must share the suffering. The patient may be unwilling to expend any further fees in order to inform his former analyst of his pain, and so the analyst continues with the illusion that the case went well and that his or her therapeutic agenda was helpful.

Today the world has changed, and what was once considered optimal is, for many patients, a painful and destructive compromise. In recent years, a number of case reports (Blechner 1993, 1994a) have been published in which the analyst claims to the patient to be neutral or accepting of homosexuality or to have no agenda to change the patient's sexuality, but the lines of interpretation indicate an obvious attempt by the analyst, perhaps unconsciously, to influence the patient toward heterosexual behavior. This adds a level of mystification and a double-bind to the treatment that is, in some ways, more problematic than the older reported cases in which the analyst was open and aware of his agenda to change the patient's sexuality.

I cannot overemphasize Rutkin's excellent point that an analyst must become aware of his prejudices and resolve them. An analyst who has not worked out his own homophobia cannot help a patient work through his own internalized homophobia. If you are a predominantly straight analyst, you must make a special effort to understand how your gay and lesbian patients experience their homosexuality and its role in their lives, and not to project onto them your own reactions to your homosexual feelings. Verghese (1994) has coined the term "homo-ignorance," which effectively characterizes many heterosexuals' lack of simple knowledge about homosexuality. We may all be more alike than different, but our differences may be very important and hard to comprehend. If you want to understand this, read first-person accounts of treatment histories, such as Martin Duberman's *Cures* (1991), or Paul Monette's *Becoming a Man* (1992). They make clear the agony of coming out and the sense of wasted time, money, and life in trying to change one's sexual orientation according to someone else's view of it.

Also, I would ask straight and married people to try an experiment: For one month, do not ever mention your husband or wife or your children in conversation with anyone. When you describe an experience that you shared with your spouse, tell of it as if you did it alone. Always say "I," even when you mean "we." These things are all done by gay men and lesbians who must keep their homosexuality hidden. I know straight people who have gone through this exercise and been astonished at how debilitating it is—to one's sense of self, reality, integrity, honesty, and cohesion. We may ask how it is that anyone who does this day in and day out, not for just one month, but for years, for a lifetime can manage not to have a feeling of loss of self, of false self.

When considering psychoanalytic writing about homosexuality, it is beneficial to try the test of "bias reversal" (Blechner 1993) to assess whether the statements are prejudicial. Try transposing the words "homosexual" and "heterosexual," and change the sexes of the people with whom the patient was involved. For example, consider the following:

> Dr. D's heterosexuality, not deeply entrenched, served mainly to ensure that

> her partner's emerging sexuality would not lead to a homosexual interest. Dr. D's idealization of her partner was partially a defense against an awareness of feelings of deprivation and the hatred of her father for failing to respond adequately to her developmental needs. . . . Her heterosexuality also served as a defense against incestuous wishes toward her mother. . . . During early adulthood, however, partly motivated by differing professional interests that involved some increased separateness from her husband and partly motivated by Dr. D's wish to experiment with homosexuality, she again made a tentative effort to resume her individuation, and she took a trip with a casual female acquaintance. Shortly thereafter, her husband abandoned her for another heterosexual relationship.

Ask yourself: How do you feel about the formulation of this case? About its clinical "success?" Would you have proceeded in the same way?

This clinical vignette comes from Hanna (1992). I have transposed the words homosexual and heterosexual, and changed the sexes of the people with whom the patient was involved. In the original reported case, the patient shifts from a deep lesbian involvement. The original text went as follows (Hanna 1992, 375–76):

> Dr. D's homosexuality, not deeply entrenched, served mainly to ensure her that her partner's emerging sexuality would not lead to a heterosexual interest. Dr. D's idealization of her partner was partially a defense against an awareness of feelings of deprivation and the hatred of her mother for failing to respond adequately to her developmental needs. . . . Her homosexuality also served as a defense against incestuous wishes toward her father. . . . During early adulthood, however, partly motivated by differing professional interests that involved at least some increased separateness from her partner and partly motivated by Dr. D's wish to experiment with heterosexuality, she again made a tentative effort to resume her individuation, and she took a trip with a casual male acquaintance. Shortly thereafter, her partner abandoned her for another lesbian relationship.

Most heterosexual analysts find the transposed version to be bizarre but have little trouble with Hanna's original version, and this indicates their bias. (Interestingly, lesbian analysts Magee and Miller have told me that when they read the reversed version, they thought, "That's an interesting formulation!") If you cannot consider heterosexual and homosexual activity and ideation to have equivalent potentials to be defensive or expressive of desire, then you cannot consider yourself neutral.

As society changes, as open gays and lesbians provide positive role models, adult gay men and lesbians increasingly are aware enough not to seek treatment from analysts who are either homophobic or insensitive to their experiences, and are better able to realize when this is true and get out of a potentially destructive treatment. For most adolescents, however, that is not the case. Every clinician should think seriously about the following questions: When you are consulted by parents upset about their teenager's homosexuality, what do you do? Do you agree to see the teenager for treatment of his or her homosexuality? How seriously do you question why the parent has condemnatory attitudes? Is the problem the child's homosexuality or the parent's homophobia?

All gay and lesbian analysts must appreciate Roy Schafer's candor about the biased clinical approach still prevalent among most psychoanalytic clinicians. Schafer writes: "I believe that, by and large, it is still that way in the analytic treatment of the great majority of patients. Heterosexual tendencies are taken for granted; it is conflict over them that is to be examined, understood, and reduced. In contrast, homosexual tendencies are considered central to psychological problems, and it is the temptation to act on them in fact or fantasy that is to be examined, understood, and reduced." A survey (MacIntosh 1994) of members of the American Psychoanalytic Association found that 97.6% do not believe that "homosexual patients can and should change to heterosexuality." Yet 34.4% believe that "most other analysts think homosexual patients can and should change to heterosexuality." This extraordinary statistic could be interpreted as a divergence between what psychoanalysts think and do. However, the letter that accompanied the survey was very directive in its implications and defensive of the profession against charges of prejudice, so it is hardly surprising that most respondents disavowed prejudice and a wish to change a patient's sexual orientation on their own part. But given the reality of psychoanalytic practice, it is not surprising, either, that most thought prejudice against homosexuality rampant among their colleagues.

Unfortunately, the level of mistreatment of gays and lesbians by mainstream psychiatry continues. A man in his mid-thirties was referred to me for psychotherapy. When he was eighteen, he went away to college and found that he was sexually attracted only to men, a fact that he had suspected but tried to ignore during high school. He knew that his religious family would disapprove of his homosexuality, and so he became extremely anxious about it. On a vacation, he returned home. His father noticed his agitation, and asked him what was bothering him. He blurted out to his father that he was gay. The family sent him to an analyst immediately. When the patient tried to bring up his homosexuality, the analyst said,

"Well, of course, doing things with girls is fun." As you can imagine, the patient was not encouraged to tell this man more. Instead, he retreated more into himself. He was hospitalized for two weeks with electro-shock treatments every other day. This had no effect on his sexual orientation, but it certainly taught him to beware of the homophobia in his parents, in psychiatry, and in society in general. He waited a dozen years to seek psychotherapy, and did so only when he could be sure to find an analyst who was openly gay himself.

I'd like to say that this was a freak, aberrant case from the bad old days of the McCarthy era. But the hospitalization with ECT occurred about fifteen years ago in a major metropolitan center, after the landmark deletion of homosexuality from the DSM. And while this is the only such case I have seen personally, I have since heard about a number of people who also were hospitalized and given ECT for their homosexuality within the last two decades. It was an important moment at The Conference when an analyst, Dr. Rita Frankiel, spoke from the audience, saying, "We analysts have to admit that we have committed atrocities on our homosexual patients." This was the first time I have heard a presumably heterosexual analyst make such a statement, although Isay (1989) and I have been saying so for years.

Frommer (1994) and Rutkin (chapter 10, this volume) discuss the serious countertransference problems of the psychoanalyst's own homophobia, a topic that has received shockingly little attention in the psychoanalytic literature, probably because of that very homophobic countertransference (but see Blechner 1992; Frommer 1994; Kwawer 1980; Mitchell 1978, 1981). Lee Crespi (chapter 1, this voume) addresses the issue of countertransference in a more global manner. It becomes apparent that values of the analyst—his or her conception of mental health, the good life, and psychopathology—profoundly influence his or her work. This has never been addressed enough in theory, although Hartmann made an important contribution, as noted by Schafer, and so did Fromm (1941). Lesser's clinical case (chapter 4, this volume) is a poignant example of an analyst coming to recognize the contribution of her own value system to defining the patient's psychopathology and the critical counteranxiety involved when a patient's way of living brings into question the validity and soundness of the analyst's own life decisions. Such questions also are too rarely addressed in the analytic literature. They have been more forthrightly addressed by artists like Ibsen (*The Wild Duck*) and Ingmar Bergmann (*Face to Face*). It is important to reiterate that the analyst can never do his or her work aside from his or her value system, and that a good match in analysis may call for the analyst's and patient's value systems to be relatively close (but not too close). The distance between them on any issue may profoundly influence the working alliance, which will also be affected by their relative differences from the prevalent belief systems of the society in which they reside.

Several writers on sexuality within psychoanalysis have declared an ardent adherence to "social constructionism" (which Paul Monette [1994] refers to as "new inventionism") and to post-modernism. We have seen over the years a gradual retreat in psychoanalysis from realism or even critical realism as an epistemological position toward phenomenalism and intersubjectivity. There is much merit to analysts' using this epistemological shift to make themselves more respectful and open-minded about what their patients believe. But I think this epistemological shift is also partly a symptom—it is a symptom of the years of psychoanalytic aversion to relatively objective data collection, and of scorn and hostility toward the data collected by non-psychoanalysts which challenged long-held beliefs of many psychoanalysts. Analysts have held many wrong conclusions that were untested and were destructive to patients. These errors were then compounded when the same analysts met their patients' protests with cries of resistance. The fault lies not in our epistemology but in our ignorance.

While I think many analysts have been too sure that their erroneous beliefs and prejudices were facts, I do not agree that the solution is to encourage a lack of empiricism and a supreme reliance on intersubjectivity and social constructionism. In my view, this trend in psychoanalytic thinking is an unfortunate by-product of the lack of scientific empiricism among psychoanalysts. Grünbaum (1984, 1993) has brilliantly addressed this lack of empiricism, and psychoanalysis has by and large not met his challenge to prove or disprove empirically the logical predictions of data trends that Grünbaum identifies.

The history of psychoanalysis and homosexuality is proof that empirical data are critical, and that analysis of intersubjectivity will not necessarily prevent a treatment from veering off into a collusion that is destructive to the patient. Many of the contributors to this volume have decried the waste of time, money, and enjoyment of life caused by analyses aimed at converting gays and lesbians to heterosexuality, and the consequent damage done to such patient's lives and the lives of their families. But it must be remembered that in many cases, such treatments were sought voluntarily. Gays and lesbians in the 1950s and '60s were brought up with the same prejudices as their homophobic analysts. An intersubjective approach would not solve this problem, since both patient and analyst shared similar internalized prejudices. We can see in the one hundred years of psychoanalytic history that many cultural mores were translated into views of psychopathology, and, in most cases, empirical studies were crucial in altering long-standing misconceptions.

The pattern is as follows: There is a cultural factor that leads to great unhappiness in certain persons. Neither the patient nor the analyst is aware of the effect of the cultural factor, and both look for the cause of the unhappiness in intrapsychic factors. Such work continues until a mixture of cultural change, political action, and a shift in scientific research lead to a shift in the understanding of the culture. Usually a factual discovery becomes the fulcrum for such change, although there is often a considerable time lag between the first publication of the discovery and the realization of its impact. For women's sexuality, Masters and Johnson's (1966) landmark research into sexual responsiveness helped revoke outdated psychoanalytic misconceptions. For gay men and lesbians, it was the important discoveries of Kinsey, et al. (1948) of the frequency of homosexual experience and bisexual practice in a surprisingly large segment of the American population. This was followed by Evelyn Hooker's (1957) remarkable study showing that gay men were indistinguishable from straight men when their Rorschach protocols were compared by experts, and that there were no differences in the level of psychopathology between the two groups.

Analysts often support their beliefs by reference to clinical experience, saying things like, "I have observed in my clinical practice. . . ." But the act of "observing" is often one of uncontrolled confirmation of specious beliefs. There is a tendency for psychoanalysts to find what they are looking for, and a fear and resistance to scientific findings that challenge commonly held beliefs of psychoanalysts. The studies which I have mentioned—Kinsey, Masters and Johnson, and Hooker—were all fought by psychoanalysts in varying degrees, and the records of their objections to the data are embarrassing to read (see Lewes 1988). Yet when organized psychiatry determines what is or is not psychopathology, such empirical findings are critical (see Bayer 1981).

One form of empiricism that seems excessively dismissed is biological data. To discuss such issues adequately, we should have biologists contributing to this book. But since biology has been mentioned so much, I must say something about it. I personally bristle when any psychoanalyst attempts to exclude biological considerations (or the findings of any field) by fiat. Such parochialism can only impoverish our theory and practice. Freud did pay attention to biology, but he did not know what we know today, so many of his biologically-based views are out of date or wrong. The solution is not to exclude biological considerations, but to update them. For example, the question has been raised of the normality or desirability of homosexuality from an evolutionary perspective, since homosexuality generally does not lead to procreation. This stereotype is changing quickly; many gay men and lesbians today are fathers and mothers. Even so, if we accept the notion that homosexual *acts* do not lead to procreation, what then? Does that therefore mean that homosexuality is not conducive to the propagation of the species? The answer is far from the simple "yes" that Freud and some of the contributors to this book have presumed.

Sociobiologists have given a good amount of consideration to this question, and conclude generally that behavior that does not foster baby-making may still foster the propagation of the species. Homosexual behavior seems to have existed throughout human history, in all cultures, as well as in animal species. Biologists are discovering homosexual behavior in ever increasing numbers of species, including nonhuman primates, female pigeons, and male octopi. It is only with great arrogance that we can leap from the notion of primary optimal reproductive fitness on an individual level to optimal fitness of a group, of a species, indeed of an entire ecosphere. Trivers (1974; see also Wilson 1975) has proposed that homosexuals have often filled special functions in society, which, while not directly reproductive, have greatly enhanced the social group, and this leads to maintenance of the genetic loading that causes such organisms to appear as homosexual some percentage of the time. It may also be that in our current world, where overpopulation is causing problems of survival, a gene favoring homosexuality might actually be sustained because of its usefulness in regulating reproduction and in controlling overcrowding and scarcity of resources.

The incorporation of empirical data into psychoanalytic thinking is not incompatible with the deconstruction of language and terminology; in my view, they are equally necessary. I am in agreement with Schafer, Schwartz, and others that psychoanalytic thinking, indeed human thinking, is excessively reliant on binary categories (Blechner 1994b). We have to admit that the polarization of sexual orientation and the common tendency to equate gender identity with sexual orientation lead to a limitation in our thinking about sexuality and gender. Yet it is very difficult for humans not to fall into binary categorizations. Indeed, neurobiologists, such as Edelman (1987), have suggested that binary categorizations may be wired into our brains. The words in Schafer's title, "Non-normative" sexual practices, create a new binary—normative and non-normative—that is similar to the more familiar "normal" and "abnormal," but less pejorative. And his phrase "nonconformist practices" suggests another binary of "nonconformist/conformist." I think this constant cropping up of binaries, even by so thoughtful a writer as Schafer in a chapter in which he is questioning our reliance on binaries, shows how they pervade human thinking.

What sexual practices are normative, we may ask? This has changed over time—whereas oral sex was once seen as a perversion, today in America it is seen as normal, although its practice is different in different subcultures. Whereas much of the population continues to consider anal sex perverted or non-normative, in some parts of American society, 19% of women have practiced anal sex (Jamott 1994). Does normative mean most people do it? More than 50%?

Like Schafer, Schwartz, Domenici, and other contributors to this volume, the great sex researcher Alfred Kinsey was also opposed to excessive reliance on binary categories. He wrote:

> The world is not to be divided into sheep and goats. Not all things are black nor are all things white. It is a fundamental taxonomy that nature rarely deals with discrete categories and tries to force facts into separate pigeonholes. The sooner we learn this concerning human sexual behavior, the sooner we shall reach a sound understanding of the realities of sex. (Kinsey, et al. 1948, 65)

Kinsey was able to avoid strict binaries in his seven-point scale of sexual orientation which depends on the relative frequencies of homosexual and heterosexual relations as well as dreams and waking fantasies (Kinsey, et al. 1948; see also Meijer 1993). Yet the gradations that Kinsey identified rarely are incorporated into psychoanalytic discourse. It remains to be determined whether this is because Kinsey did not assign words to the seven points on his scale, and thus they are not memorable, because of a rigid adherence to binary categories, or because of some other reason.

Since dichotomies are so pervasive in our language and thought, it becomes especially significant to note where human language has avoided binaries. In relation to the present topic, it has always impressed me that the English language contains the word "effeminacy," which Webster's Seventh defines as: "having unsuitable feminine qualities; marked by weakness and love of ease." This is a word without a binary. There is no masculine equivalent, i.e., a word meaning "having unsuitable masculine qualities." This may well be because in our society there is no such thing as masculine behavior that is deemed "unsuitable."

Another notable lack of a binary occurs with the term "bisexuality." Money (1988, 191) has pointed out that the antonym of "bisexuality" is "monosexuality." Yet almost no one uses the term "monosexual." Note though, that once we have such a term in mind, it is possible to problematize it and pathologize it. While no commonly used diagnostic system that I know of includes monosexuality as a pathological category (although several have pathologized "exclusive homosexuality"), Lesser's case example and Schoenberg's discussion (both herein) suggest the possibility of pathologizing monosexuality as much as bisexuality.

Several authors in this volume, including Domenici and Schwartz, have highlighted the fact that gender identity and sexual orientation are not coterminous. Scientists have clearly shown that there is a correlation between atypical gender identity and homosexuality. That is, boys who show types of behavior considered feminine tend to become homosexual adults, and girls who show types of behavior considered masculine tend to become lesbian adults. However, the correlation is far from perfect, and, more importantly, correlation is not causation. If it were true that most feminine boys become homosexual adults, that would not mean that most homosexual adults were feminine as boys.

We have, actually, at least three factors to contend with in the complicated gender/sexual orientation matrix. We have: 1) the anatomical sexes of the couple; 2) the *perceived* gender identity of the person; i.e., is he or she seen by others as masculine or feminine? 3) the *felt* gender identity of the individual. This may or may not match the perceived gender identity of the individual. An example is the male transvestite whose preferred sexual partner is a woman. Many such men are married and seem, to the outside observer, to be conventionally heterosexual. Yet they find it sexually fulfilling to dress up in a woman's clothes. Anatomically, this coupling looks heterosexual—an anatomical male copulating with an anatomical female. Some male transvestites still feel like men when dressed in women's clothes, but some do not. If a transvestite feels psychologically like a woman while dressed in a woman's clothes, is he then a psychological lesbian?

On the other hand, there exists among some lesbians a division of butch/femme (Butler 1991; Case 1988–1989; Nestle 1984). This binary categorization is also capable of infinite variegation and can change over an individual's lifetime. Nevertheless, is a woman who considers herself primarily butch who makes love to a woman who is femme, enacting a psychologically heterosexual coupling while being anatomically homosexual?[2] We see thus that anatomical sexual orientation need not coincide with psychological sexual orientation. And it is not only in psychology that sexual identities are so variegated. We also have to contend with the fact that anatomical, genetic, and hormonal differences are by no means separated so neatly in nature as the term "opposite sex" would lead us to believe (see, for example, Fausto-Sterling 1992; Imperato-McGuinley, et al. 1974; Kinsey 1948; Money and Erhardt 1972; Money, et al. 1955).

The world continues to be exceedingly complex, regardless of whether our thought and language try to reduce it to manageable categories. The terms "heterosexual" and "homosexual," as currently used, lead us to pay inordinate attention to the anatomical sex of the sexual object. One could say that psychoanalysis, and many other segments of our culture, have fetishized sexual orientation, while neglecting other important dimensions of object choice. Probably, Freud's (1905) attention to the sex of the love object has led his followers to highlight that dimension. (I cannot say how much other analysts' clinical work also fetishizes the sex of the love object. Certainly, Freud [e.g. 1900, 286–288] paid attention to social class as an important dimension of object choice.) But actually, the choice of whether one is with someone of the same sex or another sex[3] is only one of the potentially important distinctions of object choice, and possibly not the most important one as far as the progress of life is concerned. Other distinctions of object choice are important, including age, social class, intelligence, race, religion, profession, sex behavior preference, and others. Historians of sexuality tell us that some of these categories were once much more important than gender. In ancient Greece, for example, it was commonplace for males to have sexual experiences with both men and women, but there was a taboo on sexual relations between the social classes in which a person of lower status penetrated someone of higher status (Halperin 1989).

How can we expand our language to provide a vocabulary that will allow us to think of important categories other than gender as significant? This is too great a topic to consider adequately here, but I will give one brief suggestion. Currently, the terms heterosexuality and homosexuality refer to the dimension of gender. I propose that, in the future, those terms always be given a modifying prefix. When used to refer to gender, therefore, we should henceforth refer to "gender-homosexuality" and "gender-heterosexuality." We can then also speak of "age-heterosexuality" to refer to sexual couplings between people of different age ranges, and "age-homosexuality" to couples closely matched in age. Similarly, we can then speak of "class-homosexuality," "race-heterosexuality," and so on. I invite the reader to consider the many other relevant dimensions.

Of course, the binaries hetero- and homo- also restrict our thinking. Do they highlight sameness and difference excessively? Certainly, they encourage us to think of sexual orientation and sexuality as dichotomous categories, mutually exclusive, and consistent over time. Instead, it might be useful to provide a vocabulary that allows for a description of fluidity over time, since the incidence of such fluidity is much more common than popular culture leads one to believe (Weinberg, et al. 1994).

One general concern I have about many of the chapters in this book is what I would call their Freud-centrism. Most are inordinately focused on the work of Freud and his cases. This is by no means a trend unique to this group of authors; it is a trend evident in most psychoanalytic writing. I am probably less concerned with the overrepresentation of Freud than with the underrepresentation of other important analysts who wrote about homosexuality. Especially important is Harry Stack Sullivan, the founder of interpersonal psychoanalysis, and himself a gay psychoanalyst. Sullivan's own homosexuality may have contributed to his being shunned by orthodox psychoanalysis, despite his obvious genius. His most famous clinical achievement, the ward for young schizophrenics at the Sheppard and Enoch Pratt Hospital, was also an extraordinary experiment on how the removal of prejudice, homophobic and otherwise, can have a very positive effect on severe psychopathology (Blechner 1995; Chatelaine 1981). As a psychiatrist for the military forces, Sullivan attempted to remove homosexuality as a disqualifying factor for admission to military service, although he was eventually overruled by the military establishment (Bérubé 1990). For his time, Sullivan was extremely resourceful about living a satisfactory life in a homophobic world. He adopted his lover, James, with whom he could then live without undue public opprobrium. Sullivan's theoretical work about homosexuality has not yet been adequately traced and conceptualized. He made poignant attempts at integrating his own experience with prevailing psychoanalytic conceptions of psychopathology and health.

For example, he postulated that the aim of "full genitality" could be achieved by gay men through the practice of mutual fellatio ("soixante-neuf") (Sullivan 1962, 181n; see also Sullivan 1953, 293). He also did not include homosexuality among the perversions, which, at the time, was a radical statement (Sullivan 1965).

Fairbairn is one of the few analysts besides Freud to be discussed extensively in this volume. Domenici, in a thoughtful, in-depth discussion, identifies Fairbairn as anti-homosexual. While this is plausible, Fairbairn's writings on homosexuality are, to my thinking, one of the most curious events in the history of psychoanalytic thinking about homosexuality. Fairbairn said homosexuality was psychopathic, not neurotic. Although this may sound pejorative, it was, in the strictest sense, true. The definition of psychopathy (a term which seems to be falling into disuse) is based on the accepted laws and customs of society as to what is acceptable behavior (see Slater and Roth 1969). Given that at the time homosexuality was a criminal offense in the British Empire (Weeks 1977), to commit homosexual acts was, strictly speaking, psychopathic. This points up how closely psychoanalytic concepts of psychopathology and the aims of cure are linked to the prevailing laws, customs, and trends in society.

Fairbairn suggested that homosexuals be segregated from the rest of society. Of course, such a forcible segregation sounds horrible to our ears today; but at the time, homosexuals faced prison or forcible treatment with hormones to curb their sexuality. The great mathematician, Alan Turing, who is one of the fathers of computer science and was crucial in helping England prevail in the Second World War by solving secret German codes, was arrested after the war for homosexuality and forced to take estrogen to curb his sexuality. He committed suicide (Hodges 1983).

Fairbairn argued that homosexuals be rehabilitated, not treated. In doing so, he was acknowledging that the problem of homosexuality was not intrinsic to the sexuality, but to the relationship between the individual and the bigoted society. Implicitly, Fairbairn was recognizing that the problem of the homosexual is anti-homosexual prejudice. He wrote:

> Basically, he [the homosexual] despises the standards of the community of which he falls foul, and resents the attitude adopted by this community towards him; and what he seeks at the hands of the community is not care, but reinstatement. (Fairbairn 1946, 293)

> What appears to be required, therefore, is the establishment of special communities for offenders—settlements with a group life of their own, in which offenders can participate, and which is psychologically controlled with a view to its gradual approximation to the life of the community at large. (294)

This was more than twenty years before the Stonewall uprising and the development of gay liberation. It is an odd mixture of prejudice and insight. Fairbairn identifies the main problem of the homosexual as the hatred and maltreatment of him by society. His solution—the establishment of special communities—is repugnant because it would be forced by society; but without the aspect of coercion, it is not so different from the ghettoization that any group that is a victim of prejudice adopts to minimize the experience of "otherness" and prejudice—not so different from what actually has happened in America since the Stonewall uprising. In large cities, gays and lesbians have formed their own communities, with their own support organizations that are fully supportive rather than just tolerant.

The progression of thought from Freud through Fairbairn and Sullivan to the writers in this volume suggests that there is an identifiable progression of psychoanalytic and psychiatric thinking about the psychopathology of groups that suffer prejudice (see Blechner 1992; White 1992). It starts with an acceptance of society's standards, and an identification of the distress and dysfunction of the individual as a problem inherent in the individual. Gradually (often too gradually), there is recognition that the individual may be suffering not from an inherent, intrapsychic neurosis, but from the persistent perversion of living caused by unbearable requirements of surviving societal oppression. There is then a second, intermediate stage in which some theorists identify this maltreatment, and a growing recognition that the individual's problems can be cured not by intrapsychic change, but rather by changing the individual's relation to society. Finally, there is the third stage, in which there is recognition that for the ultimate removal of psychopathology, society itself must change.

Countertransference has probably led analysts not to address homophobia in general as a problematic psychological issue (while other group hatreds, especially anti-semitism, have received much attention). Donald Moss (1992) has addressed this issue in an extraordinary article, entitled "Hating in the First Person Plural: The Example of Homophobia." He writes: "Except for clinical reports on the treatment of HIV-infected people, the professional psychoanalytic journals have maintained what seems like an active silence [about homophobia]. This silence seems active in large part because, within the discursive territory of psychoanalysis, no silence is ever presumed passive. This silence is also silent about itself, its determinants not yet publicly theorized." (280)

Analysts for the most part have not asked: Why do many straight people hate and fear gay men and lesbians? The answer is complex, and I cannot go into all the possibilities. The most obvious and frequently cited idea is that straight people are uncomfortable with their own homosexual feelings, and to that degree, protect against anxiety through hatred. Lasky (1989) has argued that some male analysts' inability to identify with female patients derives from anxiety when they either take on what society calls the feminine role, as analysts often do, or more specifically when they find themselves anxiously identifying with their female patients' desire for penetration and their joy in it. This insight can be expanded to straight analysts working with gay patients. According to Lasky, if a straight male analyst is anxious about identifying with his female patient's wish to be penetrated, how much closer to home and frightening will be his gay male patient's wish to be penetrated? He may easily protect against such anxiety by any number of defenses—for example, by pathologizing anal intercourse as a regression to the anal stage and a retreat from genital primacy, rather than considering it a source of pleasure that is experienced by many gay men as genitally satisfying and expressive of the greatest emotional intimacy (see Corbett 1993).

Misinformation can be both the source and the tool of prejudice. When I was in college, a man from rural Wisconsin was staring strangely at my forehead. I asked him about it, and he told me, quite sincerely, that he had always thought that Jews had horns. Much homophobia results from similar faulty knowledge about gays and lesbians, and much homophobia results in a refusal or neglect to find out what the emotional and sexual experience of gays and lesbians is like from the "inside." How many analysts still believe that gay men hate women or that lesbians hate men? I still hear such nonsense in clinical discussions, a mix of lack of observation, sloppy thinking, and projection. And whether or not a gay man has made a narcissistic object choice, does that mean that one should consider his homosexuality itself something to be changed, or should one aim just to affect his narcissism within his intimate relations? Consider this: If a psychoanalyst marries another psychoanalyst, does that reflect a narcissistic object choice? And if it does, in the treatment of such a psychoanalyst, should the aim be to get the person to marry a non-psychoanalyst?

It takes courage and effort to admit that one's homophobia is based on misinformation and to correct it. A beautiful, straight woman told me a reason she had identified for her fear of lesbians. She felt continual sexual harassment from men, and so she valued her relationships with other women very highly. These relationships provided her time during which she could enjoy human contact without sexual pressure. And yet she had grown up believing that lesbians would pursue her sexually in the same way that straight men did. She found out fairly recently that this wasn't so, but until then she had feared lesbians and avoided them, hating them without knowing them.

When Freud (1905) shifted the focus of the cause of homosexuality from the physiological to the psychological, it was experienced as very liberating. It's also true, as Dimen points out, that when Hamer, et al. (1993) and LeVay (1993) shift the focus of the cause of homosexuality from the psychological to the physiological in our day, that is also experienced as liberating. So we see two opposite movements that are liberating. Isn't that odd? I think this tells us less about the roots of homosexuality than about the nature of anti-gay hatred. Those who hate homosexuals will use any account, biological or psychological, in the service of their hatred. Any shift in viewpoint seems liberating, because it liberates one from the old view that was pathologizing and persecutory; but in no time, the new view, no matter what it is, will be used in the service of hatred. The problem as Dimen has indicated so well is that almost any attempt to explain why someone becomes homosexual becomes an exercise in covert hatred when the unconscious motivation behind the asking is unaccepting and pathologizing.

In Europe in the 1930s, it was common for non-Jews to talk about the so-called "Jewish Problem." What a hateful term! We all know the tragic fact that the "Jewish Problem" led to the "Final Solution of the Jewish Problem." It makes a big difference whether you address the Jewish problem, or the problem of anti-semitism. Similarly, we might ask: Why have psychoanalysts devoted so much energy to the question, "Why does someone become homosexual?" and so little energy to the question that is more pressing and also more answerable by psychoanalysts: "Why do people hate and fear homosexuals, treat them badly, and deny them normal human rights when as a group they do not harm anyone?" Maybe when that is the question being asked, the problem of homosexuality will have been solved; it will have been solved along with the larger and more pressing question for all mankind, which is why people hate minorities that are different but in no way dangerous. When psychoanalysts stop acting out the problem of homophobia and, instead, address it and analyze it, our field may regain its standing as the solver of irrational problems instead of the reinforcer of problematic irrationality.

Notes

1. Schafer (in this volume) expresses discomfort with the term "straight," pointing out that its implied opposite is "crooked." Actually, I think that the word "straight" probably is used more with the implication of "straight and narrow" or "straight-laced," with the implied opposite being unconventional and adventurous. Similar objections were once raised about the term "gay," which straight people used to hear as implying the binary of "sad." It should also be noted that "heterosexual" is also an inadequate term, since it focuses too much on the sexual, and not enough on affectionate and loving aspects, nor on the total identity of the person (see Katz 1995).
2. This statement implies that butch and femme correspond, respectively, to male and female identifications. This may be true for some, but not all lesbians. (see Case 1988–1989, Feinberg 1993.)
3. As Schafer points out, the term "opposite sex" reflects a bias to the mutually exclusive, binary categories. Why do we say opposite sex rather than other sex, or, perhaps reflecting the work of Money and others, "another sex"?

References

Bayer, R. 1981. *Homosexuality and American Psychiatry*. New York: Basic Books.

Bérubé, A. 1990. *Coming Out Under Fire: The History of Gay Men and Women in World War Two*. New York: Free Press.

Blechner, M. J. 1992. Psychoanalysis, homophobia, racism, and anti-semitism: Introduction. Presented at the conference, "The Experience of Hating and Being Hated." Scientific meeting of the William A. White Society, November 18, New York.

———. 1993. Homophobia in psychoanalytic writing and practice. *Psychoanalytic Dialogues* 3: 627–637.

———. 1994a. Review of Darlene Ehrenberg's *The Intimate Edge*. *Psychoanalytic Dialogues* 4: 283–292.

———. 1994b. Projective identification, countertransference, and the "maybe-me." *Contemporary Psychoanalysis* 30: 619–630.

———. 1995. Schizophrenia. In *Handbook of Interpersonal Psychoanalysis*. Ed. by M. Lionells, et al. New York: Analytic Press.

Butler, J. 1991. Imitation and gender insubordination. In *Inside/Out: Lesbian Theories, Gay Theories*. Ed. by D. Fuss, New York: Routledge, 13–31.

Cartwright, S.A. 1981. Report on the diseases and physical peculiarities of the Negro race. In *Concepts of Health and Disease: Interdisciplinary Perspectives*. Ed. by A.L. Caplan, et al. Reading, MA: Addison-Wesley, 305-326. (Originally published in 1851.)

Case, S. 1988–1989. Toward a butch-femme aesthetic. *Discourse: Journal for Theoretical Studies in Media and Culture* 11 (1): 55–73. Also in *Lesbian and Gay Studies Reader*. Ed. by H. Abelove, M. Barale, and D. Halperin. New York: Routledge, 1993, 294–306.

Chatelaine, K. 1981. *Harry Stack Sullivan: The Formative Years*. Washington, DC.: University Press of America.

Corbett, K. 1993. The mystery of homosexuality. *Psychoanalytic Psychology* 10: 345–58.

Drescher, J. 1992. Psychoanalysis, hatred, homosexuality. Presentation at the conference, "The Experience of Hating and Being Hated." Scientific Meeting of the William A. White Society, November 18, New York.

Duberman, M. 1991. *Cures*. New York: Dutton.

Edelman, G. 1987. *Neural Darwinism*. New York: Basic Books.

Fairbairn, W.R.D. 1946. The treatment and rehabilitation of sexual offenders. In W. R. D. Fairbairn. *Psychoanalytic Studies of the Personality*. London: Routledge, 1952, 289–96.

Fausto-Sterling, A. 1992. *Myths of Gender: Biological Theories about Women and Men*. 2d edition. New York: Basic Books.

Feinberg, L. 1993. *Stone Butch Blues*. Ithaca, NY: Firebrand Books.

Freud, S. 1900. *The Interpretation of Dreams*. In *The Standard Edition of the Complete Psychological Works of Sigmund Freud* 4 and 5.

———. 1905. Three Essays on Sexuality. In *The Standard Edition of the Complete Psychological Works of Sigmund Freud* 7: 123–46. London: Hogarth Press, 1962.

Fromm, E. 1941. *Escape from Freedom*. New York: Holt, Rinehart and Winston.

Frommer, M.S. 1994. Homosexuality and psychoanalysis: Technical considerations revisited. *Psychoanalytic Dialogues* 4: 215–34.

Goldsmith, S. 1992. Oedipus or Orestes: Homosexual men and their relationships with women. Paper presented at New York University, November 7, New York.

Grünbaum, A. 1984. *The Foundations of Psychoanalysis*. Berkeley: University of California Press.

———. 1993. *Validation in the Clinical Theory of Psychoanalysis*. Madison, CT: International Universities Press.

Halperin, D.M. 1989. Sex before sexuality: Pederasty, politics, and power in classical Athens. In *Hidden from History: Reclaiming the Gay and Lesbian Past*. Ed. by M. Duberman, M. Vicinus, and G. Chauncey. New York: New American Library, 37–53.

Hamer, D.; Hu, S.; Magnuson, V.; Hu, N.; and Pattatucci, A. 1993. A linkage between DNA markers on the X chromosome and male sexual orientation. *Science* 261: 321–27.

Hanna, E. 1992. False-self sensitivity to countertransference: Anatomy of a single session. *Psychoanalytic Dialogues* 2: 369–88.

Hodges, A. 1983. *Alan Turing: The Enigma*. New York: Simon and Schuster.

Hooker, E. 1957. The adjustment of the male overt homosexual. *Journal of Projective Techniques* 21: 18–31.

Imperato-McGuinley, J., et al. 1974. Steroid 5-alpha-reductase deficiency in man: An inherited form of male pseudo-hermaphroditism. *Science* 186: 1213–15.

Isay, R. 1989. *Being Homosexual*. New York: Farrar Straus Giroux.

Jamott, L.S. 1994. HIV risk reduction among adolescents. Paper delivered to the HIV Center, Columbia University, March 17.

Katz, J.N. 1995. *The Invention of Heterosexuality*. New York: Dutton.

Kinsey, A.; Pomeroy, W;. and Martin, C. 1948. *Sexual Behavior in the Human Male*. Philadelphia: Saunders.

Kwawer, J. 1980. Transference and countertransference in homosexuality—Changing psychoanalytic views. *American Journal of Psychotherapy* 34: 72–80.

Lasky, R. 1989. Some determinants of the male analyst's capacity to identify with female patients. *International Journal of Psycho-Analysis* 70: 405–418.

LeVay, S. 1993. *The Sexual Brain*. Cambridge, MA: MIT Press.

Lewes, K. 1988. *The Psychoanalytic Theory of Male Homosexuality*. New York: Simon and Schuster.

MacIntosh, H. 1994. Attitudes and experiences of psychoanalysts in analyzing homosexual patients. *Journal of the American Psychoanalytic Association* 42: 1183–1207.

Masters, W.H., and Johnson, V.E. 1966. *Human Sexual Response*. Boston: Little Brown.

Meijer, H. 1993. Can seduction make straight men gay? *Journal of Homosexuality* 24: 125–36.

Mitchell, S. 1978. Psychodynamics, homosexuality and the question of pathology. *Psychiatry* 41: 254–63.

———. 1981. The psychoanalytic treatment of homosexuality: Some technical considerations. *International Review of Psycho-Analysis* 8: 63–80

Monette, P. 1992. *Becoming a Man*. New York: Harcourt Brace Jovanovich.

———. 1994. *Last Watch of the Night*. New York: Harcourt Brace Jovanovich.

Money, J. 1988. *Gay, Straight, and In-Between*. New York: Oxford University Press.

Money, J., and Erhardt, A. 1972. *Man Woman Boy Girl*. Baltimore: Johns Hopkins University Press.

Money, J.; Hampson, J.G.; and Hampson, J.L. 1955. An examination of some basic sexual concepts: The evidence of human hermaphroditism. *Johns Hopkins Medical Journal* 97: 301–19.

Moss, D. 1992. Introductory thoughts: Hating in the first person plural: The example of homophobia. *American Imago* 49: 277–91.

Nestle, J. 1984. The femme question. In *Pleasure and Danger: Exploring Female Sexuality*. Ed. by C. Vance. Boston: Routledge, 232–41.

Slater, E., and Roth, M. 1969. *Clinical Psychiatry*. 3d edition. Baltimore: Williams and Wilkins.

Sullivan, H.S. 1953. *The Interpersonal Theory of Psychiatry*. New York: Norton.

———. 1962. *Schizophrenia as a Human Process*. New York: Norton.

———. 1965. *Personal Psychopathology*. New York: Norton.

Trivers, R.L. 1974. Parent-offspring conflict. *American Zoologist* 14: 249–64.

Verghese, A. 1994. *My Own Country*. New York: Simon & Schuster.

Wakefield, J.C. 1992. The concept of mental disorder: On the boundary between biological facts and social values. *American Psychologist* 47: 373–88.

Weeks, J. 1977. *Coming Out: Homosexual Politics in Britain from the Nineteenth Century to the Present*. London.

Weinberg, M.S.; Williams, C.J.; and Pryor, D.W. 1994. *Dual Attraction: Understanding Bisexuality*. New York: Oxford University Press.

Wilson, E.O. 1975. *Sociobiology: The New Synthesis*. Cambridge, MA: Harvard University Press.

White, K.P. 1992. The experience of surviving hating and being hated. Presented at the conference, "The Experience of Hating and Being Hated." Scientific meeting of the William A. White Society, November 18, New York.

Contributors

Mark J. Blechner, Ph.D., is Fellow, Faculty, Supervisor, and Director of the HIV Clinical Service, William Alanson White Institute of Psychoanalysis, Psychiatry and Psychology. He is also a faculty member and Supervisor at Manhattan Institute for Psychoanalysis.

Muriel Dimen, Ph.D. is Clinical Professor of Psychology, Postdoctoral Program in Psychotherapy and Psychoanalysis, New York University; Faculty and Supervisor, Gordon F. Derner Institute, Program in Psychotherapy and Psychoanalysis, Adelphi University. Dr. Dimen is a Fellow at The New York Institute for the Humanities, New York University, and Co-Director and Co-Founder of the Seminar on Psychoanalysis and Sexual Difference. She is Book Review Editor, *Psychoanalytic Dialogues*, and Associate Editor of *Gender and Psychoanalysis*. Dr. Dimen is the author of *Surviving Sexual Contradictions* (NY: Macmillan, 1986); and *The Anthropological Imagination* (NY: McGraw-Hill, 1977). She is co-editor with Virginia Goldner of *Gender in Psychoanalytic Space* (New York: Routledge [forthcoming]) and co-editor with Ernestine Friedl of *Regional Variation in Modern Greece*, (New York Academy of Science, 1975). She is also the author of numerous essays on sexuality, gender, psychoanalysis, and culture.

Lee Crespi, C.S.W., is on the Executive Board of the Psychoanalytic Psychotherapy Study Center. She is a graduate of the Institute for Contemporary Psychotherapy, where she is a supervisor. She has authored a number of papers including "Counter-transference Love" (*Contemporary Psychotherapy Review* 3 [Spring 1986]: 86–95). She is in private practice in New York City.

Thomas Domenici, Ph.D., is a graduate of the University of California, Santa Barbara and received his masters and doctorate from the University of Southern California. He received his psychoanalytic training at New York University Postdoctoral Program in Psychotherapy and Psychoanalysis and is a founding member of the Committee on Gay and Lesbian Concerns of the Postdoctoral Program. He recently relocated his residence and private practice to San Francisco, California, and is currently writing a book on intersubjective theory, relational psychoanalysis, and the gay man.

Jack Drescher, M.D., is a faculty member and Psychiatric Consultant at William Alanson White Psychoanalytic Institute and is Co-Chair, Committee on Gay and Lesbian Issues, American Psychiatric Association, New York County District Branch. He is the author of *Psychoanalytic Psychotherapy and The Gay Man* (The Analytic Press, forthcoming), and is in full-time private practice in New York City.

Martin Stephen Frommer, Ph.D., is a faculty member and supervisor in the psychoanalytic training program at the Institute for Contemporary Psychotherapy in New York City. He is a psychologist in private practice in Manhattan.

Stephen B. Goldman, Ph.D., has a practice in psychoanalysis and psychoanalytic psychotherapy with individuals and groups. His doctorate is from Columbia University and he has a Certificate in Psychoanalytic Psychotherapy from the New Hope Guild Centers Training Program. He has been a faculty member and Supervising Psychologist at the New Hope Guild Centers for many years. He has been on the faculty of the New Jersey Insititute for Training in Psychoanalysis, and has been a Training and Control Analyst at this Institute. His recent publications include: "Bearing the Unbearable: The Psychological Impact of AIDS," which was a chapter in *Gender in Transition* (NY: Plenum, 1989), edited by J. Offerman-Zuckerberg.

Adrienne Harris, Ph.D., is a Co-Director of the New York University Postdoctoral Program in Psychotherapy and Psychoanalysis. She is Associate Editor of both *Psychoanalytic Dialogues* and a new journal, *Gender and Psychoanalysis*. She is co-editor, with Lewis Aron, Ph.D., of *The Legacy of Sandor Ferenczi* (Hillsdale, NJ: Analytic Press, 1993). Dr. Harris is in private practice in New York City.

Ronnie C. Lesser, Ph.D., is a psychologist in private practice in New York City and Westchester. A graduate of the New Hope Guild Centers Training

Program in Psychoanalytic Psychotherapy, she is a supervisor at the Institute for Human Identity and a candidate for the certificate in psychoanalysis at The New York University Postdoctoral Program in Psychotherapy and Psychoanalysis. She is a founding member of the Committee on Gay and Lesbian Concerns of the Posdoctoral Program. Dr. Lesser has written articles and book reviews on the topic of sexuality.

April Martin, Ph.D., is on the supervisory faculty of New York University's Postdoctoral Program in Psychoanalysis and Psychotherapy and Yeshiva University's Doctoral Program in Psychology. She has published and spoken extensively on behalf of lesbian, gay, bisexual, and transgendered individuals and their families in professional and psychological arenas, in the gay and lesbian community, and in the popular media. She is the author of *The Lesbian and Gay Parenting Handbook* (NY: Harper Collins, 1993) as well as other articles and chapters dealing with lesbian and gay issues.

Maggie Magee, M.S.W., is a member of the Los Angeles Institute and the Society of Psychoanalytic Studies. She is on the Clinical Consulting Faculty of the California Institute for Clinical Social Work and for many years supervised counselors in Santa Monica, California.

Robert May, Ph.D., did his clinical training at the Austen Riggs Center and the Tavistock Clinic. He is Director of the Counseling and Mental Health Service at Amherst College and is in private practice. He is the author of numerous papers in the area of psychoanalysis and psychoanalytic psychotherapy and of books on gender issues and on psychotherapy in a college setting.

Diana C. Miller, M.D., is a training and supervising analyst at the Institute of Contemporary Psychoanalysis, Los Angeles, California, and is a member of the Los Angeles Institute and Society of Psychoanalytic Studies. She is an Assistant Clinical Professor at UCLA Department of Psychiatry and Biobehavioral Sciences. She is in private practice in Santa Monica, California.

Noreen O'Connor is co-author, with Joanna Ryan, of *Wild Desires and Mistaken Identitities: Lesbianism and Psychoanalysis* (NY: Columbia University Press, 1993). She has published papers widely on contemporary European philosophy and psychoanalysis. She is on the Training Committee of the Philadelphia Psychoanalytic Psychotherapy Association, London. She works in full-time private practice.

Richard Rutkin, Ph.D., is Associate Professor of School Services, The City College (CUNY); Faculty and Supervisor, New York University Postdoctoral Program in Psychotherapy and Psychoanalysis; Faculty and Supervisor, Institute for Contemporary Psychotherapy; and maintains a private practice.

Erica Schoenberg, Ph.D., is a supervisor at The Institute for Human Identity. She is a member of the Psychoanalytic Association of the Westchester Center for the Study of Psychoanalysis and Psychotherapy and is in private practice in Manhattan and Westchester.

Roy Schafer, Ph.D., is a Training and Supervising Analyst at Columbia University's Psychoanalytic Center for Psychoanalytic Training and Research. He was the first Freud Memorial Professor at University College, London, and has been honored twice by the American Psychological Association for his contributions to psychoanalysis and professional knowledge. He is the author of, among other works, *A New Language for Psychoanalysis* (New Haven: Yale University Press, 1976), *Aspects of Internalization* (NY: International University Press, 1968), *The Analytic Attitude* (NY: Basic Books, 1982), and *Retelling a Life: Narration and Dialogue in Psychoanalysis* (NY: Basic Books, 1992).

David Schwartz, Ph.D., is a member of the Psychoanalytic Association of the Westchester Center for the Study of Psychotherapy and Psychoanalysis, is on the Editorial Board of *Gender and Psychoanalysis*, and is in private practice in Westchester County and Manhattan.

Index

NATIONAL UNIVERSITY
LIBRARY SAN DIEGO